SPATIAL COGNITION

The Structure and Development
of Mental Representations of Spatial Relations

CHILD PSYCHOLOGY

A series of volumes edited by **David S. Palermo**

SPATIAL COGNITION

The Structure and Development
of Mental Representations of Spatial Relations

David R. Olson   **and**   **Ellen Bialystok**
The Ontario Institute   *York University*
for Studies in Education

LEA LAWRENCE ERLBAUM ASSOCIATES, PUBLISHERS
1983   Hillsdale, New Jersey   London

Lawrence Erlbaum Associates, Inc., Publishers
365 Broadway
Hillsdale, New Jersey 07642

Library of Congress Cataloging in Publication Data

Olson, David R.
  Spatial cognition.

  Bibliography: p.
  Includes index.
  1. Space perception.   I. Bialystok, Ellen.
II. Title.   [DNLM: 1. Cognition.   2. Space perception.
BF 469 052s]
BF469.045   1983   153.7'52   83-5605
ISBN 0-89859-252-6

Printed in the United States of America
10   9   8   7   6   5   4   3   2   1

Contents

Preface

Had we known, at the beginning, how this volume would come out in the end, we would have either not begun at all, or at least been spared much of the rewriting, rethinking, revising that in fact made the book a huge intellectual effort. We began with some notions of the relations between the mental representation of spatial information, which we described in terms of the perception of objects and the perception of form, an idea we learned from Arnheim's writings on art and perception, and those ideas served us well for part of the book. But we also had some notions of the structure of meanings of spatial lexical terms such as *top, bottom, over, under* and were convinced that the mental representation of these terms must map onto the structure of mental representation which served spatial perception and spatial thought.

As we pursued these relations it became clear that we would require a much more explicit "representational format" for expressing the ideas we were developing. We had referred to these as rough notions of mental constituents as concepts, features, and prototypes from the beginning but, beginning with Anat Scher's experiment (reported in Chapter 6), it became clear that we could describe the *precise* structure of the mental representations involved, at least for one task, in terms of a small set of predicates and their related arguments. Miller and Johnson-Laird's book, *Language and Perception,* was a helpful approach to this propositional way of talking and thinking as was Clark and Clark's *The Psychology of Language.* Once we adopted the research strategy of trying to imagine that children and adults were literally acting upon spatial propositions made up of a particular set of predicates applied to a particular set of arguments in making the judgments they did, the research became much more deductive but, we believe, more productive and original. For as soon as we saw we could apply this analysis to one task, it was clear that we could, with minor amendments, apply it not only to every spatial task we had reported but also to many other tasks in the spatial cognition literature.

And the end product, as the reader will soon see, was a small set of theoretical ideas which make up a quite general theory of the mental representation of space which accounts both for much of spatial perception but also much of spatial thought. The system is general and economical and can be readily applied to novel problems as we illustrated in regard to Piaget's water level problem and Koler's letter recognition problem. Of course, the theory has its blind spots. For example, it makes no effort to recover the primary predicates (the primitives) from which all others are generated nor the explicit rules for relating those spatial predicates. But it does show how, if we assume humans perceive and think about space by means of such spatial propositions, they would make the judgments they in fact do.

It is worth mentioning what, for us, were the primary blind spots that most hindered our theoretical development. One, we have already mentioned, namely, the assumption, at first, that talk of mental representation had to remain vaguely expressed in categories of unspecified structural descriptions, images, patterns, forms, features, frames of reference, and the like, whereas, it turned out, the most important part of the work came from a radical explicitness provided by an analysis of propositions. This turn to explicitness was, of course, Frege's original motivation for his "Begriffsschrift", his formula language for pure thought. He attempted to construct a language for expressing logical relations such that inferences and judgments would depend exclusively on logic rather than intuition: "To prevent anything intuitive from penetrating here unnoticed, I had to bend every effort to keep the chain of inferences free of gaps. In attempting to comply with this requirement in the strictest possible way I found the inadequacy of language to be an obstacle; no matter how unwieldy the expressions I was ready to accept, I was less and less able, as the relations became more and more complex, to attain the precision that my purpose required. This deficiency led me to the idea of the present ideography" (Frege, 1970, p. 5). The representations we have attributed to our subjects and the rules they use in operating on them are somewhat less precise than were those of Frege. Nonetheless, a decisive turn in theoretical explanation in the present book occurred when we discovered we could, in fact, formulate explicit and precise representations for our subjects that would account for the behavior we had observed.

The second persistent error, in fact, motivated much of the experiential work. It was the mistaken idea that propositions were inextricably linked to words and sentences. We simply had not taken Frege, Miller and Johnson-Laird, and the Clarks seriously enough; propositions could represent pure thought as opposed to merely the meanings of sentences. Eventually we saw that we were in fact distinguishing between the structure of ideas and their expression in language, drawings, and the like, and hence, that these propositional representations could be found, indeed were found, in inarticulate subjects working on non-verbal tasks. Just because children could not express their procedures in sentences did not imply that they were not working from a basic set of propositional representations. Nonetheless, this issue is extremely important for spatial theory in particular. Spatial cognition is interesting not only in its own right but in that it provides such a clear alternative to linguistic cognition. As is well known, verbal abilities and spatial abilities are quite distinct. The conceptual trap is to infer that verbal thought is propositional while spatial thought is "imagistic" or non-verbal. In this book we do our best to show that the dichotomy is seriously misleading. Both verbal and spatial thought, we try to show, rely upon underlying propositional representations consisting of predicates and their related arguments. The difference is not in the structure of the mental representation so much as in their expressibility in language, drawing, and the like. To oversimplify, an image is a set of propositions. In fact, the process of articulation is the very process we had discussed, somewhat vaguely, at the outset of the book, as the perception of form.

The third major obstacle was our failure to acknowledge that spatial cognition was inherently relational. This problem occurred primarily because we thought we could make an analysis of spatial concepts, features, forms, and the like, whereas, in fact, what we required were relational structures which would relate particular features or particular objects to other features of objects. To cope with the relational problem we first adopted notions of frames of reference but they were limited by the fact that almost anything could be a frame of reference for almost anything else and hence they did not result in any dramatic simplification of the theory. The solution, as the reader will see, was to adopt a propositional account in which all structures are relational and to simply classify the types of arguments that could be related by spatial predicates to form a spatial proposition. The set of possible frames of reference turned out to be simple—any canonical object, that is an object with intrinsic spatial parts, including ego and the environment as particular canonical objects, could play that role. And the study then moved immediately from being one of spatial concepts to one of spatial propositions.

The fourth major conceptual obstacle was the concept of environmental space. We could readily conceive of objects having spatial properties such as tops and bottoms and the like and we could readily see that persons, egos, were special objects in that they both had distinctive spatial properties and that perceivers readily attribute these properties to objects in the environment—the top of ego corresponds to the top of the blank screen in front of a subject in an experimental setting and so on. But environmental space seemed both more fundamental and yet more difficult to characterize than either egos or objects. It would not do to simply say that environmental space was "there" and hence, known, because the whole point of the book was to argue that we make up our mental representations of ourselves and the world out of a set of mental constituents. As Pylyshyn puts it: "Perception can best be characterized as the construction of an internal description of an event using an internal vocabulary of available concepts" (1977, p. 170). What then were we to do with environmental space as a frame of reference? We finally noticed that the environment does not in fact require a special analysis. The environment is simply a canonical object larger than ego. Just as a room has a top and a bottom and a front and back and thus constitutes an environmental space, so the larger environment, a house, a block, a city, or the world is a canonical object; it has an up and down, clearly established by gravity. But it may also have a canonical front and back as a backyard does although environments rarely have intrinsic lefts or rights. The missing features or predicates in these cases are provided by some other canonical object such as ego or any other object. In general, the problem of the environment as a frame of reference vanishes because the environment is simply one among many partially canonical objects, and like any other object it can on occasion provide a frame of reference to which particular objects may be related.

The final problem had to do with level of detail. For theoretical power and clarity we adopted, as we said, explicit propositional representations as an explanation of a variety of tasks. But the problem with explicitness is the level of detail required. If you claim that a subject uses particular proposition in making a judgment you must state quite precisely what conditions must be met for the representation to apply. This, we found, frequently led us to detailed descriptions (for example the precise codings subjects assign to a random display viewed from various locations) which tend to be both long and difficult to follow. We have tried to follow a middle course; show just how such a representation and operation would work yet not lose track of the general properties of such spatial thinking. But we had the feeling that we did not always succeed in taking things both far enough and yet not too far.

This process took a considerable amount of time and a considerable amount of argument both between ourselves and Bill Ives, Joanne Rovet, and Anat Scher, it took remarkable perseverance on behalf of our secretary Mary Macri, who typed her way through many rough drafts, and it took considerable patience on behalf of our editor and publisher, David Palermo and Larry Erlbaum. We are pleased to express our thanks to these colleagues.

David R. Olson
Ellen Bialystok

SPATIAL COGNITION

The Structure and Development
of Mental Representations of Spatial Relations

1 Spatial Aspects of the Mental Representation of Objects and Events

"Has the oyster [a] necessary notion of space?"

Darwin's Notebooks.

I. ON SPATIAL COGNITION

A historical account of the conception of space and the transformations that conception has passed through—from Aristotelian to Newtonian to Einsteinian—could serve as an account of the development of intellect. These insights into physical space, as several writers have pointed out (Butterfield, 1965; Cornford, 1936; Eddington, 1958) rest upon parallel discoveries in conceptual space—the spherical but bounded Void of Pythagoras, the infinite, continuous space of Euclid and the elastic space of Lobatchvsky. The most obvious effect of these discoveries has been to alter our conception of the external world; but just as important, it has altered our conception of human cognition. If what we call physical reality is to be dependent upon certain conceptual or mental ideas, as for example the infinite, continuous, physical space of Newton is to be seen as the expression of the infinite, continuous, conceptual, space of Euclid, then it is impossible to explain the structure of human cognition by recourse to the structure of physical reality. That is, the structure of ideas cannot be explained by recourse to the structure of reality. The noted physicist, Sir Arthur Eddington (1958) made this point most strongly:

> . . . not only the laws of nature, but [of] space and time, and the material universe itself, are constructions of the human mind . . . To an altogether unexpected extent the universe we live in is the creation of our minds.

The ball, so to speak, is in our court. Can we develop some description of the operations of the human mind which will account for some of the properties of invented conceptual space and the ways in which this conceptual

1

space is employed in perceiving, recognizing and remembering objects and events? What is the structure of the cognitive processes by means of which we represent and interpret the world? What is the relation between the cognitive structures that are employed in everyday perception and action and those that are involved in our scientific representations of reality? What is the role of symbols in those cognitive processes?

Our assumption is that spatial concepts and spatial relations play a fundamental role in the cognitive structure at every level of representation from object perception to formal geometry. Furthermore, spatial structures are exploited far beyond their concrete representational functions. We may announce the topic of this book by saying it is *on* space, or that the theory is an *extension* of some earlier work, or that it is *within* the field of cognitive psychology or that it examines the processes which lie *under* or *behind* the perception and knowledge of space, and so on.

Our concern is with the problem of inner space or spatial cognition, the spatial features, properties, categories and relations in terms of which we perceive, store and remember objects, persons and events and on the basis of which we construct explicit, lexical, geometric, cartographic and artistic representations.

We shall argue that we perceive and act in our environment on the basis of concepts of objects, persons, and events constructed in large part out of features and relations which are spatial. Spatial properties may be used to recognize objects by shape, to remember locations by positions, by landmarks, and by adjacency, and to judge safety and danger by sizes and distances. But, and here again, we are at our central question, how is that spatial information coded and utilized in the service of these various activities?

Not only is spatial information critical to object, person, and event perception, but also space comes to be perceived in its own right in terms of spatial concepts—tops and bottoms, round and square, open and closed and the like, when represented in such symbol systems as ordinary language, map-making, drawing, graphing and painting. This, then, is our second question: How are these explicit spatial concepts related to the spatial information that is implicit in object, person, and event perception?

The spatial information, as we shall see, is largely preserved from object perception to spatial conception—from perceptual space to representational space as Piaget would say—but it differs in terms of the meaning system of which it is a part. But how, and this is our third question, does meaning relate to perception of objects and to our conception of space? What is the role of meaning in perception? Traditional accounts of perception, because of their lack of concern with meaning, fail in two primary ways (both coming and going if we may be excused a spatial metaphor). They fail to acknowledge that what people perceive are objects and events, not spatial/visual features—and they fail to recognize that perceptual distinctions *reflect* meaning differences rather than determine them.

We shall present our arguments in a series of stages. Firstly, we shall set out to describe a form of mental representation which jointly specifies the meaning of objects and events and the spatial information appropriate to the perception of these objects and events. Secondly, we will describe the processes whereby these structural descriptions of objects and events are "interrogated" to form explicit spatial concepts with their own distinctive meanings. Spatial concepts too are represented by means of structural descriptions but they are organized at a new level of meaning which we call representations of *form* to differentiate them from representations of objects and events.

The interplay between the implicit structural descriptions of objects and the explicit form representations of spatial concepts provides a basis for a discussion of the traditional problem of perception and representation and for outlining aspects of a theory of cognitive development.

Finally, a series of studies is presented which examines the nature of the spatial information utilized in the structural description of objects and events, the development of spatial concepts, the lexicalization of space, and the ways that these alternative forms of representation are recruited in solving some classical spatial tasks. We conclude with a general theory of spatial representation and spatial thought which can be used to explain a wide array of tasks from Piaget's motor level task to letter recognition.

II. PERCEPTION AS A SPATIAL PROBLEM

Are these pairs of items similar?

Without reflection we would tend to say that they looked very different. What was the basis for our decision as to their dissimilarity? Possibly, for A we would say that the circle is beside the square and for B that the circle is inside the square, and so on. But we would hesitate to claim that that statement bore much relation to the psychological processes involved in making that similarity judgement. Rather, they just seemed to look different.

What about these displays?

2.

    A   A¹

They appear to be very similar. Why? We may say that they both have a circle to the left of a square so they look alike. However again we would hesitate to state that our perceptual processes directly corresponded to our linguistic description. A possible alternative to the theory that we compared linguistic or linguistic-like descriptions is that A and A¹ look alike because the image of one matches the image of the second much as if one picture were superimposed upon another. But, at least in this case the explanation seems inadequate. Here is a picture of the two superimposed:

3.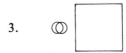

The images do not fit. Why then did we judge them as similar? The image matching view seems to fall short. No two things are identical and yet we readily judge them as similar or treat them as equivalent—This is Bill; this is a photograph of Bill. This is the Mona Lisa; this is a reproduction of the Mona Lisa, and so on. How do we judge them equivalent if they are not identical? How do we recognize a person's face as the same face if on one occasion it is smiling and on another frowning?

4.

Not only are discriminable displays seen as similar or identical but identical things are seen as different. Furthermore not all stimulus differences are equally important in deciding upon the similarity of displays. Consider the book title in 5.

5.   The fo o of Go o

Do the last letters in the underlined words look the same? In *fool* we tend to note the space between the o and l; in *God* we tend to overlook it—in order to make sense they must be seen as joined to make a *d*. If similarity judgements are based upon uninterpreted images or copies then any stimulus change should be as important as any other change. Yet in example 5, the same perceptual information, that is, the space between the o and l was perceived in two different ways. Recognition of displays seems to involve procedures that are more "intelligent" than the simple copying of visual displays. But, again, how are we to account for that "intelligence"?

What we perceive, recognize or judge as similar or identical depends, we shall argue, upon what we know, that is, on the meanings we can assign to a display. What we know—our expectancies and our interpretations in conjunction with the sensory display determine what we perceive.

The theory that meaning is a critical part of perception has had a mixed career. Two arguments, both reductionistic, have contributed to underestimating the role of meaning in perception. First, meaning is usually taken as a higher order "interpretation" of experience, while perception is a direct consequence of that experience, hence, meaning appears to have a secondary or derived status. The second was the general reductionist assumption that higher order structures could be explained in terms of lower order ones, hence, meanings could be explained in terms of the uninterpreted sensory properties captured in the act of perception. These arguments are readily traced to the British empiricists and to sense-data theorists since, including the behaviorists, who took sensation as the basis of all knowledge. The mind merely collected and associated such sensations to produce the knowledge of objects and events. If sense-data were primary in experience, complex concepts would be explained in terms of those more fundamental sense-data. Furthermore, if sense-data were picked up directly, without interpretation they could be both taken as "brute fact" and used as firm base for subsequent theoretical knowledge (Taylor 1964). Sense-data, then, reflected the world more directly and truly than did theories. Language too was to be restricted to "plain speech", an empirical object-based language with a rejection of "all amplifications, depressions and swellings of style" and the use of "an equal number of words for an equal number of things" (Sprat, 1657/1966).

Nonetheless, there have been others urging us in the opposite direction for several decades. The Gestalt psychologists provided many demonstrations that perception was not merely the preservation of a visual copy of a display but rather an interpreted structure. Various types of illusions, the Necker cube, the Muller-Lyre illusion, as well as (6) the duck-rabbit, and (7) the bird-antelope were given as examples that perception is not merely the registration of objective form but rather is "laced" with interpretation. Furthermore, the interpretation determined what was seen.

6.    7.

Rabbit or duck?   Bird or antelope?

Rock (1978) has extended these arguments by showing that the illusions of apparent motion are the consequence of what we know about the motion of real objects. Again our perceptions are informed by our knowledge of the world.

Wittgenstein (1958), in his examination of two meanings of the word "see" discussed just this problem. In one sense of "see" we mean what remains invariant in our varied interpretations of the display while the other sense of "see" we mean the various likenesses, or interpretations we put upon that display. "I see that it has not changed; and yet I see it differently. I call this experience 'noticing an aspect' " (p. 193). But he goes on to argue that these seeings are not ordered, one being perception and the other interpretation. Rather "we see it as we interpret it" (p. 193). And again, "It is a case of both seeing and thinking? or an amalgam of the two, as I should almost like to say?" (p. 197). "But how is it possible to see an object according to an interpretation? The question represents it as a queer fact; as if something were being forced into a form it did not really fit. But no squeezing, no forcing took place here" (p. 200). That is, the two meanings tend to collapse into one: "Do I really see something different each time, or do I only interpret what I see in a different way? I am inclined to say the former" (p. 212).

Hanson (1958) has applied this view of the inseparability of seeing and interpreting to modern physics. In contrast to the classical view of physics (akin to that of the British Empiricists mentioned above) in which data, facts, and observations are first collected and build up into general systems of physical explanation, Hanson examines how those theoretical systems are built into observations, facts, and data. Hanson argues that observation is always shaped by our theories and interpretations. He illustrates this view with a colorful description of a hypothetical discussion about cosmological space:

> Let us consider Johannes Kepler: imagine him on a hill watching the dawn. With him is Tycho Brahe. Kepler regarded the sun as fixed: it was the earth that moved. But Tycho followed Ptolemy and Aristotle in this much at least: the earth was fixed and all other celestial bodies moved around it. *Do Kepler and Tycho see the same thing in the east at dawn?*. . . The resultant discussion might run:
> Yes, they do.
> No, they don't.
> Yes, they do!
> No, they don't!. . . (p. 5).

Hanson goes on to argue that by possessing different theories, they see different things or at least things differently. Kepler sees the horizon dropping while Tycho sees the sun rising. Hanson rejects the argument that one first sees a display and then assigns an interpretation to it. "There is a sense, then, in which seeing is a 'theory-laden' undertaking. Observation of x is shaped by proper knowledge of x. . .'Seeing that' threads knowledge into our seeing" (p. 19–22).

In his analysis of the problem of representation in art, Sir Ernst Grombrich (1960) examined in detail the relation between what one perceives and what one knows in general and how one comes to see in a way that permits a faithful representation in art, in particular. He argues that in order to describe or portray the visible world in art one needs a developed system of schemata. These schemata are compared to a questionnaire or formulary which selects information from the visual world; only those aspects of information that are judged to be relevant or useful are registered in the schemata. The objective of the artist, that is, his conception of what he is trying to do, together with the visual forms that he already knows or can portray, will determine what information he gains from his perceptions of the world.

In his Retrospect to the book *Art and Illusion* Gombrich noted: "We have come to realize more and more, since those days, that we can never neatly separate what we see from what we know" (p. 394). We shall return to a fuller account of Gombrich's views in our discussion of development.

There are two points to notice here. Firstly, what one sees depends upon what one knows, that is on the schemata, concepts, or codes available. And secondly, what one must see to make a representational drawing is different from what one ordinarily sees in objects and events. It may be tempting to think that ordinary seeing is direct perception, that is seeing things as they really are, while artistic perception involves seeing through or seeing in terms of the properties of the codes or schema appropriate to that specialized medium of representation. That view is explicitly rejected by all of the lines of argument we have summarized here—even ordinary perception is laced with knowledge or interpretation. However, the relation between ordinary seeing and artistic seeing, what we shall call the perception of form, is problematic and we shall return to it in Chapter 2.

Let us summarize the argument to this point. The perception of an object or display and the judgement of similarity between two displays appears to be based upon some relatively rich mental representation. This mental representation, in some way, preserves or codes much sensory information, including visual-spatial qualities of an object or display. But this mental representation cannot be a simple uninterpreted copy or uninterpreted image of the display because what we perceive is as much a function of what we know as it is of the properties of the display. Our problem is how to describe the mental representations that underlie perception generally and spatial perception specifically and how to describe the relation of our "meanings" to those representations. We shall discuss the mental representations underlying perception in terms of "structural descriptions" which, when combined with meanings yield concepts. The primary relation between them is that for each distinct meaning a person entertains, he will construct or attempt to construct a distinctive structural description. Reciprocally, every distinctive structural description will either presuppose or call for a difference in meaning. Because these representations are fundamental to our analysis of space, it is necessary to consider them in some detail.

III. THE TWO SIDES OF OBJECT AND EVENT PERCEPTION: STRUCTURAL DESCRIPTIONS AND MEANINGS

Objects are perceived and patterns are judged as similar, we suggest, because they take the same *structural description*. A structural description may be considered a propositional representation of the properties or features and their relations constructed by the mind which permits the recognition of and assignment of meaning to objects. It is similar to a feature list except that the features are not assumed to be merely a list but an ordered, hierarchically organized set of descriptions. Furthermore, structural descriptions are assumed to be constructed from a set of elements that is smaller than the set of objects represented. They, therefore, constitute the language or code for the mental representation of experience.

To go back to our illustration 2, the patterns are judged as similar because they take the same structural description. They both satisfy the description "small circle to the left of the larger square". Of course, they satisfy some other descriptions as well: "circle and square", "two figures", and so on. Those structural descriptions form the basis of the perception of objects and events and, as we shall see later, of spatial relations, shapes, patterns, sizes, and positions of those objects. The alternate displays look dissimilar because they contained features in their structural descriptions that were distinctive—in one case the circle was *in* the box, in the other it was *outside* the box. By pursuing this procedure one could specify at least some of the properties and relations that enter into the structural descriptions for various displays. The spatial features of these displays would presumably consist of such properties as big/small, near/far, in/out, under/over, top/bottom and the like. Our primary concern is that of identifying some of the features and their organization that make up the structural descriptions for objects and other visual displays.

The use of structural descriptions for representing perceptual information has been outlined by Palmer (1975) in far greater detail than we shall have use for. He argues that a propositional structural description is the only form of representation that is neither so inflexible as to refer to only one display as is the case with an image, nor so flexible as to inadequately discriminate between instances, as is the case with a prototype and a feature list. Structural descriptions contain information about features, relations between features, and values on dimension, encoded at a level appropriate for recognition, discrimination, and so on.

Palmer claims that using a minimum number of parameters, propositions can be constructed to represent any visual display. The structural description for a square, in Palmer's system, requires three parameters—location, orientation, and length. This information is given by the more primitive (i.e., component) features of the lines and angles of the square which, in turn, could be specified by the component points. Thus the parts and the relationships between the parts of the figure can be retrieved at various levels. The meaning is represented by the higher order relationships, or parameters, which define the shape. The structural description suitable for the representation of a square is shown in Figure 1.1.

The advantage of a theory of structural descriptions according to Palmer, is that it can be used to represent information presented either linguistically or visually. Such a common format would seem to be necessary to perform cross-modality tasks, such as verifying pictures against sentences. Further, these propositions can encode an analogue image upon which analogue operations can be performed. Thus, mental rotation tasks (Shepard & Metzler, 1971; Cooper & Shepard, 1973a) can be performed by means of propositional representations rather than imaginal transformations, as traditionally argued. Palmer suggests that a structural description containing a feature for the angle ϕ is constructed, and the task is solved by following changes in the proposition as a function of successive increments to the angle ϕ.

The cognitive system constructs the structural descriptions appropriate for various types of information, from simple points to complex scenes. Objects, for example, are represented in terms of their shapes and other properties such as color, size, orientation. A proposition decomposed into its most primitive features can be used to generate an image, a suggestion we shall follow up presently. Hence, structural descriptions are not to be seen as an alternative to images and prototypes; rather they are to be seen as an underlying form of representation from which both images and prototypes may be generated. We shall consider how these are related presently.

Pylyshyn (1973, 1977) too has argued extensively that the mental representation of objects and events must be in the form of propositions or "structured descriptions" rather than images. As they are usually defined, images are taken as uninterpreted copies of perceptual events. Yet is is extremely improbable, Pylyshyn argues, that mental representations are stored as raw images. For example, in recalling a scene one may directly address such meaningful aspects as furniture, characters, and so on which suggests that the representation must have been interpreted before it was stored. Further, some aspects of a scene are clearly non-pictorial, such as relationships of causality. For these and other reasons, Pylyshyn rejects the viability of unanalyzed mental imagery for memory and cognition and

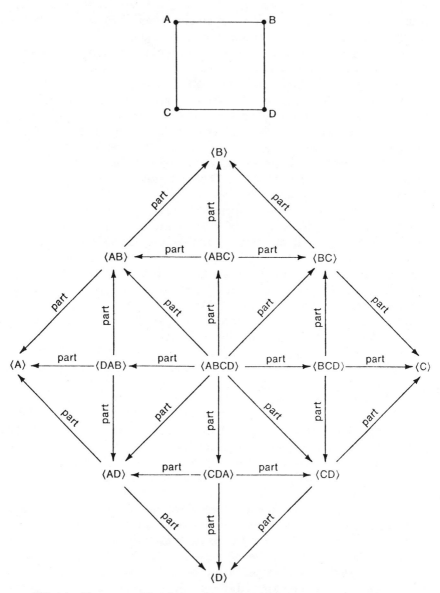

FIG. 1.1   The structural description of square ABCD. Nodes represent the component
POINTs, lines, and angles of the square (from Palmer, 1975). Parameters of the component
parts are not shown.

posits instead "structured descriptions", which are analyzed interpretations
of mental events. Images, while they do exist, are non-pictorial in character,
just as structured descriptions are non-linguistic. These structured descrip-

tions are constructed by selecting from a "vocabulary of available concepts" to form an appropriate representation. Complexity is defined in terms of the symbolic structure of the representation of an event, that is, of the structured description, rather than in terms of geometry of the event being represented. Pylyshyn uses this concept to analyze spatial problems such as mental rotation, and argues that a computational model using such propositions can account for existing data at least as well as can theories which postulate analogue mental images. Also important is his observation that the problem with the traditional concept of mental imagery and analogical representations is that it does not adequately distinguish perception and representation nor show how either may be mapped into language. Pylyshyn (1978) adds: "Whatever merits the proposals for imagistic or analogue representations may have they clearly do not help the language-perception interface problem since sooner or later the representation must be analyzed in such a way as to be commensurable with natural language terms" (p. 176). We shall return to Pylyshyn's discussion of images in Chapter 12.

Although we shall adopt the notion of structural description for our theory of spatial cognition, we must now qualify it in three important ways. Firstly, it is tempting to attribute to the structural description of a display all of the features that one could ever come to correctly attribute to the display and thereby grossly overestimate the richness of a structural description. This is in our view the fundamental flaw in image theory. Structural descriptions are not fully constructed upon the first exposure to an object or event but are progressively elaborated in the course of development. More importantly, much of the information about a display may be constructed when it is needed rather than simply stored as a direct consequence of exposure to a display. To illustrate, let us suppose that a child's structural description for a square consists initially of, say, two sets of parallel lines meeting at right angles. Then suppose that in some other quarter for some other reason he begins to perceive the number of individuals in small collections and by one means or another learns a set of transferable number symbols: 1, 2, 3, 4. Now he may take these new descriptions and apply them to the old structural descriptions of the square to yield the new properties of four-sidedness and four-corneredness. Presumably, many such features of a square are not stored initially as part of the structural description but are constructed on demand. Once constructed, they may or may not be added to the structural description.

Secondly, it is tempting to assume that these representations are "articulated" into known constituents for the perceiver. While structural descriptions are constructed from a limited set of features and relations and therefore possess an implicit structure, the resulting structural descriptions function as integrated units which cannot ordinarily be decomposed into an articulated set of properties and relations. Thus, although the structural descriptions for the display in 1. would represent the shapes and relations involved, those shapes and relations may not be perceived independently of the whole description of which they are part. This is particularly true for objects but may also be true for relations between objects. Thus the explication and articulation of these features is, we shall argue, a major achievement in the development of spatial knowledge.

Thirdly, these structural descriptions are often described in a single symbolic form—a square, for example, in terms of Euclidean dimensions—whereas, we shall argue, they are composed of a set of non-commensurate codes, some preserving topological relations, others preserving angles and distances; some relating object to viewer, others relating objects to each other. Hence, although we shall often talk in Euclidean terms we do not wish to suggest that mental spatial cognitions are exclusively Euclidean.

Finally, we may note that the properties in terms of which situations are represented are not the properties of the objects per se any more than the representations of the objects are copies of the objects per se. Rather, they are constructions build out of the representational resources of the cognitive system. As Count Korzibsky would say, they are maps not territories, and they are accurate in so far as they give a correct account of the events they symbolize.

These structures constitute the fundamental part of one's empirical knowledge, and spatial information is implicit in these structural descriptions of objects and events. That is, spatial cognition is embedded, originally, in one's knowledge of reality. When these spatial structures are pulled out of their embeddedness in the structural descriptions of objects and events, we have the beginnings of spatial knowledge.

But these cognitive structures, incorporating spatial information, are constructed for a purpose. These purposes are reflected in the *meaning* system, to which we now turn.

The Meanings of Objects and Events

Any object, we have suggested, may be mentally represented in terms of a structural description composed of properties and relations, which is sufficiently general to group together objects and events that can be safely regarded as equivalent, and sufficiently detailed to distinguish those which it is important to differentiate. If an object or event or display can "take" a particular structural description, that object or event is assigned the meaning associated with the structural description. Bartlett (1932) described this process of relating a given pattern to some known schema as "the effort after meaning" (p. 20).

These meanings, then, are somewhat different from the structural descriptions with which they are associated. They mark the significance of any particular object or event and determine the roles the mental representation may play in any means-end analysis. Significance could mark, for example, what x may do to me, what I may do to/with x, what role it plays in a routine or format (Brunner, Roy, & Ratner, in press), and so on. Secondly, meanings, unlike structural descriptions are articulated, that is they are subject to mental manipulation such that they may be inserted and recombined in attempts to achieve a goal, and we suppose, they are subject to consciousness.

More importantly, meanings and meaning differences provide the occasion for the construction and differentiation of structural descriptions. In this way the perceptual recognition routines we have outlined as structural descriptions are motivated. If it becomes important to differentiate, for example, celery from rhubarb, the structural descriptions will be modified accordingly. We shall consider this interplay between structural descriptions and meanings more fully in the next chapter.

Perception, then, involves both meanings and structural descriptions. If an object or event "satisfies" a particular description, that is, if all (or a majority) of the properties of a structural description are satisfied by the stimulus display, then the meaning associated with it, as we have said, is assigned to that object or event. Perception, then, involves both the pick-up of stimulus information and the assignment of meaning.

Finally, the differentiation of meanings from structural descriptions is particularly important in that it provides a possible means of relating perception to language. Meanings and significances provide the associative links between concepts and hence between words: Meanings provide the basis for the "sense" of a word; Structural descriptions provide the ground for the reference by specifying the intension of the concept, the set of properties common to the members of the class or concept. This too would require a good deal of unpacking so we can do little more than mention Frege's famous distinction at this point (see Lyons, 1977) and promise to return to it in the next chapter.

This view of the role of meaning in perception is not dissimilar from the traditional associationistic one. In the essay "Towards a new theory of vision", Bishop Berkeley (1966) pointed out that the sensations resulting from the sights and sounds of an approaching object come to be associated. Once associated, any sensation picked up auditorially or visually can yield the perception of that object because they have been repeatedly encountered together. Meaning, therefore, defined the difference between sensations and perceptions. The sensation of redness of a certain shape, when meaning is added, can be perceived as a stop light. Titchener (1910, p. 174) made this idea explicit in his core-context theory of meaning. Meaning is the context that accrues associatively to the sensory core of a perception. The codings of these sensory events to which a meaning is attached makes up the structural description for an object or event. The problem with this view, as we have seen, is that it assumes that sense-data is picked up prior to and independently of the interpretation one assigns. Rather, we suggest that the meanings are often prior to the structural descriptions—in that case that structural descriptions are differentiated after one constructs a meaning difference. On other occasions, an object or event which fails to "take" a structural description may lead to a new description and subsequently to a search for meaning. But it is necessary to consider in more detail the relation between our proposed form of mental representation and some of the more promising current alternative proposals.

2 On the Formation of Structural Descriptions and Meanings for Objects and Events

"No doubt the perception of shape depends on certain universal neurophysiological characteristics of the perceptual system."

Miller and Johnson-Laird

In the preceding chapter, we gave some arguments as to the role of mental representations and some suggestions as to their form. In this chapter we look more specifically at the rules for formation of both the structural descriptions and the meanings which make up any particular mental representation of space. We conclude the chapter by comparing our proposals with some alternative hypotheses.

I. ASSIGNMENT OF STRUCTURAL DESCRIPTIONS

To reiterate our basic assumptions, spatial displays or spatial relations generally are cognized by means of assigning a structural description to that event; to learn about an object or event is to construct a structural description for the event; to recall an event is to retrieve the appropriate stored structural description. Further, each distinctive structural description possesses a distinctive meaning; indeed the latter is an important condition for the construction of the former. Two events that take the same structural description are considered the same, and two events, if it becomes important to differentiate them, that is, if they have different meanings, must be assigned distinctive structural descriptions.

What determines the structural description that is assigned to a particular display? That depends on the characteristics of the display—the properties of the display that satisfy or fail to satisfy particular structural descriptions—the context in which the display occurs and on the character of the perceiver—his prior knowledge, his stage of development, his purpose, expectancies, and most basically on the nature of the mental code. Let us consider some of these more fully.

The properties of objects and displays. The properties of objects or displays whatever their intrinsic properties may be, must be honored by the structural description that is assigned to that object or display if that representation is to have either validity or utility. Regardless of the goals or biases of the perceiver the displays shown in Chapter 1 *cannot* be represented for example as a "square inside circle". Since clearly there is some correspondence between reality and our mental codings of reality, it is tempting to simply hypostatize the features of reality *as being* the features of the mental code as we mentioned earlier or the inverse—to attribute the features of the mental code on to reality. While such a "copy" theory is convenient explanation it is unsatisfactory in that it makes unwarranted claims about reality—that the world consists of features collected together to make objects and the like (Russell, 1946). Rather it seems necessary to say that the world can be correctly described or represented in certain ways—the moon can be correctly described or represented as round, a flag can be correctly described as rectangular, aftershave lotion can be correctly described as a beverage (by some people) and so on. This expedient permits us to honor both the facts that some descriptions are correct while others are incorrect, and yet permits the important possibility that any one representation may subsequently be shown to be wrong and that no description exhausts the features of the objects or events it describes (Goodman, 1978). Thus, there are a vast number of true descriptions for any display. For 1, they may consist of such things as: ball and box, little ball near larger box or changing the level of description from concrete object to geometrical form, as circle outside square, circle to the left of square, and so on.

If there are such a large number of true structural descriptions that may be assigned to a display what then determines the form any particular structural description will take?

The context of the display. The context of a display is one important factor that determines the assignment of a particular structural description. Consider again the alternative displays shown in Chapter 1. After viewing the alternatives in figure 1, the alternatives in figure 2 are perceived as similar. For figure 1, the code or structural descriptions *in* and *out* served to differentiate the alternatives. Applying these descriptions to 2, both figures satisfy the same structural description and so they are perceived as same.

1.   ○ ☐   ○ ☐   2.   ○ ☐   ○ ☐

        A   B   A   B

The code has the effect of making even visually distinct options appear similar. As shown, if we employ structural descriptions differing in their features of *in* versus *out,* alternatives in 1 would be regarded as different and those in 2 as same. If it becomes important to differentiate the alternatives in 2, then the structural description could be elaborated to include some distance feature such as *near* versus *far.* If the code now consisted of a pair of features *out + near,* again some alternatives would be perceived as similar, as for example those in figure 3.

3.

A   B

If it were important those could again be differentiated by elaborating the structural description: out-near-left. The new elaborated code would now exclude the second alternative of 3 but admit the alternative shown as 4. Again, the code would be elaborated: out, near, left, on the midline.

4.

Gibson (1969) has amply shown experimentally the progressive elaboration of such featural descriptions for a variety of perceptual patterns.

The endless variety of alternative displays would seem to require an extremely large number of structural descriptions to differentiate them. However, if features were binary, the number of alternatives that could be differentiated even if the objects related (the circle and the square) remained constant, would be extremely large—20 such features would differentiate over 1,000,000 alternatives. The more typical case is that differences and sometimes even substantial differences go unnoticed. One function of perception is to treat things which could be differentiated if necessary, as if they were equivalent. What then determines the elaboration and differentiation of structural descriptions? That is, when will two objects or events be assigned the same structural description and when will different structural descriptions be constructed? This process, we suggest, reflects the purposes and meanings of the perceiver.

Dispositions, Purposes, and Meanings of the Perceiver

The structural description assigned to any object or event is a function of the relation of that object or event to the purposes or goals, broadly conceived, of the child or adult. Our view is functionalist after James, Dewey, Bruner, and Piaget. Structural descriptions are constructed and elaborated not as copies of the stimulus but in the service of adaptive action. Generally, cognitive structures depend upon the activities that those structures are to regulate. To illustrate, a human, being a mobile animal, would require and construct a more elaborate system for representing space than would a barnacle. The structural description a human assigns to objects, events, and layouts will reflect the activities in which he is engaging, planning to engage, and prepared by nature to engage in. Predominant in these activities are such things as balance, locomotion, prehension, recognition of recurrent events, and the like. To perform these tasks successfully would require some sensitivity to gravitational vertical, to invariants of shape across changes in position, to the spatial ordering and spatial relations—as well as to sizes, distances, and so on.

The functions which are served by cognition put their imprint upon those cognitive processes in two ways. Evolutionarily, we may expect that an organism specialized for such physical activities as locomotion, prehension, and manipulation of objects, would be correspondingly specialized to form appropriate mental representations for regulating those activities. Thus if the foot was specialized to support vertical posture and bi-pedal locomotion, the brain could be expected to be similarly specialized to serve the function of maintaining that posture and directing that locomotion. Considerable research is currently being directed towards recovering just such biological predispositions or "preparedness" in animals (Jenkins, 1973; Seligman, 1970) as well as in human infants (Bower, 1978; Leslie, in press; Meltzoff & Moore, 1977; Trevarthen, 1980).

Such predispositions for representing events in a particular way are the bias that a child or any organism brings to experience. Yet these biases anticipate and reflect the functions that these representations are to serve. As a result the representations are restricted by the predispositions of the organism rather than being neutral, objective, copies of reality.

Consider how this could happen. Certain cues structured in certain ways, for example, the sensitivity to vertical orientation required for maintaining erect posture, or the sensitivity to relations between elements within an object or between objects in a spatial layout, may because of their functional significance, come to be the biological basis for structural descriptions of objects and events. These aspects of descriptions make up at least a part of the internal "vocabulary" of representations out of which the structural description for any particular object or event or layout is constructed. But if the infant has available such a "vocabulary", he may apply it to virtually any perceptual event with the consequence of constructing a structural description even in the absence of an immediate purpose, significance or goal.[1] Primary features of this "vocabulary" of forms would appear in many structural descriptions. Features common for more than one structural description would help explain verbal overextensions. A child's calling a moon a ball, or calling a "ball" of spinach a moon (Bowerman, 1977; E. Clark, 1973a) would seem to indicate that the feature *round* is an important constituent of the structural descriptions for the representation of balls, moons, as well as of rolls of spinach.

Evolutionarily, therefore, we may expect that the human species will have a bias to code spatial relations in a way appropriate to action, objects, and events which serve the kinds of activities in which they engage. Moreover, we may expect that structural descriptions may capture some differences between objects and events for which there is not yet any known functional difference.

On any particular occasion, however, what the child or adult is attempting to do will determine what information, including spatial information, is selected and how it is represented. If, for example, it becomes important to treat two relatively similar displays as different, as for example if one leads to a reward while the other does not, then structural descriptions will be differentiated; an object or event in question which satisfies one of the structural descriptions will not satisfy the other. In the short run, then, meaning differences dominate the construction and elaboration of structural descriptions.

Consider a non-spatial analogy. In linguistics, it is conventional to define phonemes as units of sound which are correlated with differences in meaning. Thus the difference between /pin/ and /bin/ is phonemic and /p/ and /b/ are different phonemes because the difference in sound corresponds to a difference in meaning. But not all detectable sound differences are phonemic. A phoneme such as /p/ is actually pronounced somewhat differently depending upon its phonological environment. These sound differences are ordinarily not heard because they are not correlated with meaning differences. These sound differences are called allophones. The /p/ in pin is aspirated, that is, it is accompanied by a burst of wind, while the /p/ in spin is not. Yet these sound differences are ordinarily not heard because they do not correspond to meaning differences. Equally slight sound differences, where they do indicate meaning differences, that is, when they are phonemic, are easily heard. The point to be drawn from this example is that not all sound differences will be represented in a structural description but rather a structural description will be elaborated in the service of meaning differences. That is, we are reversing the usual cause-effect (stimulus-response) relation between a stimulus and representation. Rather than say

---

[1]Robin Campbell and Melissa Bowerman helped us see this point.

that stimulus differences result in differences in structural descriptions and meanings (the naive realist view) we are arguing the reverse: two events which "take" the same structural description (and hence have the same meaning) will look alike. We do so because of the role that meanings play in the construction and elaboration of structural descriptions.

However, we may take our phoneme analogy one step further. Sound differences which are phonemic will be heard as constitutive of "possible" words even in the absence of a meaning. So too, basic elements of the "vocabulary" of structural descriptions, if activated, suggest the presence of a distinctive object or event in advance of the assignment of meaning. If, for example, no known word or associated meaning is available, young children, as mentioned earlier, take as a hypothesis for the meaning some concept with an overlapping structural description.

Even in the short run, however, in which the structural descriptions directly reflect the goals, purposes, meanings, and significance of events, we would argue that the structural descriptions will be constructed from the same basic set of spatial properties and relations. To give an example that we shall encounter later, even adults in making judgments of spatial orientation in which position is completely irrelevant cannot avoid processing, and being misled by the position in which that line occurs. This suggests that position is a fundamental constituent of the mental representation of space.

To summarize, while structural descriptions indirectly honor the character of the objects they represent, as a map does a territory, they directly reflect the mental resources of the perceiver—the biases and structures of his mental representational apparatus from which he constructs his structural descriptions — the perceived or inferred context in which an object or display is encountered, and the meanings, purposes and goals of the perceiver. The result, ordinarily, is a structural description plus a meaning, both of which are attributed to the stimulus that occasioned the perception. (So when we see a cow, we say "There is a cow" and not "I'm entertaining a mental representation which has an associated meaning of the concept cow".)

There is, nevertheless, considerable variability in the structural descriptions that may be assigned to a single display and to alternative displays. Some presumably are simple such that objects corresponding to them are easily recognized, discriminated and remembered while others are so complex that they take years of study and practice to master and even then the assignment of objects and events to them may be slow and calculated. It is the nature of these structural descriptions, their progressive elaboration and subsequent explication, that is our primary concern. But before we proceed to analyze them, it is necessary to give a more adequate description of the role that *meaning* plays in the construction of structural descriptions.

II. MEANINGS AND STRUCTURAL DESCRIPTIONS

In the foregoing we have argued that meanings are decisive at every point in the construction, elaboration, and differentiation of structural descriptions. Whenever a meaning difference occurs, we have suggested we shall find differences in structural descriptions. Thus if some apples are found to be inedible, a search begins for perceptual features which may be added to the existing structural descriptions which will permit the assignment of those apples to the new meaning categories—edible apples/inedible apples. Further, we have argued that whenever an object is perceived it is perceived as a meaningful object *by means* of a structural description. From those considerations it may be concluded that the meaning of an object is the structural description for that object; that the meaning is simply the collection of formal and functional features which make up the structural description for that object.

Our suggestion, however, is that the meaning system is represented and organized somewhat independently of the structural descriptions for objects and events. Although an adequate treatment of meaning would make up a book on its own right (which we couldn't write), we suggest that meanings represent the intentions, purposes, and goals of the perceiver, while the structural descriptions of objects reflect the properties appropriate to assigning that object to a meaning category. Meanings are not represented as part of the structural descriptions of objects but rather they are the criterion in terms of which features are selected, detected and added to a structural description.

Consider the meaning of an apple as something to eat. The meaning is not a part of the structural description; rather it is the criterion in terms of which the child or adult assembles distinguishing features into a structural description. The perceptual features which enter into the implicit structural description are the sensory features which are cues to significance as an edible object—its color, size, texture, shape, tartness and the like. The features which get into the structural description are those which are reliable perceptual clues to its meaning as an edible fruit. The search for distinguishing cues will end, presumably, as soon as the edible object can be readily recognized and discriminated from the inedible and the non-fruit ones. But the meaning of edibility is not a part of that structural description, it is part of the meaning system, the system of significances—things to eat, things to wear, things to expect in a barnyard, and so on.

We have, then, two terms in our explanation of subjects' knowledge or concepts. A concept is a structural description plus a meaning. The concept "apple" has the meaning of edibility, portability, purchasability in a supermarket, plus the structural description by means of which apples are assigned that meaning. And we have given meaning a priority in that it is the criterion in terms of which structural descriptions are formulated.

That emphasis on meaning, however, is misleading in one important way: It overlooks the putative fact that both nature and technology have conspired to make the experienced world perceptually distinct on just those lines that are useful for distinguishing meanings. Consider smell. An infant need not do deep detective work to find out the perceptual features that differentiate wholesome from rotten food; the child is particularly sensitive to smells and the differences between smells are highly related to the differences in edibility. Generally, perceptual sensitiveness of the child are "attuned" to differences which are important to meanings. While in the above we emphasized that the child has a meaning criterion in terms of which he or she initiates a perceptual search for distinguishing perceptual features, it is important to note that the opposite can also occur, namely the child may form a structural description on the basis of the features he or she is particularly predisposed to process and only secondarily look for its meaning.

We may imagine that the child is in the process of constructing two types of analyses while looking for ways of mapping one on to the other. On the one hand the child is constructing and elaborating the meanings and significances of objects and events, and on the other he or she is constructing and elaborating structural descriptions to permit the reliable recognition and discrimination of those objects and events. As Bransford and McCarrel (1974) have shown, one could learn to recognize relatively unknown tools designed to perform very specialized functions without knowing what any of those functions were. In our terms the construction and elaboration of structural descriptions can occur without the corresponding elaboration of meaning. On the other hand, one could have developed a fairly elaborate meaning without the corresponding structural description for recognition. Putnam (1975) describes just such a situation: he suggests one may have a meaning for "beech" trees but no procedures for recognizing or discriminating them. This is the converse of the case mentioned earlier of having recognition routines for objects without corresponding meanings. Ordinarily, the two systems develop together; the formation of a structural description leading to a search for meaning, and the formation of a meaning leading to the attempt to construct an appropriate structural description. Put this way, it is clear that these two activities are similar to those described by Piaget (1952) as assimilation and accommodation, the former involving changes in structural descriptions without corresponding changes in meaning; the latter involving changes in the meaning system without corresponding changes in structural descriptions. And as Piaget points out, these two are ordinarily in equilibrium.

Two recent cognitive theories have set the problems of meanings at the center of their accounts of perception and knowledge. Neisser (1976) building upon Gibson's (1966) theory of "affordances", has argued that the meanings of an object or situation are directly perceived. Rather than treat meaning as something which is added to object perception, meanings are perceived directly as an affordance of the stimulus—what the stimulus will afford or permit the perceiver to do. Perception involves the pick-up of the significances of objects and events. But since any one object or event affords many forms of activity, Neisser suggests there is some schematic control over perception which selects between seeing a chair as something to sit on, something which permits the changing of a light bulb, the blocking of a door, the walking of a toddler, and so on.

The strength of the theory is that it allows for the pick-up of meanings in a way complementary to the pick-up of formal features of displays. It, as we said, puts meanings back into the center of perception. But it does so, we suggest, in a somewhat incorrect way.

We objected earlier to the theory that perceptual features were simply picked up from the environment as copies; if the theory then states that meanings are also simply picked up from the environment as copies, we must also reject it. Rather as we argued, structural descriptions are never copies of environmental events—as Arnheim (1974) has said, representations are "their equivalent in a given medium." The same point is made in contemporary philosophy of science: "Our best scientific results to date thus provide knowledge merely of the structural properties of physical objects, states, and events; the question as to what are their intrinsic properties must be left entirely open" (Pucetti, 1978, p. 66).

In other words, again we are objecting to attributing to the objects our interpretations of them. Rather than project our meanings back onto the objects, we would assign meanings to the intentions of the knower and then use these meanings as the criteria for constructing structural descriptions for recognizing those objects. Then the meanings are in the heads of the knowers (where they belong) rather than in the stimulus.

The second major proposal incorporating meanings into perceptions comes from Miller and Johnson-Laird (1976). Their concern is to show how perception relates to language. To do so they differentiate percepts from concepts and add: "...Much more than perceptual paradigms must be acquired before a label can be used as a word" (p. 234). They point out that labels are tied to concepts and one may have a concept without having the corresponding perceptual routines. In addition, they suggest that concepts have the distinctive property of being related to other concepts and hence of specifying how words are related to other words to form semantic fields.

Again, Miller and Johnson-Laird's views on the relation between perception and meanings are close to our own and as we shall see later their analysis of the structure of space is highly relevant to our enterprise. However, they are somewhat unclear as to how a perceptual predicate (a structural description) relates to a concept. Our suggestion is that the meaning system originates in the plans and intentions of the child and that the meanings serve to organize the construction and elaboration of the perceptual routines which we call structural descriptions. But the meaning system as it becomes articulated serves as the basis for language learning. That is, we do not assume that the organization of the meaning system depends exclusively upon the acquisition of language. But like Miller and Johnson-Laird we assume that the relations between words are determined by the relation between the concepts of meanings and not through the perceptual predicates.

We have, therefore, four properties of meanings which indicate both their differences from and relations to structural descriptions. First, they mark the significance of object and events, they are the articulated constituents of goal directed intentional actions, and they serve as the criteria for the construction of recognition routines we called structural descriptions. Finally, we suggest, they provide a level of structure, commensurate with the structure of language, indicating, for example, the ways in which words are related.[2]

III. REPRESENTATION OF SPATIAL INFORMATION

We are now ready to address the problem of the mental representation of spatial information. Some spatial information, we shall argue, is implicit in the structural description of objects. That is, the spatial cues are used as part of the recognition routine for particular objects and events. The nature of this spatial information used in object and event perception is one of our concerns. Whatever its organization, there seems little doubt that size, form, orientation, as well as various spatial relations, are implicit in the structural descriptions of objects, layouts, and events. Yet because this spatial information is implicit in structural descriptions, it is not known *as such* by the perceiver.

What is known *as such,* we suggest, are systems of meanings. How does the spatial information implicit in the structural descriptions of objects and

---

[2]Ian Howard has pointed out that the distinction we draw between structural descriptions and meanings may be too severe because the same feature may appear in the concept as either a structural description or a meaning depending on a set of contextual and other variables. He prefers to refer to these as different "descriptive domains", maintaining the distinction but loosening their categorical difference (Howard, 1982).

We would agree that there is nothing "semantic" about the difference, they may both involve the same features, but we consider it to be important to mark the implicit and automatic nature of the former and the intentional, conscious nature of the latter.

events come to be known as spatial meanings or spatial concepts. Our suggestion, which we shall outline presently, is that it is the meaning system that is expanded while the spatial information remains much the same. In a word, spatial concepts are implicit in our structural description of object concepts. The elaboration of meaning systems, primarily the elaboration of symbolic forms, is the means whereby we may "interrogate" our structural descriptions to produce spatial concepts. It is, we shall argue in the next chapter, an enterprise in the explication of spatial cognition.

IV. ALTERNATIVE THEORIES OF MENTAL REPRESENTATION: CODES, PROTOTYPES, AND IMAGES

Structural Descriptions and Coding Theory

We have adopted the more complex term "structural descriptions" rather than the simpler and more familiar term "code" because of our assumption that the representations of events have an internal componential structure. Whereas a code implies a set of descriptions with an homogeneous internal structure, structural descriptions imply a more complex and principled internal structure. To illustrate, whereas the code "top" would be an unanalyzed entity, the structural description for "top" would be one of a set of values on one of a set of dimensions, thus (vertical +, polar +). That is, the code is assumed to be analyzable into a set of properties and/or features. Furthermore, these features are organized, not simply as a list, but as a structure composed of sets of elements or arguments related by a spatial term or predicate thus: in (circle, square), i.e. the circle is in the square.

A further reason for adopting the term structural description rather than code is because the latter, in addition to being unspecified, are ad hoc, new codes can always be added or invented, and so on. New structural descriptions, on the other hand, are generated from the same set of underlying features and dimensions. We assume therefore, that development consists not of the ad hoc accumulation of codes but of the elaboration of structural descriptions generated, at least largely, from the same underlying set of features and dimensions. This criticism is less true of the theory of codes presented by Bruner et al (1966) which differentiated enactive, iconic, and symbolic forms of representation. The advantage of that theory was that the first two codes could be seen as private and pre-linguistic, somewhat like the ones proposed herein. The limit of that proposal is that the distinctions are difficult to maintain. If images are like pictures they are just as symbolic as sentences as Gombrich (1974) has shown. If they are not like pictures, but just sensory memories, they still are problematic as we have noted (and shall again note). And finally, they are unanalyzed in terms of their structure hence they give no clue to the continuities in development which are of concern here. For example, even enactive representations may preserve such relations as up/down, above/below that bias the pick-up and use of spatial information, and our interest is in capturing those relations. Hence, we present our views not in opposition to a theory of codes but as an extension or elaboration of such a theory. Gombrich (1960) stated the perspective that is shared by code theory and a theory of structural descriptions:

> The individual visual information...is entered as it were, upon a pre-existing blank or formulary. And, as often happens with blanks, if they have no provision for certain kinds of information we consider essential, it is just too bad for the information. (p.73).

Our question is what is the structure of that formulary?
Pylyshyn makes the same point this way:

> ...what is occurring in perception can best be characterized as the construction of an internal description of an event using an internal vocabulary of available concepts. The internal vocabulary arises from a number of sources and is being continually refined and reorganized. It arises from inherent properties of our biological equipment (these might perhaps be called innate concepts), from our culture, from our linguistic environment, and from interactions among these. (p. 170).

Our one reservation is with Pylyshyn's use of the word "concept"; we reserve that term for the explicit meaning based representation and not for the implicit features of which they are composed.

The concept of a "structural description" is borrowed from the analysis of language. In linguistics, structural descriptions are the underlying relations that hold between sentence constituents. In language it is clear that the meaning of a sentence is not the simple summation of a set of word meanings, in the famous example, a venetian blind is not a blind venetian, or Wittgenstein's, "Don't regard a hesitant assertation as an assertion of hesitancy" (1958, p. 122). Further, in language it is clear that new sentences are not merely new symbols but rather novel yet permissible or rule-governed combinations of meaning constituents. We suggest that both of these properties characterize the structural descriptions employed in perception generally, and spatial cognition specifically. We admit, however, that we have not gone far in unravelling the structural descriptions employed for the representation of space let alone for "mentalese" generally (Fodor, 1975; Pylyshyn, 1981), yet, perhaps, they can be characterized sufficiently to outline the roots of spatial knowledge.

Schema Theory and Structural Descriptions

We intend that our proposals regarding structural descriptions be taken as an elaboration of schema theory advanced by Bartlett (1932), Piaget (1952), Nelson (1974) and most recently Neisser (1976). A schema is the basic organizational unit of knowledge. It is the mental unit which coordinates perception and action by representing both what is known about an object or event and the meaning or significance of that object or event to the knower. It, therefore, represents an amalgam of knowledge, skill, and values. Piaget states:

> Every schema of assimilation constitutes a true totality, that is to say, an ensemble of sensorimotor elements mutually dependent or unable to function without each other (1952 , p. 244).

Neisser adds:

> A schema is that portion of the entire perceptual cycle which is internal to the perceiver, modifiable by experience, and somehow specific to what is being perceived. The schema accepts information at sensory surfaces and is changed by that information; it directs movements and exploratory activities that make more information available, by which it is further modified (1976, p. 54).

Most helpful to the present account is Nelson's (1974) discussion of early concepts. Nelson explicitly differentiates the functional aspects of a concept which bear on the meaning of that concept from the formal properties or features of the concept which are used for the identification of the members of that conceptual category. Concepts are formed on the basis of function (or meaning) and new members are assigned on the basis of hierarchically organized features: "new concept instances [are identified] by noting the salient stable ("invariant") characteristics of members included in the concept on functional grounds and forming a hierarchy of identificational attributes therefrom" (p. 276).

Common to all of these descriptions is the view that schema combine both procedures for recognition and action as well as specify a functional meaning or significance. Like them we have argued that objects or events are known as functional or meaningful wholes not simply as collections of features; conscious knowledge is organized largely in terms of meanings. The structural descriptions in terms of which those meanings are represented are *not* subject to awareness; they are not known as such. Neisser adds in this vein:

> In most cases we are unaware of the fine structure of our own perceptual activity. We do not usually note the successive views of an object that eye movements provide or the individual pressures at the skin that occur as we explore it with our hands: what we experience is the object. Similarly, we are aware of the meanings and affordances that the perceptual cycle reveals, not of the detailed phases of the cycle itself. What we later remember is also the object (or event) and its meaning... (p. 75).

Two differences in emphasis between the view we have advanced herein and those described above may be mentioned. Firstly, our interest is primarily in the architecture of this implicit knowledge. In that respect our theory is more similar to that proposed by researchers in cognitive science whose work we mentioned earlier. Secondly, our emphasis is on the nature of the spatial information which enters into those structural descriptions or schema for objects and events. We have suggested that the spatial information which enters into structural descriptions for various objects and events may possess a somewhat similar form, and further, that the spatial structures which subsequently become explicit in symbols again reflect this common form.

Our analysis of the nature of structural descriptions permits us to account for two other important analysis of the perception of objects-prototype theory and image theory.

Prototype and Structural Descriptions

A possible alternative to the view that objects (and forms) are represented by means of structural descriptions is offered by prototype theory. In that theory, a best or typical example serves as the basis for a representation rather than a set of properties or features. Judgments of similarity and the recognition of new instance would be made by comparing that display to the best example or prototype.

The theory of prototypes has three important roots. Putnam (1975) in his analysis of the meanings of natural-kind terms argued that formal definitions (logically related criterial features) were not plausible candidates for the representation of lexical meanings because ordinarily one is never too certain of the extension of a concept—is that yellow metal that the jeweller shows you really gold? Determination of the extension of a term by means of formalizing and testing for the presence of the critical features is the task of an expert, not of an ordinary speaker of the language. As an alternative Putnam suggested that ordinary meanings are represented as stereotypes; the typical set of beliefs held about the object in question: "stereotypes capture features possessed by paradigmatic members of the class in question" for example "stereotypical tigers are striped" (p. 250).

Just such typicality effects have been found in experimental studies which measured the length of time it took subjects to decide on the truth of statements involving typical members of a class "A dog is an animal" and non-typical members of a class "A monkey is an animal". Smith, Shoben, and Rips (1974) found that such judgments involved two stages. The first appeared to involved the comparison of the example to a prototype; if it was clearly similar to the prototype or widely divergent from it, subjects make a quick yes or no response. However, if the example was near the boundary, subjects made a more careful, analytical, and slower response presumably on the basis of the criterial or defining features which Putnam described as being more specialized.

The role of prototypes in the recognition and memory of perceptual attributes and concrete objects have been shown even more clearly by Eleanor Rosch. Building upon Berlin and Kay's (1969) finding of a universal set of "basic" color terms, and of the Gestalt psychologists demonstrations of "basic" or "good" visual forms, Rosch (summarized in 1977) showed that those complex objects such as birds and furniture which were judged to be most typical of a class were also most easily learned, recognized, and remembered. Rosch concludes:

> the categories appear to be coded in the mind neither by means of a list of each individual member of the category nor by means of a list of formal criteria necessary and sufficient for category membership but, rather, in terms of a prototype of a typical category member. The most cognitively economical code for a category is, in fact, a concrete image of an average category member. (p. 30)

These findings are important for several reasons. Firstly, they show that category systems are not completely arbitrary but reflect the cognizing structures of the mind. And secondly, they give some indication of the form of the mental codes by means of which we represent objects and events. Finally, the show that these mental representations are not analyzed into explicit formal constituents. But what is the status of a prototype? Is a prototype the particular object or event which best exemplifies a particular concept as Rosch at times suggests? Or is a prototype a mental representation which closely matches particularly typical instances? It cannot be the former for as both Bransford and Franks (1971) and Rosch (1977) have shown, subjects may form a prototypic representation for a class of displays without having ever encountered the most prototypical member. Rather a prototype must be a mental representation constructed by the viewer as a representation of a particular display or series of displays. What then is the internal structure of a prototype? Presumably it consists of what we call a structural description. Hence we would argue that prototypes are not mental representations at all. Rather objects and events will be taken as typical or prototypical if they are highly congruent with a particular structural description. Applying this notion to comparison tasks, we would say that objects and events which satisfy all or most of the properties of the structural description will be quickly recognized and easily remembered while those that match only a part will be assigned more slowly, on the basis of an explicit analysis of two or three features which were previously implicit in the structural description for that class of objects.

The theory of prototypes, then, differs from the theory of structural descriptions plus meanings that we have offered here in three ways. First, whereas Rosch claims that attributes are "in the real world", we have argued that they are "in the mind" and simply represent or stand for whatever it is that is out there in the world. Secondly, the role of significance, function, and meaning, generally in the construction of structural descriptions, is at the center of our account whereas it is somewhat peripheral to Rosch's account of how categories are formed. Rosch argues that basic categories are constructed for reasons of cognitive economy in that (1) class members have a maximum number of attributes in common, (2) class members are the recipients of common motor movements, and (3) class members have maximally similar shape. We have argued that structural descriptions are constructed and elaborated to honor significance and function as Brown (1958) and Nelson (1974) and others before us. And thirdly, Rosch argues that the mental representation is "an image-of an average category member" whereas we have argued that the mental representation consists of an unanalyzed structural description plus a meaning. As mentioned above, we would say that a prototypical instance is one that best satisfies a particular structural description. Conversely, the activation of a structural description would produce a mental image corresponding to a typical member of the class. Thus the notion of a structural description could account for both prototypes and images as well as provide a structure suitable for unpacking in the course of the development of the perception of form as we shall see in the next chapter. Like the theory of codes, the theory of prototypes is not an alternative to the theory of structural descriptions, but rather an important exemplification of it.

Images and Structural Descriptions

A number of cognitive theorists have recently begun to provide evidence of the importance of mental images in a variety of cognitive tasks. Mental images have been found to serve as memory aids for remembering such things as the contents of a room or of lists of words (Paivio, 1971); they have been found to conflict with patterns of visual search (Brooks, 1968), and they have been found to be used in mentally rotating different visual displays into congruence (Shepard & Metzler, 1971), and in retrieving various facts about known objects (Kosslyn, 1975). While some earlier image theories hypothesized that these images were direct copies of visual displays, constructed independently of and prior to the assimilation, interpretation or the assignment of meanings to those displays, most of these more recent views agree with Pylyshyn that such images are interpreted; they consist of interpreted descriptions of objects and events, and they may contain nonvisual relations such as causal ones.

In spite of this, most of these theories hold that mental images form an alternative mental code for the representation of knowledge. Posner (1973) for example suggests that letters of the alphabet may be represented in a visual code based on a stored image or template of the appearance of the letter, in addition to the more conventional meaning or name code. He bases this conclusion on the facts that if a subject is shown, for example, an upper case A, she will be able to judge a second letter as having the same name more quickly if it also is upper case than if it is lower case. The first letter not only sets up a representation of the meaning of the letter but also of the physical appearance and the latter facilitates the comparison.

Again, what is the status of the "visual code"? It is tempting to assume that the template or visual code is an uninterpreted image which is assigned prior to meaning. But that is somewhat misleading in that the template is formed for a meaning category, the known letter *a*. Rather, the template must correspond to a recognition program for the letter. As Neisser (1976) puts it, "...images are anticipations...to have a perceptual set for something is to have an image" (p. 144-5).

While we agree with Neisser that images are basically not different from object schemas and cognitive maps which are employed in ordinary perception, it is important to add that one may have a schema, or as we prefer a structural description, and yet be unable to activate it in the absence of an object. Thus we suppose that dogs have a structural description for bones but we doubt that they can activate that description in the form of an image. The difference between schema for recognition and schema for imaging marks an important development in Piaget's theory of intellectual development. It may be that different schema are involved, or it may be, as we suspect, that while the schema are the same, the means for activating them are lacking in the first case.

We relate images to structural descriptions in the following way. As we have said, representations consist of meanings plus structural descriptions. For most perceptual purposes, the meanings are conscious and the structural description employed in the assignment of meaning remain implicit. Imagery involves the process of bringing some aspects of those structural descriptions into consciousness in their own rights. As we shall argue later, this is both a matter of using meanings to retrieve structural descriptions and of developing symbolic forms for "interrogating" these structural descriptions. For the moment it is sufficient to note that concepts composed of structural descriptions plus meanings provide an alternative to the two code theories. We shall return to the problem of images and spatial representation in the final chapter.

3 Representations of Spatial Form

"Objects are unobservable. Only relationships among objects are observable."

Marshall McLuhan

In the preceding chapter we argued that our knowledge of the world was stored in terms of sets of structural descriptions. Recognition of an object occurs when that object matches some stored structural description. Further, we suggested that the object concept consists of both this structural description, or recognition procedure, and a set of intentions or meanings which motivates the construction of and search through the stored structural descriptions. This conceptual system of structural descriptions plus meanings is organized at the level of everyday objects, what Brown (1958) calls the "level of usual utility" and Rosch (1977) calls "basic level objects." A lollipop, for example, is recognized as such because it can take the particular structural description for lollipop which includes visual/spatial properties such as portable, sweet, and so on, and satisfy the significance or intention or meaning of "things to eat".

Descriptions at the level of ordinary functional objects is, we suggest, the primary level of representation in that it permits both the recognition of well-known objects and events as well as the assignment of novel objects or events to established categories. As Neisser (1976) has argued, they serve primarily as anticipatory schema for ordinary perception and action. The basis of this level of representation is our purposeful, goal directed interactions with objects and events; the structural descriptions reflect the significance of those objects and events to the organism that constructs those representations. The meanings most appropriate for these interactions with the environment are primarily those which designate and differentiate these objects on functional grounds. Although the code primarily describes general classes, such as dogs, pennys, trees and the like, particular instances, such as "my toothbrush", "mommy", and so on may be represented when they possess distinctive significance by elaborating the structural description to the level appropriate for recognition and discrimination.

The information in the structural description by which we recognize objects, we have argued, is largely implicit; the colors, shapes, sizes, locations and so on that provide the basis for object identification and discrimination are usually neither known nor attended to as such. Yet it is these perceptual features which are responsible for our identification of objects. We recognize a stop sign because it is red, round, and mounted atop an upright support; we may recognize a lollipop because it is round and mounted atop a vertical stick. Yet because of their meaning differences, they are not perceived as the same; we are not tempted to lick the stop sign nor to slow-up upon seeing a lollipop. But on further analysis, stop signs and lollipops do have a similar form. The central question of this chapter is: If objects having different significances are seen as different, how does one come to see that they still may have the same form? What is the relation between object perception and form perception? Again, what is the difference between the perception of objects and the perception of features of those objects?

One solution is to say that we perceive both objects and their features. That view harks back to the one we have already discounted, namely, that we perceive both a "given" stimulus and an interpretation of it; all perception is already interpreted in terms of significances, we argued. Furthermore we may note that we are frequently in the position of recognizing an object but are unable to recover the particular visual features by means of which we identified it. How do we recognize a face or the letter "a", for example? Many experiments have provided evidence that we recognize such things by means of sets of visual features of which we are unaware. A good illustration of this comes from some studies of children's perception and copying of a model of a diagonal which were reported a decade ago (Olson, 1970). Children aged 3 to 4 years would look at such a display and say 'No, it is not a crisscross" (see display 1), yet they could neither tell why nor point to the part of the diagonal that was in error. They recognized the display as a whole, by means of features of which they were largely unaware.

1.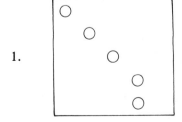

In general, we suggest that perceptual features must be implicit in the structural descriptions for objects. Several studies in this book are, in fact, attempts to recover the specific features and their relations that make up the structural descriptions and permit the recognition of such visual displays as lollipops, obliques and visual scenes. However, given the similarity of features in the structural descriptions as in the case of lollipops and stop signs, how is it that we see these as distinct objects? The answer, we suggested, is that each is associated with a unique intention or significance, that is, it has a meaning. The entertainment of meanings provides the occasion for the examination and construction of structural descriptions. Differences in meaning, in the range of functions the object serves, or the ways in which one responds to the object or display, or their distinctive names, provide the concept differences which are then honored by the construction of distinctive structural descriptions. And while the object meaning is explicit, that is, known as such, the structural descriptions by means of which objects are assigned to that meaning category remain *implicit*. That is to say that the perceptual features by means of which objects are recognized provide information as to the meaning category that the object or event should be assigned to; the information is not identical to the meaning of the object. There is an important difference between perceptual information and meaning (Proffitt, 1977). Moreover, the two together, the perceptual information and meaning, comprise the concept.

The implicitness of structural descriptions is particularly important in regard to space. Spatial information, forms, locations, relations between objects and the like are implicit in the structural descriptions of objects and events. In this sense, spatial knowledge is part of the implicit, structural description by means of which we perceive objects and events. How then do we come to see the similarity between stop signs and lollipops, given that they have different meanings? While spatial information may be used to assign objects and events to meaning categories, it is not, at least initially, perceived in its own right. To illustrate, the depiction below could be perceived as a lollipop or as a circle with a vertical line beneath it (see 2). To

2.

perceive the depiction as a lollipop we utilize the spatial information regarding its circleness and its vertical line to assign the display to the meaningful category of lollipops. That is, we utilize spatial information but we perceive the lollipop. But in the latter case we have perceived the circle and the line in their own right, not merely as clues to object identification. This second type of perception we may call *form perception* and the structural descriptions that make form perception possible we call form representation. The distinction then is one of object perception as opposed to form perception or of knowledge of objects as opposed to knowledge of forms. Notice that exactly the same visual information is utilized in both cases, but the perception is assembled at different levels of meaning and results in different categorization of the displays. Thus the perception of form is embedded in the perception of objects. Our central hypothesis is that *forms* are merely aspects of structural descriptions of objects made explicit.

Perception, the assignment of structural descriptions and meanings, can occur either (or both) at the level of objects or at the level of spatial forms. For both object and form perception, the relationship between the concept—its meaning and structural description—is identical: the concept is explicit and is comprised of an implicit structural description and a unique meaning. The explicit concept for form representation, however, is equivalent to information that was implicit for object representation. The development of form representation, therefore, requires that information implicit in object representation is made explicit and assigned a meaning, thereby becoming a concept in its own right. In this way, it may be said that the differences between object and form representation is marked by a difference in the level of meaning. At the level of forms, different objects may be treated as equivalent provided that they are similar at the explicit level of form, such as the class of round objects. Children's spatial cognition develops both by elaborating structural descriptions so as to permit the recognition of new objects and by the progressive explication (making explicit) of the implicit structures that make up the structural descriptions for the representation of objects.

When meaning is assigned at the level of form, the structural description for that form contains all the lower-level features implicit in the perception of the form. Consider, for example, the structural description for a lollipop which is represented schematically in Figure 3.1

When meaning is assigned at the object level, that is, lollipops, then the structural description includes all those features of lollipop which are implicit in our concept. Thus, objects which are small, round, attached to sticks, sweet, and satisfy the meaning "edible", may be categorized as lollipops. One set of these implicit features refers specifically to the characteristic shape of the object, in this case, roundness. When attention is directed (however that is managed), specifically, to this shape feature it may be assigned a meaning, namely, the concept roundness, and hence assume its own structural description. The form feature then becomes differentiated from the object as shown in Figure 3.2 and may itself become an invariant concept to which new instances are assigned. The class or form "round", is now explicit, has a distinctive meaning relative to the class of shapes, and is defined by all the component features that were below it in

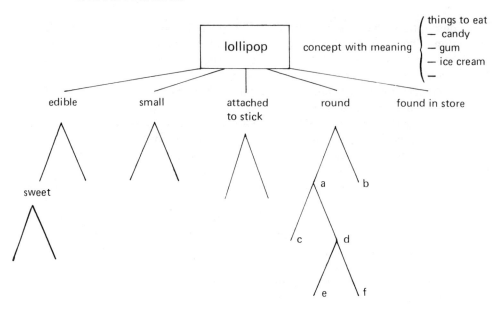

FIG. 3.1   A pictorial representation of the structural description and meaning for the concept *lollipop*.

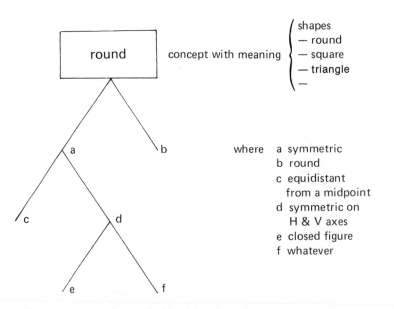

FIG. 3.2   A pictorial representation of the structural description and meaning for the concept *round*.

the original hierarchical structural description for the object. These subordinate features remain implicit for form perception, that is for the meaning of "round", and would include features for symmetry, closedness, and curvature by which we identify roundness. In this way, the structural descriptions for objects may be recursively explicated by assigning meaning at lower levels of the structural descriptions. At the end of the next chapter we shall recast these featured descriptions into propositional ones.

Our suggestion, then, is that there are two levels of spatial representation, one at the object level and one at the form level. But rather than suggesting that these are merely different "codings" localized in different cerebral hemispheres, for example, we have suggested that they are embedded. Object recognition is primary and is based on structural descriptions consisting of spatial form features, which, like the other perceptual features, remain implicit, and unperceived as such. Form features serve merely as one means to the end of object identification. To become conscious of forms themselves, that is to perceive form, involves a whole new set of concepts and meanings different from those required for object perception.

The development of form perception involves explicit attention to part of the structural descriptions employed implicitly in the recognition of objects. To see that a lollipop is indeed composed of a circle and a straight line standing in a certain relation to each other requires the explicit activation of a part of the structural description of the lollipop. When the child sees that relationship for the first time, she is not constructing new spatial images, but is becoming aware of aspects of the structural description that she was already automatically (implicitly) using for object recognition.

The relations between objects and forms is particularly important for spatial cognition. Although ordinary object perception has utilized spatial information as part of an implicit structural description, it is only when distinctive meanings are assigned to the spatial forms per se that we can talk of the perception of space. Such perception is derivative from object and event perception and, we suggest, comes to be employed primarily when we are dealing with human artifacts such as Euclidean geometry, Vygotsky blocks, map-making, and the visual arts.

Our suggestion, then, is that spatial information is implicit in the structural descriptions of objects and events and underlies the perception of objects and events but is not initially perceived in its own right. Our concerns then, are two. What is the structure of the spatial information that is utilized in the perception of objects and events? And why does the child come to perceive spatial form and to assign meaning to form in its own right?

Recall that the perception of form does not necessarily involve the detection of new information but the attention to form per se. The development of form perception, or spatial knowledge, would then merely require a means for making the child conscious of what she already knew implicitly, that is, of recovering the categories and relations that were inherent in the structural descriptions for ordinary object perception. Thus, the structures of explicit form perception in adults, as represented in language, art, geometry, and so on, should indicate the properties that were implicit in the perception of objects and events by children. In this way cultural inventions reflect the structures already present, perhaps innately, in the perceptual process. Hence, ordinary language can be a means of explicating the relations that are already implicit in the simple perceptual processes. The difference is merely one of implicitness, in the case of object perception, and explicitness, in the case of form perception, linguistic description and the like, in adults.

From this perspective Euclid did not invent the square. Nor is the concept of square derived from nature. Lines, angles, symmetries, and presumably, squares, were constituents of the structural descriptions constructed for the perception of ordinary objects. Euclid's contribution was to make those properties explicit. The man-made environment, including artifacts, are explicit representations of implicit spatial cognitive structures. But how are they explicated?

As an aside, it must be admitted that this line of argument may lead one to attribute too sophisticated structures to the cognitive processes of children. It is at best an hypothesis requiring empirical test. That is, we cannot claim that the spatial structures we turn up in our examination of the language of space, roughly our spatial terminology, or those that we turn up in representational art, will in fact precisely reflect the child's structural descriptions for the recognition of objects, but we have good reasons for using spatial language and drawings as models for structural descriptions implicit in ordinary perception. Several tests of this model are presented in later chapters.

One means of learning to extract the forms from objects is through the arts. In fact, Arnheim, in his work on perception in the arts, first differentiated the levels of representation dicussed here. To account for the difficulty children had in drawing or copying the shapes of objects and other visual displays, which they could perfectly well recognize, that is to account for the discrepancy between perceiving and performing, Arnheim (1968) wrote:

> Tentatively I would suggest that the incapacity exists because perception is not primarily the apprehension of shapes or colors. Rather, to perceive is mainly to receive the expressive or dynamic effects of shapes and colors. Early experiments of mine have taught me that when the average person looks, say, at a human face he sees its tenseness or plumpness or slyness or its harmony rather than the shapes and colors producing that effect. Apprehension of shapes as shapes and colors as colors does exist, of course, but its level of discernment develops gradually from the simple to the complex.
>
> The difference, then is not primarily between perception and representation, but between perception of effect and perception of form, the latter being needed for representation (p. 206).

Representational systems in general, such as language, may have a similar effect of focusing attention on certain aspects of structural descriptions for objects. It is only with the construction of an explicit representational system for the spatial features of object structural descriptions that we can properly talk of the perception of space per se.

The differences between objects and forms is known in the visual arts as the relation between form and function. At times the attempt, as in design, is to develop a form that visually suggests its function; the appearance of the chair makes you feel like sitting in it. At other times, as in the paintings of Ben Nicholsen, the attempt is to split the form from the function to make the form the subject of perception in its own right.

A neglect of different levels of meaning involved in objects as opposed to forms, has led to many empirical confusions. We shall mention two. Earlier we criticized the view that a child's word meaning may be represented by the list of features used in identification of the objects that make up the extension of the term. The sum of those features, we argued, constitute the structural description or the recognition routines for an object or event but not its meaning. Following Nelson (1974) we have argued that the meaning is derived from the set of intentions or the functions or significances of these objects to the knower. Those meanings often are responsible for initiating the construction of a structural description for the correct recognition of instances. Nelson overlooks the possibility, however, that structural descriptions could be set up for objects or displays in the absence of a meaning (what Piaget would term massive accommodation). However, even in this case the features of that structural description would remain implicit. In neither case is there ground for saying that spatial, perceptual features are explicitly known. Much of the controversy, however, appears to revolve around the sense of "known". Both featural and functional theories say that features are involved: they differ in the status of the features—explicit versus implicit—and whether or not those features constitute the meaning of the concept as opposed to its recognition routines. It is important to the present theory to emphasize that spatial perceptual features are implicit in the structural descriptions of objects in order to contrast the role those same features play when they become explicit as spatial concepts. As we shall argue, the features used implicitly in perception are used explicitly by artists in attempts at representation.

Secondly, the old discrimination literature often involved the same error. Features were treated as if they had meanings in their own right—as if they were entities independent of objects they composed. Hence, objects were described as if they were nothing other than a set of logically related abstracted features. Thus an animal or a child may be taught to respond to the value "black" on the color dimension while ignoring size and shape features. Once the discrimination was achieved the problem was switched so that the alternative value "white" on the same dimension was the correct response. The finding was that children over 8 years or so, solved the problem after a single error, while younger children and higher primates did not (Kendler & Kendler, 1962). Younger children and some lower primates found it easier to solve the size problem after a color problem. However, when Cole, Gay, Glick, and Sharp (1971) reanalyzed this data, they found that children had not learned to respond to such abstracted features as "black" or "large" at all. Rather, they had learned to respond to two specific *objects*, both of which the experimenter described as "black" or "large" but which the children apparently did not. Hence when the task was changed from a "black" to a "large" problem, the children did not learn to respond to an abstracted feature of size, rather, they preserved the correct response to one of the former *objects* and began anew to learn the correct response to the other *object*. If it was changed from black to a white problem, they had to begin from chance to learn correct responses for both of the objects (cf. Posner, 1973, p. 64).

Notice that the child or the animal is using color and shape information to arrive at the identity of the block. Our claim is simply that she does not perceive color or form per se, that is assign meanings to or construct distinctive structural descriptions for such properties as color or shape; rather she perceives the *blocks* by means of an implicit structural description composed of properties including size and colors. She may subsequently develop "meanings" for and construct distinctive structural descriptions for such perceptual properties as color and form but those are both more "abstract" and more sophisticated than the object representations from which they are extracted. And they involve a new level of meaning. The theory of structural descriptions constructed for the representation of objects and for the representation of forms permits us to address three other issues prominent in the study of spatial cognition—images, hemispheric specialization, and the lexicalization of space all of which, in our view, remain confused because of a failure to draw the distinction between objects and forms.

I. SPATIAL IMAGERY

As we have argued in the previous chapter, an image involves the activation of an implicit structural description of an object concept and does not constitute a separate code or processing system. As Neisser (1976) has pointed out, the images are instances of perceptual readiness. It is worth citing this account of how these anticipations turn into images:

> . . .consider how actual rotating objects are perceived. Suppose, for example, that we want to look at an acrobat's face as he spins in a somersault. This requires a schema that accepts information about the speed and direction with which the acrobat is turning, and directs the pickup of information from the position where his head will be at

the next moment. Any perceiver who can do this successfully will also be able to imagine such a spin simply by activating the anticipatory schema in the absence of the
acrobat. His image then consists of a readiness to pick up certain kinds of information from a given part of a moving body (p. 148–9).

This account perhaps underestimates the difference between anticipating an
object and imagining that object in its absence, a difference Piaget has
discussed. Nevertheless, images involve the activation of the implicit structural descriptions of objects and events. This activation of the appearances
of the object does not require that one make explicit the representation of
form. As we argued, the perception of form requires the explication of the
spatial properties that were implicit in ordinary perception by means of
assigning distinctive meanings to those forms. Once explicated, of course,
forms may also be imaged as readily as objects. In either case, however, images involve the activation of their respective implicit structural descriptions.

We can readily see the distinction between an explicit description and an
image by reference to a well known task utilized by Clark and Chase (1972).
Superficially, the sentence is a description or representation of the meaning

+

The star is above the plus.

of the visual display. In fact, Clark and Chase offer the hypothesis that the
mental representation of the visual display and the sentence are identical:
above (star, plus). This assumes that the linguistic representation and the
picture representation are equivalent which, of course, they are for that particular proposition. However, as Donaldson (1974) has noted, someone seeing the display would ordinarily have coded in the implicit structural
description more information that is represented in that linguistic description or in that single proposition. The viewer would know, for example,
that the star and plus are symmetrical figures, of a certain size of the same
color, separated by a particular distance—a distance roughly equivalent to
the size of the two figures and so on. Only in the most constrained conditions would subjects construct structural descriptions of the visual display
which preserved only the specific proposition in question.

The more elaborated form of the structural description, consisting of
many such propositions attached to a meaning or concept, if activated
would be called an image. Once the image has been generated from the
structural description, it is subject to the same cognitive operations as is any
other mental representation; it may be recalled, described, transformed,
and so on. Tasks which bias subjects towards forming this type of represen-

tation, such as those used by Shepard and Metzler (1971) or Kosslyn (1975) may well have been solved by some other means, since a structural description could have been assigned at any level of meaning to represent aspects of the same display. However, the level of meaning and the structural description chosen in any one case will depend on the features of the displays and on the requirements of the task.

The image, in our view, is not independent of a notational, or linguistic description in the manner suggested by dual coding theories (Paivio, 1969; Posner, 1973). In these accounts, a display is assigned a representation in one or both of the linguistic or imagery systems, each being specialized for encoding different aspects of the display. In Posner's letter-matching task, for example, the visual system is assumed to process the physical features of the stimulus letters while the notational system is assumed to assign them to a meaning category. But how can meaning be assigned without some indication of the physical appearance, or conversely, how can the lines and angles be perceived as a known letter without recourse to some organizing meaning category? We suggest that the two types of representations are not independent but reflect the two aspects of the same concept, the structural description and its meaning. The structural description anticipates the appearance of the display while the meaning specifies the relationship of that display to the other letters of the alphabet, that is to the other members of a semantic field.

Kosslyn and Pomerantz (1977), in their argument for the retention of visual imagery as a viable form of mental representation, suggest two sources for the formation of images—independent dual coding, and generation from an abstract proposition. After reviewing a number of studies which involve processing of spatial images, they suggest that the explanation in terms of direct dual coding of the image is most plausible. They acknowledge, however, the possiblity that the image could have been generated from a proposition. Reed (1974) resolves the problem in another way. He argues that both a structural description and an image are formed to represent a display, but that a problem can be solved in one of three ways—by means of the structural description, the stored image, or a new image generated from the structural description. The structural description is the preferred representation, and he presents reaction time data to show that solutions based on these descriptions are faster than those which involve scanning or generating an image.

We suggest that the contrast is not between images and structural descriptions. Rather, a single structural description of considerable specificity or depth is assigned to a "known" object and constitutes a basis for perceiving and imagining the object. However, some of those features may be represented by explicit form features, for example known geometric shapes (a spruce tree is triangular shaped), while other features are completely implicit and yet represent specific and detailed features of the appearances of the display. Ordinarily, an image would involve the activation of essentially the entire structural description. Some simpler tasks may involve the activation of only the most general and abstract or higher level features of a structural description (as for example judging typographically different *a*'s as exemplars of the class of lower case *a*'s) while some more complex tasks, such as judging if a second *a* is an exact copy as opposed to a forgery would involve the activation of the entire structural description (or call for detailed formal analysis). Similarly, for some problem solving tasks the retrieval or activation of only some of the predominant features, if they are represented explicitly as form representations, may be sufficient as in transformations involving rotation of an object or movement of the observer. For example, someone knowing the oppositional form representation frontback could derive the consequences of movement from the code rather than from visualizing the entire spatial transformation.

The view that there is a single structural description with different levels of meanings (i.e. objects and forms) has some other advantages. For one, there is no problem in accounting for the transfer of information from one "type" of representation to another such as from the name of a letter to its general physical appearance. In our view both the word and the display activate the same concept—one via the meaning the other via the structural description; hence they may interfere with or facilitate each other.

II. HEMISPHERIC SPECIALIZATION

Theories which maintain a distinction between images and descriptions often argue that the differences between them map onto different processing strategies associated with the left and right hemispheres. Thus evidence has been presented which suggests that at least some spatial images are processed more readily by the right hemisphere while verbal descriptions are processed more readily by the left (Bogen, 1969; Milner, 1971; Ornstein, 1972; Sperry, 1964).

Illustrative is Bogen's report that "split brain" subjects were able to write English with their right hand (left hemisphere) as well as they were before, but could no longer draw. A square may be copied as four corners stacked together; the nominal attributes of the object were preserved but their spatial interrelations were lost. With the left hand, (right hemisphere) the same subjects could copy the square but not copy written English. Kimura (1973) reported that the task of locating an object in space, either in a plane or in depth, was performed by the right hemisphere more easily than by the left. Thus, it appears that the left hemisphere is specialized for linguistic tasks while the right is more specialized for spatial-visual tasks. The extension of this observation is the argument that these tasks are represented and processed in qualitatively different ways. Further, it would be argued that structural descriptions are appropriate only for left hemisphere functions and it may be noted that Reed (1974) uses the concept exactly this way leaving images the task of representing "appearances".

To obtain evidence of this specialization, however, it is usually necessary to invent visual-spatial forms that prohibit the ready assignment of object names or simple form descriptions, such as roundness, pointedness or the like. Witelson's (1980) study is interesting in this regard. She presented children in the early school years with spatial displays of sufficient complexity to prevent verbal descriptions (we would say explicit representations in terms of forms) for tactile recognition. While girls could recognize the forms equally easily with either hand, the boys were more successful with the left hand. From this Witelson concludes that for boys the right hemisphere is specialized for spatial information processing.

However, why does the right hemisphere come into play primarily for *complex* spatial displays? Does information cease to be spatial if it is represented in terms of explicit forms (or lexically)? If one did know those forms explicitly, would simpler spatial displays still be handled in the right hemispheres? There seems to be no boundary in terms of content between spatial and linguistic representations. Rather, we would again suggest that *any* distinctive display is assigned a structural description. If the critical parts of that structural description can be made explicit as form representations, the latter may be used for problem solving, recognition, description and the like. If it is too complex for such form representation, subjects revert to the activation of the entire structural description in the form of a spatial image, as in Witelson's study. The right hemisphere, therefore, appears to be specialized for operating upon unanalyzed structural descriptions while the left is specialized for explicit representations *including* spatial ones.

If, as we argue, recognition is based on the assignment of structural descriptions, then some such description must be generated for any to-be-recognized display even those processed in the right hemisphere. Our explanation is that a display too complex or unfamiliar to be assigned an explicit form representation is represented in terms of a more complex or richer structural description which may be called an image. These images preserve more of the features of the display than do the explicit form representations since many details relevant to the image may not be captured by the known, explicit features of form representations. Forms could, of course be "imaged" but to do so would involve adding such perceptual features such as size and color which are incidental to the abstract form.

Again, this is the case with the figures used by Shepard and Metzler (1971)—no known simple form representations were appropriate and so an extremely rich structural description was required. Such an activated structural description may be called a visual image.

The interesting point is that when the highly elaborated structural descriptions are employed, the cognitive processes of comparison and recognition appear to be somewhat different than when the spatial displays are assigned simpler explicit form representations. These complex structural descriptions for which no aspects of form can be extracted are nonetheless recognized, transformed and so on, primarily by the right hemisphere and presumably as "images".

Again notice that it is not necessary to say that the code is different in the right hemisphere. It is rather that aspects of the code that can be represented in terms of explicit form descriptions or explicit object descriptions are normally transferred to the left hemisphere for processing. Those that have not yet been transferred, that is spatial information for which no known form representation exists, continue to be represented and processed in the right hemisphere. Thus it would only be complex, novel, undescribable patterns for which the right hemisphere remains dominant, a conjecture consistent with the existing evidence. If a known form description can be assigned to a display, the task becomes easier and is reassigned to the left hemisphere. Ives (Chapter 7, this volume) shows how this "notationalizing" of a spatial layout facilitates the child's solution to Piaget's famous three mountain task.

Another line of evidence which argues in favor of a dichotomy between visual/spatial and linguistic systems comes from research demonstrating that verbal representations may interfere with verbal forms of response while spatial representations may interfere with spatial responses. In a series of experiments Brooks (1968) gave subjects either a spatial task in which they answered questions about the physical properties of the letter "F", or a verbal task in which they counted the number of nouns in a sentence and were asked to respond in each of a spatial-pictorial or verbal mode. The finding was that spatial responses interfered with the spatial task and verbal responses with the verbal task, but that crossing modalities facilitated performance. The explanation was that each modality utilized different representation and processing systems; interference occurred when one system was being used for two functions. Thus it was not possible to use the spatial system both for visualizing the letter "F" and for responding to spatially arrayed information on a page.

Brooks (1970) later argued, however, that interference was not caused by the use of the same modality, but by the requirement to operate on two representations that are semantically incompatible with each other. In our terms, the structural description for the letter "F" involves certain spatial information about positions, directions, and so on. Similarly, the spatial response involves the spatial features of the answer sheet that also includes positions and directions. The two representations, however, are incongruent—the spatial features of the answer sheet do not correspond to the spatial features of the letter "F". It is this conflict of information that is the source of interference. Presumably, if the spatial features of the answer sheet corresponded to the "F", that is, if the responses were arranged in the shape of the letter "F" rather than the random array used, then response would be facilitated. Thus, interference is not attributed to differences in the representational modality or processing hemisphere, but to conflicts in the information represented in the structural description.

A third line of evidence comes from the interference effects of processing verbal and positional information simultaneously. Palef and Olson (1975) and Palef (1978) showed that adult subjects had difficulty pressing a response key to the word "above" if it occurred on the lower part of the display, a phenomenon called a "Spatial Stroop." But if position is processed in terms of a Right hemisphere visual/spatial code and lexical items in terms of a Left hemisphere verbal code, why do they interfere? Rather it seems necessary to say that both position and spatial word meaning are represented in the same spatial cognitive systems. It could be suggested however that if the lexical item involves an explicit form representation while the position involves an unanalyzed structural description, the former would be better handled by the left hemisphere while the latter would be better handled by the right. That hypothesis remains untested.

Again, then, we suggest the images associated with the right hemisphere are not different codes from the formal explicit representations of the left hemisphere. Structural descriptions, of which we remain largely unaware, constitute the representation for the object and events with which we deal in our every day lives. Some small part of these structural descriptions become explicit, that is known as such, as form representations that permit the perception of forms across objects. Those aspects of structural descriptions which become explicit as form representations, become subject to conscious control in speech, drawing, and so on. But those aspects of structural descriptions which do not come to be explicated as form perception, are not lost or ignored. They remain as part of our implicit knowledge of objects and forms, they can be activated as images, they can be transformed somewhat as the real objects of which they are structural descriptions, and some of them can be made explicit by new developments in language, mathematics, art, and so on. These later cultural activities make aspects of structural descriptions explicit and again subject to conscious control. And, finally, it is those aspects of description which are explicit and subject to control that are assigned to the left hemisphere.

III. THE LANGUAGE OF SPACE

Our discussion of the levels of representation in which we contrasted an object level and a form level, the latter being an explicit representation of the primary aspects of the former, provides a framework for a consideration of the language of space. First, it should be clear that while spatial information is extremely important in the construction of structural descriptions for objects, the perception and explicit cognitive representation of space per se is derivative. That is, children presumably do not perceive space as such, rather they use spatial perceptual information in their structural descriptions of objects, relations, layouts, and the like. The progressive explication or "unpacking" of the spatial information implicit in those structural descriptions is what is involved in the development of perception of space. Language, being an explicit set of representations of spatial information is one of the primary means for making that spatial information explicit and hence, for the development of spatial cognition. Conversely, the study of the language used for explicitly representing space provides us with some evidence of the nature of the structural descriptions that were implicit in ordinary perception of objects, relations, events, and so on. The structure of language, therefore, is a window to the structure of the recognition routines we have called structural description.

The language of space has been examined by Bierwisch (1967), Teller (1969), Leech (1969), Clark (1973a) and Olson (1975). An interesting property of the language of space is that to understand the meaning of spatial terms you must know something about space. The question is: does the linguistic structure learned by every speaker of the language determine how he "codes", "organizes", or "perceives" space, a Whorfian notion, or is the causual relation operative in the opposite direction—the structure of perception of space determines the subsequent structure of the language of space. The "deep structure theorists" such as Bierwisch (1967) and Clark (1973a) opt for the latter. We argue, in terms of our theory, the spatial lexicon is simply the explicit spatial forms of implicit structural descriptions.

English has a fairly large number of spatial terms that fall into the form classes of adverbials: here/there; prepositions: up/down; on the left/on the right; at the front of/at the back of; in/on; by; above/below; adjectives: big/small; long/short; wide/narrow; thick/thin; deep/shallow; and nouns: top/bottom; left/right; front/back; side/end. These spatial terms have several common properties. Firstly, they all assume a point of reference—the speaker or some other object. Secondly, they are organized around particular dimensions such as verticality or length. Thirdly, these terms come in contrastive polar pairs specifying the dimension as in the following:

Dimension	Contrastive Pair
where:	here/there
vertical:	up/down; high/low; above/below
horizontal:	right/left
frontal:	front/back
length:	long/short
distance:	far/near
height:	tall/short
width:	wide/narrow
depth:	deep/shallow
thickness:	thick/thin

Finally, these contrastive pairs have the property of "marking". The "unmarked" number of the pair normally occurs in the neutral question form, "How high is the airplane?" and it is generally the positive form. The marked form is generally defined in terms of the negation of the unmarked number, e.g. short → not long, while the converse does not hold (Webster's Dictionary).

Let us now consider the relation between spatial language and the nature of spatial information more generally. Clark (1973a) describes two representational systems which he calls P-space, or perceptual space, and L-space, or linguistic space. These two systems are highly correlated and can be shown to mark the same distinctions—both are organized around the concepts of dimensions, values on dimensions, reference points, markedness, and so on. Clark argues that this congruity occurs because they both map onto the same physical and biological reality, that is, they both describe the same world. That formulation, however, hides an ambiguity. P-space is not, at least for children, perceived as such; rather, P-space is implicit spatial *information* utilized in the representation of ego, objects, rooms, and the like. Hence, we suggest, that the congruity between these systems is more simply attributed to the idea that L-space is derived from P-space, as in a set-subset relationship. Whereas for Clark, these were two independent but highly correlated representational systems, for our purposes, they are not independent systems at all. Rather, as we have said, L-shape is an explicit representation of part of the structure of P-space used in ordinary perception.

What determines the selection of the features that will be assigned explicit form or linguistic representations? Three factors which may contribute to this selection are the perceptual and functional biases of the organism, the restrictions of the linguistic system itself, and the particular purposes recruited by the task.

We suggested earlier that the original selection of features from the environment for the construction of structural descriptions for object perception was determined by the nature of the organism and its usual interaction with the environment. Thus, it was argued, humans are differently biased to perceive the distinctions necessary for their usual activities—vertical dimensions to sustain upright posture, and so on. If we are to assume that the language of space is simply an explicit representation of part of the structural descriptions of objects and events, then the effects of perceptual biases are indirect. The activities one engages in, however, may be directly responsible for determining the features that will be made explicit in language. That is, human perceptual biases determine what features of the environment it was possible to encode in the structural descriptions; the usual activities of the organism may determine which of these are important enough to be assigned an explicit linguistic representation. This importance may then be reflected in the speech habits of the linguistic community.

The second factor which restricts the explicit representation of the features of the structural descriptions is the nature of the linguistic system. In general, the linguistic system may be described as a discrete, notational symbol system, as opposed to a continuous, non-notational system (Goodman, 1968; Gardner, Howard, & Perkins, 1974). Whereas perceived space may be structurally described in terms of an infinite number of finely differentiated points and lines, the language of space tends primarily to represent discrete alternatives. The bias of the linguistic system is to represent information in a contrastive, binary fashion (Ogden, 1932). Perceptual information not suitable to that format cannot be assigned a simple lexical description. In many cases a more elaborated linguistic description which represents information in terms of compound descriptions, such as "up to the right" or "very, very long" can be formulated, but for perceptual features which are not inherently binary, or descriptions so complex that such a componential analysis is prohibitive, linguistic representation may be impossible and a person may revert to imaging the more general structural description. Similarly, representations in drawing or painting—the systems of the visual arts—allow for different aspects of the structural descriptions to be made explicit than are made through ordinary language.

Finally, the task demands determine the particular features that will be made explicit in language. Just as alternate structural descriptions could be assigned to a display as a function of the perceptual requirements, so alternate linguistic representations can be extracted from structural descriptions as a function of communication requirements. Aspects of the structural descriptions can be noted, differentiated, and explicated as it becomes important to do so (Ogden, 1932; Olson, 1970b). In a study by Ford and Olson (1975), descriptions of a block in various contexts were elicited from children 4 to 7 years of age. Subjects modified their descriptions to suit the immediate contexts, explicating in language those features particularly relevant to the set of alternatives. More generally it is reasonable to expect that the spatial lexicon will be more elaborated in some cultures—such as those involving carpentry—than in others—such as those not so involved. These are both indications that the features made explicit by language are determined in part by situational and communicational demands.

What are the features of the structural descriptions that language makes explicit? Various accounts of these features are offered (Bierwisch, 1967; Clark, 1973; Leech, 1969; Teller, 1969), and most theorists argue that these comprise a set of "linguistic universals". It becomes necessary to postulate the existence of such a set in order to deal with the correlation between perceptual and linguistic space. Clearly, if we reject the Whorfian notion that perceptual organization is a consequence of linguistic structures, then the only alternative is to attribute to language a similar but independent set of semantic features as was attributed to perception. The present theory, however, would not ground the universals in the language because in our view, the features of language are simply the explicit representations of the structural descriptions of objects and events. If universals exist, it is the perceptual constituents and relations from which the structural descriptions are generated. They are, as Fodor (1975) would say, the "language of thought."

Let us examine two features made explicit in language to see how they are represented in our spatial lexicon and what they indicate about the underlying implicit structural descriptions of objects. These are the features for dimension and referent.

Our perception of the world is organized in part in terms of a system of three coordinated dimensions, each perpendicular to the others. Clark (1973a) has described the representation of these dimensions in the language. The first dimension is the vertical axis defined by a gravity and represented in language by terms such as "up/down", "top/bottom", "over/under", "above/below", "high/low", and so on. The second can be described by the plane extending through the centre of our bodies and corresponds to the descriptions "front/back", "ahead/behind", and so on. Finally, the plane which is perpendicular to this and symmetrically bisects our bodies maps onto the linguistic descriptions "left/right". These three dimensions, then, constitute one of the bases for the structural descriptions assigned to ourselves and other objects and it is these basic features that are made explicit in the spatial lexicon.

Linguistic representations of space reflect a second factor, the nature of the referent, that is the object or event relative to which a spatial description is specified. Spatial descriptions (verbal descriptions of space) may, for example, make explicit either the constituent properties of objects such as the top or bottom of a cup, or the relationships between objects, such as above or below a cup. These differences in referent influence among other things, the form class of the spatial term that is applied to a particular spatial property or relation. While the dimensional properties of space are somewhat invariant across various referents, the differences in the referent result in alternative lexical representations differing in their syntactic form class. Thus, while "top" and "above" both mark vertical positive spatial properties, the former is a noun which refers to a part of single object while the latter is a preposition which refers to the relation between two objects. Consider, for example, the set of lexical items containing the feature for the vertical. Some of these, such as "tall/short" are used to refer to aspects of objects, that is, relations within an object. Similarly, the pair "top/bottom" describes a spatial arrangement internal to an object. Thus, adjectives and nouns may be said to represent spatial aspects of objects. These spatial terms, therefore, may be called "structural." Descriptions such as "over/under", "above/below", "far/near", on the other hand, represent relationships *between* at least two elements, or spatial relationships external to an object. The features implied by these descriptions generally make reference not to an object, but to the relationships that hold between objects. These are represented in language primarily by means of adverbs and prepositions. These spatial terms, therefore, may be called "relational". Both structural and relational terms, or predicates, shall be examined more fully in Chapter 5. Again notice that these features are presumably implicit in our ordinary perceptions of objects and their relations.

The example of the two features for dimension and referent demonstrates how the spatial lexicon utilizes perceptual features in a systematic way, and how an examination of these features can be used to infer the nature of the implicit structural descriptions underlying the perception of objects and events. An exhaustive account of the linguistic features underlying the language of space would provide a rich description of the implicit perceptual structures from which they were extracted.

In fact, this assumption was central to the ideas of Frege who was the first to uncover the logical forms of thought through his "Begriffsschrift", a formula language for pure thought. Frege argued that "The world of thoughts has a model in the world of sentences, expressions, words, signs" (1952, p. 123). Hence, the logical analysis of sentences would provide a model for the structure of non-verbal thought. As many reviewers have pointed out, Frege made several decisive steps in his attempt to formalize that structure. First, he argued that the appropriate level of analysis was that of a proposition, not that of a concept, because only the former could lead to a judgment, or what today would be said to specify truth conditions. To illustrate, Frege pointed out that the idea "house" is only a part of a proposition and therefore could not become a judgment while "The house of Priam was made of wood" could. Hence, the appropriate level of analysis of thought was at the level of sentences or propositions, not words or ideas. Secondly, Frege pointed out that sentences did not reveal their propositional structure directly. Since subjects and predicates of sentences did not clearly specify the basis for judgment, he substituted predicates and arguments as the appropriate elements of propositions. A proposition consists of a predicate plus one or more arguments. And it was these predicates plus argument constructions that Frege offered as a model of thought. These predicate-argument constructions have become extremely important in studies of language and in cognitive science. Parisi and Antinucci (1976) for example, in their analysis of grammar, state:

> *Predicate* must be understood as a component in a thought structure, not yet tied to its linguistic expressions as a verb, as a preposition, or as any other grammatical category. *Predicate* is anything which is attributed to something else (if the predicate has only one argument) or any relationship instituted between two or more things (if the predicate has more than one argument). If we accept this broad definition, it then becomes evident that the words *on* and *for*, when they appear in sentences..., express relations and therefore are predicates (1976, p. 34).

Propositional analyses are not only popular, they have certain advantages of explicitness which more general talk of structural descriptions does not and hence, as we approach our experimental work, we will adopt a Fregian form of expression. A structural description consists therefore of sets of propositions, each proposition consisting of a spatial predicate such as on, or above, and one or more arguments. We can economically describe these propositions by stating the predicate followed by its arguments, thus:

tall (house), that is, The house is tall.

Other spatial predicates, take two arguments, thus:

on (food, table), that is, The food is on the table.

In this case, the proposition admits of a truth judgment; it is either true or false.

Once we adopt these notions, the central questions become those of determining the precise propositions that make up the structural descriptions we have discussed to this point. What set of propositions built around what set of spatial predicates can we find in the mental representation of object, and events and how are these representations used in the process of spatial thinking. These are the central questions for the remainder of the volume.

To summarize, we began by differentiating the form of mental representation that would be required for the ordinary perception, memory, and imagining of objects, events, layouts, and the like. These mental representations we suggested consisted of an implicit structural description composed in part of spatial properties and relations, plus a meaning. In this chapter we described how particular features and relations of these structural descriptions can be "explicated" and perceived in their own right as form perception. We claimed that the development from objects to forms was managed by the assignment of meanings at a new level. Whereas objects have their meanings in the role they play in ordinary activity—the lollipop, for example was one thing among the set of alternative things you could eat such as gum, candy, ice cream, lollipops, and so on—the forms have their meanings in terms of the set of alternative shapes—round, square, oval, and so on. Yet because the latter is derived from the former, we may examine the latter to draw inferences as to the structure of the former. We may use, for example, spatial language to suggest what the implicit structural descriptions were composed of. Hence, we concluded the chapter with a description of the spatial lexicon and showed how the lexicon provides a model for the propositional representation of implicit structural descriptions.

In the course of the chapter we attempted to show that our distinction between implicit structural descriptions and explicit forms could be used as an alternative to the more traditional distinctions between verbal and visual codes, between the verbal and the spatial hemispheres and between spatial perception and spatial concepts. Finally, we have suggested that at any one time, some spatial knowledge will be implicit in the structural descriptions of objects and events while some will be explicated as spatial forms, always with distinctive meanings, and often with an explicit lexical form. The implicit propositional structure for the representation of spatial information is the primary problem for a theory of spatial cognition. And the transformation from implicit knowledge of space to explicit knowledge of space is the primary problem for a theory of spatial development. To these problems we now turn.

4 The Development of Spatial Cognition

As we have pointed out, the origins of spatial concepts lie in the structural descriptions constructed to represent objects and events. Spatial information pertaining to the internal forms of objects, to relations between objects, and between objects and their environments constitute part of the implicit structural descriptions which underlie the perception and representation of objects and events. The progressive explication of that spatial information is involved in the development of both structured categories such as shape, and relational categories such as location and direction. The extraction or explication of these categories, themselves spatial propositions such as those representating simple Euclidean shapes, permits the detection of invariant features in the structural descriptions across many different objects or events. Similarly, explicitly known spatial relations, as marked in the lexicon for example, are an abstraction of the relationships that hold between and within objects. When meanings can be assigned to these spatial aspects of the structural descriptions of objects, making in effect, the forms and relations explicit objects of thought, then spatial cognition, the perception and representation of space per se, becomes possible. This process of explication of implicit structure is recursive and may be carried out at any level of abstraction. Our concern in this chapter is to set out the primary aspects of the development of spatial cognition.

Spatial development may be attributed to two concurrent processes—the increasing elaboration of the spatial aspects of the structural descriptions of objects, and the gradual explication, or "representation" of the features of those descriptions. The first refers to the development of the implicit structures used for object perception, permitting the child to recognize increasingly complex displays, to make new discriminations, and so on, a process admirably described by Eleanor Gibson (1969). The meanings of these structural descriptions are assigned at the level of the objects rather than at the level of the features by means of which that object is recognized. However, since the features remain implicit, that is, not consciously represented, development of increasingly elaborated structural descriptions can only be detected through increased skill in discrimination and recognition of object and events. To illustrate, one can demonstrate that the child's structural descriptions for an A is more elaborated if he can now, but could not before, discriminate it from an H. He may however remain unaware of the perceptual information by means of which he makes the discrimination.

The second, and more important aspect of development, is the progressive explication of the structural descriptions of objects as "representations" of space. Whereas in structural descriptions the spatial features are implicit and completely tied to the objects they signal, in "form representations" they come to be explicit and known in their own right. These explicit representations make possible the perception of *form* whereas structural descriptions permitted the perception of *objects*. It is these explicit representations which are captured in the development of symbolic systems such as language and which, we suggest, permit the execution of certain spatial cognitive operations such as transitive orderings, classifications of objects by such spatial properties as shape and size as well as such constructions and performances as drawing, modelling, and the like.

Spatial thinking requires that the structural descriptions are assigned at the level of forms and relations rather than at the level of the objects with which they were originally associated. That is, the spatial features of the display must be explicitly represented to permit the solution of some spatial problems. In this sense, spatial thinking does not assess the processing of spatial information implicit in structural descriptions but rather explicit spatial representation. In the former, the spatial features of a display may be implicit; in the latter, they must be assigned an explicit representation and a distinctive meaning. We may illustrate this difference by means of the classical conservation task. If the problem is solved perceptually, i.e., on the basis of implicit spatial features, the child will fail; perceptual differences between the stimuli are inadequate for solving the problem. The correct solution requires explicit attention to the two spatial dimensions, length and width and an analysis of their compensatory relations. Thus spatial tasks depend upon the spatial forms and relations being extracted from object perception; spatial cognition then, refers to the thoughts and operations permitted by these explicit representations of space. It is our hypothesis that the explications of the spatial features of structural descriptions of objects are responsible for the development of spatial cognition including the development of spatial representations in such symbolic media as art and ordinary language.

The emergence of this explicit representation from the implicit spatial structures which underlie object perception, may be examined from two perspectives. The first of these is the nature of the activity that is responsible for making the spatial structure of objects explicit; generally, such activities as speaking and drawing. The second concerns the order in which various explicit representations are extracted from the structural description. If we can assume that the child is exploring with pencil, paint, his blocks, his speech, and so on, can we specify the principles that determine the order of explication of these forms? Knowledge of these principles should permit us to predict the spatial representations and operations that have become explicit and that can therefore influence the child's performance. To illustrate, if roundness has been extracted from an object's structural description to become a form representation, the child should be able to group objects on the basis of their roundness and learn the lexical representation for that form.

Let us consider first the ways in which structural descriptions are made explicit in the representation of forms and relations, and then the order in which various aspects of the structural descriptions become explicit.

I. THE EXTRACTION OF FORMS AND RELATIONS

A. Symbolic Representations of Space

The formal representations extracted from the structural descriptions must be solicited, encouraged or sustained by some particular form of activity. Thus a vertical arrangement, a highly invariant feature may be extracted earlier than a horizontal arrangement, but only when conditions dictate. The question then is what encourages the extraction of these form representations from object representations. In other words, how do the spatial properties and relations of objects come to be given explicit representations as spatial forms and what is required to transform the spatial information in a structural description into these spatial concepts or meanings? In concrete terms, how do children come to see that a lollipop is, in fact, round? We suggest that the process of explicating these features begins through the child's own practical activities and becomes greatly specialized through the adoption of cultural symbol systems such as language, cartography, geometry, and art.

It is worth noting in passing that most cognitive theories gloss the distinction being drawn here. That is, it is simply assumed that form representation is as much an immediate consequence of experience as is object representation or that children know roundness even before knowing the lollipop. Both conjectures imply that spatial forms can be known independently of objects. However, if meaning is the organizing factor in the construction of structural descriptions as we argue, an important difference between objects and forms becomes apparent. Objects, such as lollipops have a meaning in that humans act upon them in distinctive ways while forms are by definition common across objects—roundness is a property of several objects and has no independent meaning in that context. Thus meaningful structural descriptions could be assigned for objects but not for forms. Once extracted from objects, however, forms could be assigned a meaning at a new level of description, that is, they could be treated as "objects" containing their own set of implicit properties.

Some theoretical traditions have noted this difference and described the construction of form representations in terms of abstraction (Goldstein & Scheerer, 1941). Piaget and Inhelder (1956), differentiate perceptual space from representational space roughly along these lines: "There is therefore an interval of several years between *perceptual* and *conceptual* construction [of space], despite their pursuing a similar path of development" (1956, p. 451). Piaget's theory of representation also emphasizes that in one sense the imaginary activation of the object in its absence is not a totally new construction but rather a *re*-presentation of what has been known perceptually.

However, the theory leaves unspecified the primary distinction we propose herein, namely, that representation is not merely the activation of the object in its absence but the representation of that object in terms of a set of forms or other underlying structural features. But these forms and relations as we have repeatedly insisted, are not different from the structural descriptions of objects but rather are an explicit representation of the very properties that were implicit in object perception. Thus, we accept Piaget's insistence on the difference between perceptual space and representational space but we explain that difference primarily in terms of explicitness of the structural descriptions. The late emerging conceptual space to which Piaget refers requires the construction of what we have described as explicit representation of form. Perceptual space, however, develops early since explicit attention to the structural description is not required.

Piaget and Inhelder (1956) do relate the development of representational space to such symbolic activities as drawing:

> A drawing is a representation, which means that it implies the construction of an image, which is something altogether different from perception itself, and there is no evidence that the spatial relationships of which this image is composed are on the same plane as those revealed by the corresponding perception. (p. 47)

We would agree with Piaget that the spatial constituents of the image are not "on the same plane as those of . . . perception"; we suggest, however, that they are nevertheless implicit in the structural description for ordinary object perception. But how do they become explicit?

The classical theory of abstraction, such as offered by the British Empiricists was that the comparison of particulars led to the detection of common features. The comparison of balls, moons, balloons, and lollipops resulted in their particular identities of objects being somehow cast off leaving only the abstracted form of roundness. Concept formation research of a decade ago made the same assumption: people could acquire concepts merely by comparing instances and forming hypotheses about critical features. However, how can a feature such as roundness be hypothesized, that is, manipulated in consciousness, if it is merely an implicit feature of a particular object?

This line of criticism led Cassirer (1957) to deny the validity of abstraction theory. In the first place, he argued, forms did not emerge gradually from objects: "The discovery of spatial forms marked a genuine crisis in spatial consciousness". He argued that percepts must be differentiated from concepts; the latter have their power by virtue of the fact that they are represented by a symbol or symbol system. Thus a world of symbols intervenes between percept and thought. Cassirer states:

> The phenomenon of perception, taken in its basic and primary form, in its purity and immediacy, shows no such division. It presents itself as an undivided whole, as a total experience, which is, to be sure, articulated in some way but whose articulation by no means comprises a breakdown into disparate sensory elements. This breakdown occurs only when the perception is no longer considered in its simple content but is viewed from a definite intellectual standpoint and judged accordingly. (p. 27)

Thus one candidate for the origin of the forms (as opposed to object concepts) is the acquisition of a symbol system for representing space, the primary example being ordinary language. The language consists of a set of artifacts created over the generations which the child encounters in his experience and which he learns to utilize for the representation of his own experience.

Spatial concepts are therefore considered in terms of a conceptual or symbolic system that arises through analysis and reflection and not directly by viewing nature: rather, their meanings must be "wrested from the world of language." Cassirer argues that spatial knowledge does not reflect concrete data but reflects, instead, the process of symbol formation. The concrete knowledge of space, "the space of action", is replaced by the symbolization or representation of space, "the space of intuition", which breaks up the stream of successive experiences and organizes it into conceptual systems. The conceptual system one employs to represent space depends upon which spatial determinations and relations one postulates as invariant. Thus according to Felix Klein cited by Cassirer (1957, p. 157) every special geometry is a theory of invariants which is valid in reference to a set of transformations. Whether a square and a rectangle are considered as similar or different depends on which transformations you choose to admit.

There is much similarity between Cassirer's views on this development and those of Piaget. Both make a clear distinction between perception and representation, the latter of which is the primary component of thought and intelligence. They differ primarily in that Cassirer attributes the development to the culture while Piaget attributes it to the internalization of the child's actions. We suggest that it is neither. Neither action nor language create the structural descriptions. Structural descriptions reflect the basic coding processes of the human mind. From these resources, descriptions are constructed which are invariant across actions for example and which can be explicitly represented in the form of a symbol, but they originate in neither. Although we disagree as to the origins of spatial categories, we agree with both Piaget and Cassirer as to the implicitness of perceptual space and the explicitness of conceptual space.

However, not all the constituents of spatial structural descriptions are represented lexically in ordinary language. Some are too complex and the language specifies these structural descriptions at a particular level of generality or abstraction. Furthermore, these lexical descriptions are appropriate primarily to some forms of activity, such as differentiating objects and displays but not so appropriate for other activities, such as drawing or copying. Other forms of symbolic activity make other features of structural descriptions explicit. To these we now turn.

B. Visual Representations of Space

The problem of "representation" in art has been examined by Gombrich (1960) and Arnheim (1974). In art there is no doubt that there is a difference between one's perception of nature and one's representations of nature. The questions then becomes what is the relation between what one sees and what one draws or constructs. The first relates to the features implicit in our perception; the second to those explicit represented in art and artifice.

Gombrich's (1960) conclusion is quite compatible with the views presented above: "...the correct portrait, like the useful map, is an end product on a long road through schema and correction. It is not a faithful record of a visual experience but the faithful construction of a relational model" (p. 90).

What is the relation between the development of those representations such as maps and perception in the first case and between conceptual or representational space in the second case?

Gombrich (1960) states that in order to describe or portray the visible world in art one needs a developed system of schemata. The schemata are compared to a questionnaire or formulary which select information from the visual world: only those aspects of information that are relevant or useful are registered in the schemata. The objective of the artist, that is, his conception of what he is trying to do, together with the constraints of the medium in which he is working and the visual forms that he already knows or can portray, will determine what information he gains from his perceptions of the world. Gombrich provides interesting illustrations of the important effects of an artist's schemata on what he sees in nature. Carland assumed that the Cathedral of Notre Dame was a Gothic structure so although he was "drawing it from nature" he gave it pointed arches when in fact it had rounded windows. Similarly, Goltzius, a master of Dutch realism, in portraying a whale washed ashore, apparently mistook the flipper for an ear and hence made it look remarkably like a cow's ear and placed it much too close to the eye. In both cases the artist's schema or conception or expectancies regarding the event influenced both his perception of the event and its subsequent portrayal. The act of portrayal itself involves the choice or guess of an appropriate schema or form and correcting it by repeatedly comparing the production with the object it represents. Gombrich writes: "The artist who wants to represent a real (or imagined) thing does not start by opening his eyes and looking about him but by taking colors and forms and building up the required image" (p. 395).

He argues, moreover, that these schemata are invented, not discovered simply by looking intensively at nature. Two further examples drawn from Gombrich document this point. An early art historian had described how Masaccio had "loved to paint drapery with few folds and an easy fall just as they are in natural life." Before Masaccio no one did; after Masaccio many artists did. Gombrich then asks, "What difficulty could there have been in this simple portrayal which prevented artists before Masaccio from looking at drapery for themselves" (1960, p. 12)? A second example comes from Constable's experiments with color, such as his use of yellow paint to represent sunlit green grass, which , although it at first looked odd, was adopted by a whole generation of artists. Art develops by the progressive development of "a vocabulary of forms"; what can you see in nature and what you can "say" in art depends on the limitations of your vocabulary of forms and colors. That vocabulary is expanded by such inventions as we have mentioned above and it is transmitted primarily from looking at the record of these inventions, that is from looking at other paintings, not directly at nature. It is because of this invented, conceptual property that art has a history at all.

But what is the relation of this "vocabulary of forms", what we call the explicit representation of space, to the spatial information implicit in the structural descriptions of objects. Gombrich claims that the former are invented and that their invention permitted the artist and his audience to see nature in a new way. We suggest, however, that these inventions are not *sui generis* but an explicit representation of aspects of implicit structural descriptions. That is, forms are not invented but explicated.

Arnheim's (1974) account of the development of children's art is quite compatible with the view that pictorial representations are determined by the vocabulary of forms described above. What the child draws is not any printout of the real world, but the visual world recast in terms of the pictorial schema that the child has learned. While there is a discontinuity between perception and representation, Arnheim points out several parallels between the perceptual development of children and the progressive elaboration of their drawings. For example, despite their similar visual projections, a 6 foot man at 10 feet *looks* larger than a 3 foot child at 5 feet, and children's drawings tend to preserve this fact. Similarly, there is a corresponding pattern of progressive differentiation in the child's perceptual world and the pattern of differentiation in a child's drawing. However, children undoubtedly see more than they draw. To account for this Arnheim also relies on the concept of representation. "Representation never produces a replica of the object but it's structural equivalent in a given medium" (p. 132). The evolved system for representing objects or events depends on the medium in which the artist is working. But within any medium the "vocabulary of forms" demonstrates a continuous evolution. For children's drawings it involves differentiation and integration of simple lines to circles, to angles, to obliques, and so on. Whatever the child draws will be constructed out of the forms available to the child at the time. Arnheim presents a convincing set of drawings composed entirely of straight lines and circles made by preschool children in which the same set of elements, or forms, are rearranged to represent such diverse object as a hand with fingers, a flower, a face, and a sun, or even the teeth of a saw. The evidence is compelling that the child draws in the manner that Arnheim and Gombrich describe; any object is represented by, or within, the set of elements, operations, or forms available. Improvements in drawing occur by virtue of refinements and precision in the use of these schemata or forms, and innovation occurs through the development of alternative sets of forms.

The relation between ordinary object perception and artistic (form) perception has been clearly stated by Arnheim (1974):

> There is a basic difference between the vision of the artist and everyday behavior. In practical orientation we concentrate on identifying objects. (p. 236)

> Psychologically we can say that although we move freely in space and time from the beginning of consciousness, the artist's active grasp of these dimensions develops step by step, in accordance with the law of differentiation. (p. 218)

Two points of divergence between Gombrich and Arnheim may be mentioned. First, Gombrich criticizes Arnheim for assuming that the relation between perception and representation in art is so close that once we are sufficiently exposed to such revolutionary works as those by Picasso and Klee we see that they "look exactly like the things they represent." Rather, Gombrich emphasizes the varying objectives an artist may have in his portrayals, and the inventiveness he may use in achieving these objectives.

The second concerns the origin and cultural transmission of these forms. When a child draws a circle, has he learned it from looking at balls, moons, and wheels, or from experimenting with his own pencil drawings, or from looking at other people's portrayals or representations of balls and circles? Only (some) psychologists believe the first; Arnheim favors the second, and Gombrich emphasizes the third. Arnheim (1974) states, "Again we are not dealing with an imitation but with an invention, the discovery of an equivalent that represents the relevant features of the model with the resources of a particular medium" (p. 169). Gombrich, on the other hand, emphasizes the role of the culture, that is the effects of looking at other artists' works on the development of representation. In regard to the development of a child's ability to represent things in art there is some anecdotal evidence that children's drawings of houses are markedly facilitated by looking at other children's drawings, as opposed to looking at the houses themselves. It is also well documented that it is easier to copy a painting than to paint from nature. The implication is that in copying the painting, the biggest part of the work is done by the previous artist, namely that of providing, or at least suggesting, the appropriate schemata for representation. This suggests that one learns to represent nature in art more by looking at art than at nature.

The divergencies between these views reflect the fact that Gombrich as an historian is attempting to find the continuity in the culture whereas Arnheim like Piaget is more interested in the origin of forms in an individual's experience.

The extent to which a cultural media such as drawings and maps evolved has been indicated by McLuhan (1964; cf. Ivins, 1946):

> The art of making pictorial statements in a precise and repeatable form is one that we have long taken for granted in the West. But it is usually forgotten that without prints and blueprints, without maps and geometry, the world of modern sciences and technologies would hardly exist.
>
> In the time of Ferdinand and Isabella and other maritime monarchs, maps were top-secret, like new electronic discoveries today. When the captains returned from their voyages, every effort was made by the officers of the crown to obtain both originals and copies of the maps made during the voyage. The result was a lucrative blackmarket trade, and secret maps were widely sold. The sort of maps in question had nothing in common with those of later design, being in fact more like diaries of different adventures and experiences. For the later perception of space as uniform and continuous was unknown to the medieval cartographer, whose efforts resembled modern non-objective art. (p. 145)

In all of the theoretical contexts we have considered, systems of representation of an abstract, conceptual, or symbolic nature have been postulated as an important constituent of explicit knowledge. It is these mental representations that are used to account for the possibility of thinking, or intelligence, and for the development of human culture. It is important to notice, however, the slightly different meanings of "representation" in two contexts. For Gombrich and Arnheim, representation is the performance in a medium such as pencil, paint, or clay. For Piaget and Cassirer, and for us on the other hand, representation is a conceptual, imagined, or conscious mental event that lies behind these activities. In our view, it is the former that makes possible the latter.

To distinguish perception from representation is not to solve the problem of how they are related. As we suggested earlier, the clue to the problem is that representations are not in substance different from the structural descriptions that permit the recognition of objects. Rather they are aspects of structural descriptions that have been made explicit either through language, drawing, or any other activity in some symbolic medium. We have thus come around to Arnheim's suggestion: "The difference then is not primarily between perception and representation, but between perception of effect (what we have glossed as object perception) and perception of form, the latter being needed for representation" (1968, p. 206).

Visual or pictorial forms, both Gombrich and Arnheim have argued, are invented in the course of explorations with pencil or paint. The forms once invented can be seen as appropriate, with corrections, for the pictorial representation of ordinary objects. But again it should not be surprising that these forms are appropriate to the objects they are used to represent. They are appropriate precisely because those forms are the constituents of the original structural descriptions of objects constructed for the purposes of recognition. In a word, that is why a drawing looks like the object it represents. Artistic productions, then, whether with pencil or paint, provide the medium less for the discovery of reality than for the discovery of the structural descriptions of objects. Only this time, with symbolic forms of representation, the structural descriptions are known explicitly, but not of course exhaustively, as forms. Language does much the same. The development of the word "above" in the invention of speech and in its acquisition by children constitutes the representation as form of what was previously merely part of the implicit structural descriptions for objects and events and their relations. Hence, in one sense children acquire new knowledge, in the other sense, they already knew it. Many theoretical debates have been waged on just this ambiguity.

It may be added that artistic productions do not only make explicit what was already "known" and coded in the structural descriptions of objects and relations. Frequently, the attempt at drawing or making, or for that matter describing, makes one examine the object again to detect features that went unnoticed in the course of ordinary perception. Thus art is a means of greatly elaborating our structural descriptions as well as bringing those descriptions into consciousness as forms. This dual role is a primary justification for education in the arts. (See Goodman, 1968, 1978).

II. THE ORDER OF FEATURE EXTRACTION

The second issue in the development of spatial representations concerns the order in which the implicit features of the structural descriptions can be made explicit. It is important to recall that children have spatial information included in their structural descriptions of *objects* and *events*. But their concepts and their meanings are restricted to a practical, functional level of reality; the spatial information in the structural descriptions for those concepts remains implicit. The progressive explication of that spatial information as conscious forms and relations, and the assignment of meaning to these forms may also be described as a rule-governed developmental process.

The order in which these predicates are made explicit and assigned meaning will be reflected in the child's spatial cognition and the spatial lexicon. Two principles are postulated to account for this ordering. These principles describe the restrictions on the child's early spatial representations by identifying two sources of complexity. Assuming that simpler descriptions will be assigned earlier than complex ones, an analysis of the complexity of the features of the structural descriptions enables one to predict the order in which children should be able to explicitly represent various types of spatial information. The two principles are the Principle of Invariance and the Principle of Information. We will begin, however, by describing our propositional structure for the representation of spatial relationships.

Constructing Spatial Propositions

Spatial relations which provide locative or structural information about some element with respect to some other comprise a large part of the possible spatial propositions. Linguistically these are represented by prepositions, such as "over", "under", "to the left", "beside" and nouns, such as "the top", "the front", and so on, and contribute to sentences which express spatial relations such as "The car is to the left of the tree". To better see the structure of these spatial concepts and relations we shall adopt a Fregean analysis of sentences, meanings, and ideas in terms of the underlying propositions expressed by these verbal expressions.

These spatial propositions may be stated in terms of a predicate-argument relation. The spatial term serves as the predicate and the referents or objects serve as the argument or arguments of the relation. Thus "a big man" would be represented as a one place predicate: big(man). The comparative "the man is bigger than x" would be a two-place predicate: big (man, x) that is, the relation bigger holds between the man and x where x represents some other person, object or norm. Similarly "the biggest man" would be a three (or more) place predicate: big (man, x, y) where the spatial relation holds between the man and at least two other people or things. For our purposes here, however, it is important to notice only that these propositions have both a predicate and one or more arguments.

Two features characterize these propositions. First, each predicate is based on a particular spatial dimension, such as horizontal or vertical, and second, each argument contains a point of reference, what Miller and Johnson-Laird (1976) have called the "relatum". And both the spatial predicate and the referential arguments contribute to the spatial relation. The propositions represent the spatial relation but they indicate little as to the particular properties or features of either the predicates or the arguments that contribute to their complexity. We will first propose two principles that account for some of the complexity in each of these terms of the propositions and then examine aspects of the predicates and arguments of spatial propositions by means of these principles so that we may attempt to order these spatial relations for difficulty.

Principle of Invariance

Spatial propositions differ in their extent of generalizability. A proposition constructed to represent the position of the coffee cup with respect to the desk, for example

on (cup, desk), that is, the cup is on the desk

serves as an accurate description from any position around the desk and, indeed, would be equally appropriate were the speaker to walk around the desk. A similar expression relating the chair to the desk, however,

in front (chair, desk), that is, the chair is in front of the desk

depends critically on where the speaker is standing and where we assume the "front" of the desk to be. In this sense, we would say that the former proposition is more generalizable than the latter since the construction of a single proposition preserves the relations across a variety of spatial positions. We call the generalizability of the spatial proposition the invariance of the relationship.

Invariant predicates remain appropriate when assigned to different aspects of the environment, in spite of changes in the relationship between the speaker and the environment. For example, predicates based on a vertical dimension, such as *up, over, top,* are relatively impervious to changes in the position of the speaker; the propositions constructed on those bases generally continue to provide an accurate description of the world. Predicates such as *in front, behind, to the right,* and so on, exhibit this property only when applied to "relatum" which maintain intrinsic side features, such as the speaker as an ego relatum (the role of various relatum will be discussed shortly). Otherwise, a change in perspective often requires an adjustment in the predicate of the spatial proposition, for example, the transformation from *in front* to *behind.* Similarly, most of the predicates indicating topological space, such as *inside, adjacent to,* and *between* also demonstrate this aspect of invariance which permits a single proposition to represent an event across changes in the speaker's activity or position.

The invariance of the spatial proposition is considered to be an important aspect of complexity in that spatial relationships which remain constant across activities are by hypothesis simpler to represent and operate upon than are those which alter as a function of activity or changes in spatial location. The selection and representation of invariant spatial relationships of objects and events, for example, presumably facilitates their identification across situations and contexts; variable relationships must be reanalysed in each situation and hence provide weak evidence for the presence of known objects. The detection of invariant spatial properties, then, should be simpler than the detection of variable relationships; as a consequence spatial predicates representing these invariant relations should be less difficult than predicates representing variable relations. Invariant spatial propositions assure the consistent applicability of spatial descriptions across various encounters by an individual or by individuals assuming different perspectives than the speaker. Linguistically, too, it should be easier for a child to acquire a description which is invariant and therefore common to both the child and adult than to acquire descriptions which vary with the position of the speaker.

Principle of Information

A second aspect of the complexity of a spatial relation is in the amount of information required to represent an object or event. The spatial proposition reflects this quantitative difference in two ways: first, the proposition may require more than one predicate-argument construction to represent a particular spatial relation thus increasing the number of predicates in a given proposition; and second, predicates themselves vary in the number of arguments they require in a given proposition.

The first point may be illustrated with reference to the problem of assigning representations to line segments in different orientations. (This problem is discussed at length in Chapters 10 and 11.) Horizontal and vertical line segments are each based on a referential system requiring only one dimensional axis, and therefore, only one predicate-argument structure in the proposition:

> *on* (line (H-axis)), that is, the line is on the horizontal
> axis, or the line is horizontal.

These lines are easily constructed, represented, and described by children. Diagonal lines, however, must be related to two axes and thus require two predicates in the proposition:

> *right* (line (V-axis))
> & *up* (line (H-axis)), that is, the line is up to the right, or, a
> right oblique.

These line segments are problematic for children to recall, discriminate, and construct (Olson, 1970a).

The second point is that predicates such as *between* which require two arguments to complete a proposition should be more complex than similar predicates, such as *beside* which require only one. We may illustrate this difference using our formal propositional notation as follows:

Sentence	Proposition	Form
The front of a car	*front* (car)	f(x)
A man in front of a car	*front* (man, car)	f (x,y)
A man behind a car	*behind* (man, car)	f (x,y)
A man beside a car	*beside* (man, car)	f (x,y)
A man above a car	*above* (man, car)	f (x,y)
A man between a car and a truck	*between* (man,car,truck)	f (x,y,z)

The principle of information states that cognitive complexity is a function of the number of arguments taken by the spatial predicates in question. Indeed in an informal experiment which compared the two place predicates *above, beside,* and *behind* and the three place predicates *between,* we found that 4-year-old children made more errors in comprehending and producing the three place predicate. (Note however that the child's position relative to the display was invariant; had he been allowed to move the invariant relation *between* may have been simpler. It is not clear whether invariance or information is the overriding principle in acquisition.) Two factors, therefore, contribute to the amount of information in a spatial proposition: the number of predicates required and the number of arguments taken by each of those predicates. These analyses of the complexity of spatial terms are generally congruent with what is known about the difficulty children will have in acquiring them.

This quantitative explanation of complexity in spatial relationships may be used to re-interpret some of the evidence offered by Piaget and Inhelder (1956). Psycholinguistic studies, too, (Slobin, 1973) have found that children acquire topological spatial terms such as *on* and *in* before they acquire more dimensional spatial terms such as *over*. In their scheme, the child begins by representing information about topological space and later learns to represent Euclidean relationships. Other researchers, however, have either failed to replicate the original studies or have isolated other critical factors not accounted for by Piaget and Inhelder (E. Clark, in press; Fisher, 1965; Lovell, 1959; Walkerdine & Sinha, 1981).

A more parsimonious explanation would be to attribute difficulty not to the topological or Euclidean nature of a relationship, but to the amount of information required to specify the relationship. This point is illustrated by another informal experiment. In a card matching task, 4-year-old children were shown a card with a dot in the centre and a circle set in one of four positions relative to that dot, and situated either near or far from the dot. Thus the proposition required two predicates:

> *right* (circle, dot)
> & *far* (circle, dot), that is, the circle is to the right of
> the dot and far from it.

The children were asked to select a match from two alternative cards, one of which preserved the proximity of the circle to the dot, the topological feature, and the other preserved the dimension of separation between them, a Euclidean feature. If the children were operating on a code which systematically deleted Euclidean features, we would expect their choices to match on the basis of the topological similarity between the two cards. The results showed, however, no preference for either feature, and no difference in the children's ability to describe the basis of their choice in either case. We would expect, however, that increasing the number of features, rather than their topological or Euclidean distinctiveness, would create problems with representation for certain relationships. In Piaget and Inhelder's study, the Euclidean relationships were consistently more complex in that they required at least two dimensions and therefore two predicates, while the topological relations required only one.

Other evidence for the importance of amount of information may be taken from studies by Huttenlocher and Presson (1973). To compare the processes involved in solving orientation and perspective problems, they standardized the two tasks so that the tasks differed from each other in only one critical way. For the orientation problem, subjects had to anticipate the appearance of a display after a rotation; for the perspective problem, subjects had to predict the appearance of the display to an observer positioned at some vantage point other than their own. Therefore, while the rotation problem involved only two arguments—ego and the array, the perspective problem required simultaneous consideration of three arguments—ego, array, and other observer. We would say that a relatum, namely, observer, was added to the arguments of the proposition. Perspective problems proved to be more difficult than rotation problems, and Huttenlocher and Presson suggest that this additional element may have contributed to the complexity of the problem. In Chapter 8 we shall discuss these propositional relations more fully.

Finally, Fishbein, Lewis, and Keiffer (1972) found that with only one object, children as young as 3 1/2 years could identify the perspective of another observer. As the number of display objects increased, so did the errors. Again, an increase in the number of arguments in the proposition increases task difficulty.

In various tasks, then, children's ability to solve problems is limited by the amount of information that must be represented and operated upon in the spatial proposition. Consequently, relationships which require the representation and manipulation of more information will develop later than those which can be more simply represented.

The two principles described above could be used to predict the order in which spatial features are assigned to the structural description of objects and events. We have, however, used them primarily to predict the order in which these spatial features are made explicit as spatial predicates. These then are the basis for representing space in language, drawing, and other media. The predictions for this ordering depend upon an analysis of the complexity of this spatial information. Let us, then, examine each of the predicates and arguments of a proposition for complexity in terms of these principles.

Dimension of the Predicate

In this section we shall consider the dimension of the spatial predicate and some of the factors that contribute to their complexity and ultimately to children's difficulties in dealing with them.

The primary dimensions for representing these relations are the three axes—Vertical (Up-Down), Frontal (Front-Back), and Lateral (Left-Right). These may be further collapsed to define two dimensions—Vertical and Horizontal. Even these two major dimensions are not of equal significance. Whereas gravity specifies a vertical orientation common across activities, no counterpart reliably describes a horizontal.

Spatial tasks which require subjects to make judgements in these two dimensions show differences attributable to the vertical/horizontal dichotomy. Rock (1973, 1974) claims that while objects and their inverted image are easily distinguished, mirror image, left-right discriminations are difficult. This may be attributed to the difference between the dimensions in each case. Similarly, symmetry about a vertical axis has been shown to be more salient than that about a horizontal (Corballis & Beale, 1976; Corballis & Roldan, 1975; Rock & Leaman, 1963). Ghent (1961) observes that written languages, although varying in many respects, all are read from top to bottom. Tilted objects are righted to a vertical (Perkins, 1932) and horizontal objects are often recalled in the vertical although the converse is not true (Takala, 1951). Lumsden and Poteat (1968) find that children initially define "big" according to the extent of the vertical axis although Maratsos (1973) adds a preliminary stage in which a non-dimensional assessment of size is used. Huttenlocher (1967) found children were more successful in copying vertical patterns than horizontal ones. In an object concept task, Butterworth (1975) found that infants had a response bias to "up" in searching for a disappeared object. We report in Chapter 11 that of the eight compass points used in an oblique matching task, response time was fastest for north and second fastest for south positionings of the stimuli. There seems to be ample evidence, therefore, that horizontal and vertical axes are not equally salient or economical dimensions for representing information.

A number of factors serve to assist in the explication of vertical features from the unanalysed structural descriptions prior to that for horizontal ones. The bilateral symmetry of the human body is important in this regard: whereas the left-right symmetry of our bodies makes horizontal discrimination difficult (Corballis & Beale, 1976; Howard & Templeton, 1966; Schaller & Harris, 1975), the top-bottom asymmetry of our bodies facilitates vertical discrimination. Thus, vertical information may be more simply represented because it corresponds to our biological and perceptual biases—to the code out of which we construct our mental representations.

A critical difference between vertical and horizontal relationships is that vertical relationships are invariant to the perceiver while horizontal ones are not. Given locomotion in a horizontal plane, relationships arranged vertically remain invariant across actions; those arranged horizontally do not. Language reflects the same invariance—words which refer to vertical directions ("up", "top") are shared across speakers occupying different positions; words which refer to horizontal directions ("front", "left") are not. This relative invariance of vertically based predicates compared to those that are horizontally based should result in the verticality predicates being explicated from the structural description earlier than horizontal ones and consequently used to express relationships in spatial propositions earlier than are horizontality predicates.

Thus, vertical relationships are less complex than horizontal ones, and the predicates corresponding to each of these are similarly ordered for complexity. This ordering should be duplicated in the child's linguistic development—words referring to vertical relationships ("top", "over") should be acquired before words referring to horizontal ones ("front", "in front" or "left" and "right").

There is also a linguistic argument which makes this prediction plausible. For the vertical there is a word which refers to the top part, "the top", and a word which specifies a location relative to that part, "over". For the horizontal, however, the two meanings are collapsed onto the single term "front" to mean both front part as in "on the front", and a spatial location, "in front". The collapsing of two discrete forms onto a single lexical item is evidence of markedness (Greenberg, 1966). This would make the horizontal relationship marked with respect to the vertical which preserves two separate forms. Generally it is the case that unmarked concepts are acquired before marked ones, and this would result in the primacy of descriptions for vertical arrangements.

Both in constructing structural descriptions for objects and events and in explicating these structural descriptions in the form of explicit spatial propositions, then, we may expect to find that vertical relations are more basic than horizontal ones. Both, however, are fundamental constituents of mental representations.

The Relatum of a Spatial Proposition

Although it has been noted that a spatial relation necessarily implies the existence of a relatum or frame of reference (Clark, 1973a; Leech, 1969; Olson, 1975), the consequences of the nature of that relatum for the representation of spatial relations, has been less well documented. This feature of the spatial proposition has typically been called the "referent" in studies of spatial comprehension and development. Clark (Clark, 1973a; Clark, Carpenter, & Just, 1973) describes the "conditions of application" of various spatial terms (adjectives and prepositions) and explains how the selection of the lexical item is controlled by the properties of the referent as, for example, in the number of spatial dimensions presupposed by certain objects. The role of the referent in children's ability to solve spatial problems involving the concepts "in", "on", and "under" has been demonstrated by E. Clark (1973b), Grieve, Hoogenraad, & Murray (1977), Hoogenraad, Grieve, Baldwin & Campbell (1978), Wilcox & Palermo (1975). In these studies, performance varied, not with the spatial term, but with the referent; a container as referent elicited the relationship "in" while a supporting surface as referent elicited that for "on" regardless of the spatial preposition used in the instruction. Donaldson and McGarrigle (1974) showed a similar phenomenon for the terms "all" and "some" by demonstrating that the response was determined by the referent rather than by the instruction. In another study with adult subjects, we found that descriptions of the location of either a pig or an "X" changed as a function of the referent. When an "X" was drawn on the bottom of an inverted cup, the relationship was described as "The X is *on the bottom* of the cup"; when a pig was placed in the same position, the relationship became "The pig is *on top* of the cup". The change in the relatum from a part of an object to a supporting surface altered the spatial description. Thus the relatum controls the nature of a spatial relation and therefore should control as well the difficulty associated with constructing and representing particular spatial relations.

In our theory, a set of spatial predicates which originate in the mind are assigned to a set of arguments, or relatum, in constructing a propositional representation for various objects, events, patterns, and orientations. Given the importance of the relatum to the spatial proposition, it is necessary to systematically examine the range of possible relatum to determine their effects on complexity, similarity, and so on.

The concern in this section is in elaborating the nature of the arguments or relatum, which accept the spatial predicates, and provide the basis for the construction of spatial propositions. We propose three categories of events which can serve as the relatum in a spatial proposition, each of which has different properties which are reflected in the resulting spatial proposition. The three categories are egos, canonical objects including observers, and noncanonical objects, including frameworks.

Although predicates are assigned automatically to all three of these classes of relatum, the assignment to ego is especially central. As with any other relatum, the assigned predicates indicate tops, bottoms, fronts, and so on, as well as providing the basis for generating over, in front, behind, and the like. A distinctive quality of ego space, however, is that it subsequently provides a means for assigning spatial descriptions to other objects and events in the environment. As we shall see presently, spatial predicates are also assigned to other objects in the environment, such as trees, cars, and so on, but the assignment of these descriptions nonetheless honors the spatial structures established for ego space.

The second class of relatum is canonical objects. These are objects such as desks, cars, rooms, houses, villages, countries, that by virtue of their usual orientation in space, have parts that are described as being intrinsically tops, fronts, backs, and so on. The origins of these parts, we claim, is the same as the origins of the parts of ego space, that is, they were assigned spatial predicates from the same set and in the same manner as was used to determine ego space. Once these have been assigned, the fact that these objects have particular spatial orientations and have distinguishing features which correspond to those orientations, the spatial descriptions, such as top, back, etc. become intrinsic parts of the object description, just as motor, trunk, and roof are intrinsic parts of the car. Because these intrinsic spatial descriptions have become part of the object, their specification no longer depends on the position of ego, although the correspondence between the ego top and the car top may have been responsible for the initial assignment of that description. Thus this spatial system behaves independently and, as a consequence, may come into conflict with the spatial system established by ego. If the intrinsic front of a car defines a space projecting from the part to specify "in front of the car", then depending on the location of ego, there may be a conflict between the representation using the car as relatum and that using ego as relatum. In this second case, the front would merely be the side closest to ego, and the proposition "in front of the car" from the point of view of ego, could easily conflict with the same proposition constructed using the car as the relatum.

In many ways, observers, that is, other people, are treated just as canonical objects. They are assigned spatial features which become intrinsic properties of those people, and they provide the basis for constructing spatial relations. The use of observers as the relatum, however, is more complex than is generally the case for canonical objects, and we shall return to this problem.

The third class of relatum is that of noncanonical objects. These are objects in the environment, which have no particular spatial orientation, and likely have no distinguishing features that mark spatial position. These objects, such as boxes, balls, balloons, can be assigned spatial predicates, again from the same set, and again on a basis to correspond to ego space, but quickly lose those descriptions when the situation changes. That is, the spatial predicates are assigned temporarily, and during that time, the object may be treated as if it were canonical. For example, if it is important to locate something with respect to a tree, one might say that the ball is *in front* of the tree, choosing as the front the side closest to the speaker. In that context, the tree now has a front, and certain minor alterations of the position of ego may not even affect that description. A major disruption in the spatial arrangement, however, as would happen if the speaker moved around to the opposite side of the tree, would invalidate that description. In any new proposition, the front of the tree would need to be reassigned on the basis of ego.

An important difference between canonical and noncanonical objects is that canonical objects can assign space independently of the ego, but noncanonical objects must take account of the position of ego. While noncanonical objects may thus appear more complex since more features of the environment need to be attended to, namely, the position of ego, they are also simpler, since there is no possibility of conflicting descriptions as was the case for canonical objects.

A special case of noncanonical objects is provided by frameworks or displays. These are confined spaces to which the spatial predicates top, bottom, and the like, may be assigned in much the same way as they are assigned to any relatum. Like noncanonical objects, once assigned, these displays are treated as canonical for the purpose of solving the particular problem, or encoding the particular event. They frequently become relevant in experimental tasks such as the rotations problem (Chapter 8) or the line orientation problem (Chapter 11) where it is necessary to keep track of changes in spatial relations by relating a stimulus object to some fixed system of reference.

To return to observers as relatum, we find that these are complex because they can be used either as canonical objects, or they can be used as frameworks to assign representation to noncanonical displays.

The difference between the observer as a canonical object and observer as a framework is in the degree of elaboration required to specify a spatial relation. For the former, spatial relations may take the form:

front (x, observer), that is, x is in front of the observer.

In the three mountain task, for example, this would involve noting which of the mountains was directly in front of the observer, for example,

front (blue montain, observer), that is, the blue mountain
is in front of the observer.

For the latter role of the observer, a spatial relation between two or more entities is interpreted in terms of the space imposed on the display by the observer, for example,

front (x, y, observer), that is, x is in front of y for the
observer.

In the three mountain task, this would involve noting that, for example, the blue mountain is in front of the red mountain, from the point of view of the observer.

The distinction between these two roles for the observer is analogous to the distinction between two problem types in the Huttenlocher and Presson (1979) study discussed in Chapter 8. In that study, item questions, which could be solved only on the basis of what was in front of the observer, were easy, while appearance questions, which required the construction of an entire spatial layout from the point of view of the observer, were difficult. We would account for this difference in terms of the two different roles for the observer as the relatum, and the requirement to construct elaborated spatial descriptions in the second role. This problem is discussed more fully in Chapter 8.

Hence, it is gravity and human sensitivity to gravity which provides the ultimate meaning for the predicates of verticality, *up, down, over,* and so on. These predicates are used to establish canonicality for self and objects, including larger canonical objects such as the room or a building or the world. Hence, permanent canonicality of objects is assigned not on the basis of ego space or of any other canonical object space, but rather on the basis of the sensitivity to gravity.

In contrast to the use of gravity for the assignment of an invariant canonicality, spatial predicates may also be temporarily assigned to noncanonical objects, but here the assignment may proceed from a different basis. The temporary assignment of predicates to noncanonical objects may be on the basis of ego, or other canonical objects, including the world. The one chosen for this assignment may depend on such factors as the relative salience of these relatum in the situation.

Just as gravity is the primary cue to the assignment of verticality, so direction of motion and positioning of perceptual apparatus are the cues to the assignment of the front-back dimension (Clark, 1973a). The third dimension is logically determined once the first two have been specified since no degrees of freedom remain in three-dimensional space.

A similar theory which also takes account of the basis upon which spatial structures are assigned is proposed by Harris (1977). He argues that spatial descriptions may be assigned from two points of view: egos and landmarks. Spatial development involves learning to control both these systems and learning to coordinate them for certain purposes. On the basis of conflict between these two systems, and the child's initial inability to adequately coordinate them, he accounts for children's difficulty on such typical spatial problems as object search in infancy, and the solution to perspective problems and the acquisition of the spatial lexicon for older children. While we agree in principle that a great deal of the difficulty on such tasks is attributed to the need to use these two conflicting systems, our own explanation attempts to elaborate on this position in two ways: first, by treating in a more detailed way the distinguishing properties of the various spatial relatum (three, in our account), and second, by elaborating the notion of competing spatial systems and detailing more precisely the factors which lead to failure in the various spatial tasks we discuss. These analyses are presented in Chapters 5 and 11.

Complexity of Spatial Propositions

Since we assume that predicates are assigned to all relatum in a relatively automatic manner, and that in all cases the predicates originate from the same set in mind, there is no a priori reason to expect systematic differences in the difficulty of assigning these predicates to various relatum. Nonetheless, the two principles proposed earlier indicate that there are essential differences among these relatum. For example, since the predicates assigned to ego and canonical object relatum are invariant across spatial transformations, these should be simpler than noncanonical relatum according to the principle of invariance. As we have seen, however, this invariance is not necessarily an advantage in that the inherentness of the descriptions may produce conflict when there is a competition between relatum for expressing a particular relationship. Thus the assessment of the complexity of a spatial proposition must include as well other features of the spatial relationship, in particular, those that describe the predicate. Specifically, we propose that complexity of a spatial proposition is determined by the interaction between the relatum of the argument and the spatial dimension presupposed by the predicate for a particular proposition. Complexity should influence adult's ability to comprehend and operate upon certain spatial relationships, and children's ability to learn certain spatial relationships in both cognitive and linguistic development.

Rather than consider the problem of complexity exhaustively, we will provide an analysis for only six types of spatial propositions. The order of acquisition of these six types of propositions is the subject of the study reported in the next chapter.

The six propositions are constructed from two types of predicates—vertical and horizontal—and three types of objects as the relatum. The first object is a canonical object which typically has intrinsic spatial parts on all dimensions—top, bottom, front, back, left, and right. A second type of object shares some properties from each of the canonical and noncanonical categories. These are objects such as cups, bottles, trees, tables, coat racks, which have intrinsically specified tops and bottoms, but are noncanonical with respect to fronts and backs and lefts and rights. It is interesting to note that there are very few objects which have canonical fronts and backs but no tops and bottoms. Some examples, however, are mirrors, arrows, carbon paper. The third class of objects are those which are noncanonical on all dimensions, such as rocks, balls, boxes.

Rather than attempting to propose an absolute ordering of these six relationships, we will use the two principles to determine the ordering of specific groups of relationships within the set. Our analysis of an interaction between the effects of the predicate and those of the argument on complexity, prevents us from proposing more detailed hypotheses.

First, according to the principle of invariance, those relationships based on a vertical predicate should be simpler than those based on a horizontal one. Hence, for all relatum, the vertical propositions should be simpler than the horizontal ones.

Second, the presence of intrinsic side parts for the complete canonical object should make horizontal predicates simpler to assign to these than to the other two types of relatum which do not possess intrinsic fronts or sides.

Finally, the relatum which is canonical on only one dimension should present conflict for the construction of spatial relations; for vertically-based predicates the proposition will be as readily constructed as for canonical object relatum, while for horizontally-based predicates, the propositions will resemble those for noncanonical object relatum.

More specific proposals for analyzing these six types of spatial propositions are presented in the next chapter with a study of their development by 3 to 4-year-old children.

It has been argued that spatial cognition develops as the child is increasingly able to assign explicit representations of forms, locations, and relations to the spatial information which was previously only implicit in the structural descriptions of objects. As these forms are assigned a distinctive meaning, they come to be articulated independently of objects. The spatial forms are thus extracted from objects and known in their own right, as conceptual objects at a new level of meaning. It is this divorce of form from object that permits explicit spatial cognition; the new forms which can be operated upon, reassigned, or represented in language or drawing.

The emergence of form from object depends upon the articulation of the propositions implicit in the structural descriptions for objects. The means of extracting these features can be attributed to the child's activities and his adoption of cultural symbol systems; the order in which they are extracted can be attributed to the complexity inherent in the spatial propositions themselves.

By defining spatial cognition in terms of underlying structural descriptions made up of spatial propositions which are explicated in a particular order, it is possible to understand the difficulty associated with certain spatial tasks. The difficulty of a problem should be determined by either or both the availability to the child at any particular stage of development of the appropriate structural description of the object or of the explicit formal or spatial predicates. If problems can be altered such that they can be solved either by means of known structural descriptions or by means of known explicit spatial relations, their solution should be facilitated. We shall see how this proceeds in the subsequent chapters.

5 Aspects of the Development of the Spatial Lexicon

The development of mental representations of space has been described as the progressive explication of the implicit features of the structural descriptions of objects (Chapter 4). Spatial concepts develop when these implicit features become detached from their former object meaning and are assigned their own distinctive meaning with their own distinctive structural descriptions. That is, although "top" had been an implicit feature in an object concept such as "table", the explication of "top" as a meaningful unit in its own right and with its own set of implicit features is required for the development of the spatial concept "top". Once explicated it may be used intentionally as a spatial predicate in the construction of new spatial propositions. The order in which these implicit features are assigned independent meanings to become spatial concepts is assumed to be constrained by the two principles postulated in the previous chapter.

To study the order in which these spatial concepts emerge, it is necessary to have a means for assessing which features are being made explicit. The most appealing way of examining these features is to construct displays in which spatial features are uniquely represented: big/small; round/square, etc. However, as we have seen, this experimental expedient confounds the problem in that the meaning of the feature becomes synonymous with the meaning of the object. The feature, say large, may be either part of an implicit structural description for block *or* it may be known as such apart from the object. But a correct discrimination response would give no indication of whether the child is responding to the object or to the feature.

One way of circumventing the problem is to study the development or explication of these spatial features as meaningful concepts in various conventional symbolic media. The most important of these symbolic systems is language. We may, then, examine the progressive explication of spatial features in the acquisition of spatial language. The spatial terms to be considered in this chapter are the nouns "top", "bottom", "front", "back", and the prepositions "over", "under", "in front", "behind".

To account for the order of explication of spatial properties in the form of spatial concepts, the previous chapter claimed that both the predicate, *top* and the argument table, of the spatial relation had to be specialized: *top* (table). The dimension specified by the predicate is relevant, it was argued, in that vertical relationships (e.g., top) are more invariant than are horizontal ones (e.g., front) and thus should be acquired first. And the argument or relatum to which that spatial relation is applied is relevant in that the classes of relatum are differentially complex in terms of the two principles. To this end we distinguished three types of relatum: ego, canonical objects, and noncanonical objects. Further, we suggested that some objects can serve in both the latter two categories in that they specify canonical features for one dimension only, usually the vertical.

We argued that the complexity of a spatial relation arises from an interaction between the properties of the predicate and the properties of the argument of the spatial proposition. Thus the dimension presupposed by the predicate and the canonicality of a particular feature of the relatum may influence the assignment and acquisition of spatial terms.

If we distinguish the spatial predicates from the types of referents to which these predicates apply we derive a four-fold classification relevant to the present study. The spatial predicates may be on a vertical axis or on a frontal axis (the lateral axis was not relevant to the present study) and they may be predicated of either canonical or noncanonical objects; the relationships are hence vertical-canonical (VC), vertical-noncanonical (VNC), frontal-canonical (FC), and frontal noncanonical (FNC). Can these spatial relations be ordered for complexity in any principled way?

Two issues are involved in the examination of the explication of the structural descriptions of these four types of relationships. The first concerns the nature of the structural description relevant to each of these types of objects. How, for example, do we decide what the "front" of an object is? And how does its intrinsic front relate to the position in front? Are the same criteria used for all objects in all conditions? The existence of alternate frames of reference provides conflicting solutions to these problems. The second refers to the order in which these concepts will be made explicit by children. Are spatial concepts which refer to some dimensions for some referents acquired before others, and how does this order relate to the underlying structural description? These considerations are not independent since the order of acquisition of the term is assumed to be constrained by the nature of the spatial representation implicit in the representation of objects.

The spatial propositions are applied to objects or events for two different purposes which we may identify as structural and relational. In their use as *structural* propositions, the spatial predicates are applied to the internal structure of egos, objects, rooms, and so on in order to relate the constituent spatial properties of these relatum by means of such predicates as top, bottom, front, right, and so on. The spatial relation involved is that between a proper part and a whole object; such spatial propositions describe the internal structure of that object. For canonical objects, these descriptions are initially based on the object's usual orientation in space; the top of a car is its uppermost part in environmental space. These descriptions continue to apply even when the object is disoriented. Thus the *top* of the car is generally taken to be the roof, even if the car has rolled over and the wheels are in the uppermost position. Moreover, for canonical objects such as faces and asymmetrical objects the recovery of these intrinsic spatial components is critical to their recognition (Corballis, 1981; Ghent, 1960; Rock, 1973). In ordinary language, these structural spatial descriptions are represented by nouns: the *top* of the car, the *front* of the house.

Spatial propositions may also be used *relationally* to describe the relationship between objects, between ego and object, and so on. In these cases, such as "The airplane is *over* the lake", "The man is *in front of* the tree", the proposition defines the location of one object with respect to another object or relatum. Such relationships are expressed in ordinary language by means of prepositions.

Consider in more detail the spatial terms used to describe the structural properties of objects. These are expressed propositionally as one-place predicates and, as we have said, linguistically as nouns.

The top of the car	*top* (car)	where top $\Rightarrow$ over (Ppt, H-midline)
The bottom of the car	*bottom* (car)	where bottom $\Rightarrow$ under (Ppt, H-midline)
The front of the car	*front* (car)	where front $\Rightarrow$ in front (Ppt, V-midline)
The back of the car	*back* (car)	where back $\Rightarrow$ behind (Ppt, V-midline)

The meaning of the structural spatial descriptions, then, is given in terms such as "the top is the proper part over the H-midline", "the bottom is the proper part under the H-midline", and so on. But since the designation of a particular H and V midline is not specified in these propositions, their meaning may in fact be ambiguous. Changing the criterion to a different set of H and V axes will change the meaning of the spatial proposition.

The conflict is particularly apparent for canonical objects. The usual interpretation of these axes is to use the environmental space which through gravity indicates an asymmetrical vertical axis. For canonical objects in their usual orientation and for all noncanonical objects, this strategy clearly provides a means for interpreting the appropriate vertical axis and hence assigning meaning to the structural vertical relationships. *Top,* in these cases, is both the uppermost surface and the intrinsic top of the object. When canonical objects are disoriented, the object space although originally given by their usual orientation, is preserved as an intrinsic structure of the object and this object space may now provide an alternative means of specifying a vertical axis: The surface adjacent to the roof. There is a conflict, then, between using environmental space and using object space to establish H and V axes. While the environment will indicate the top to be any upper surface, the object will indicate the top to be a particular part of the object which is environmentally uppermost only when the object is in its canonical orientation (see Figure 5.1). In a word, the structural, canonical *top* may conflict with the more general environmental *top* when the object is in a novel orientation.

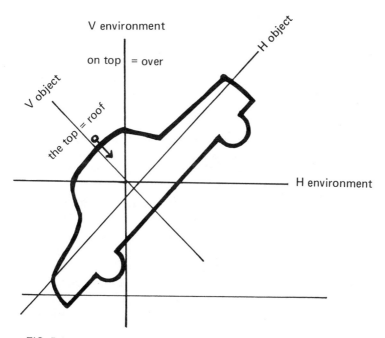

FIG. 5.1   Object space and environmental space may come into conflict.

Ordinary language makes some differentiation between interpretations in that the structural parts, that is, those intrinsic to the object tend to be marked by the definite article. The article in *the top* tends to mark the intrinsic or structural *top* not the current environmental *top*. However, the ambiguity arises more strikingly when this noun phrase is embedded in a prepositional phrase, yielding *on top* and *on the top*. We assume that there is a tendency to interpret *on top* on the basis of environmental space and *on the top* on the basis of object space, partly because of the presence of the definite article in the latter expression. In an experimental test of this hypothesis, however, 17 4-year-old children failed to show this pattern. The children were asked to place an adhesive dot both *on top* and *on the top* of an upside-down car: "Put the dot on top (on the top) of the car." The results, reported in Table 5.1, showed both that they failed to distinguish the two instructions on the basis of the definite article, and that they predominantly used an environmentally based interpretation for both instructions. Informal observation with adults, on the other hand, gives some support to the expected pattern: *on top* refers to a relating in environmental space and *on the top* is determined by the intrinsic top of the object.

TABLE 5.1
Number of Subjects Using Environmental Space
to Decide on Placement of a Dot (Structural)
or Boat (Relational) with Respect to an
Upside Down Car

		on top	on the top
structural:	dot	12	10
relational:	boat	17	14

A similar conflict exists in determing the horizontal structural relations for canonical objects. In these cases, however, the ambiguity involves the use of object space and the use of ego space, since the environment does not clearly signal a front/back or a left/right horizontal axis. Using the object space interpretation, *the front* of the object is the part so designated in the object's usual orientation and use, that is, the headlights of the car, the main entrance to the house, and so on, and is described as *the front*. Using the ego space interpretation, however, the front of the object is the side closest to the speaker. Thus *in front* of the car may be the side door of the car if the speaker and the car are situated in a particular way. Again, however, we expect that adults typically resolve this problem by taking the definite article to specify object space, that is, to designate the location of structural spatial parts of canonical objects, thus *the front* marks a front in a dimension specified in object space while *in front* may specify either object space or ego/viewer space.

We expect that other factors contribute as well to the interpretation of the propositions which are potentially ambiguous. Some of these factors are the likelihood of encountering the object out of its usual orientation, the use of the spatial term as the name for an intrinsic part of the object (compare the bottle *top* with the *top* of the chair), and the degree of difference between the two frames of reference. Small discrepancies may be ignored and transformations sharing some aspects of predicates, such as those of 90°, 180°, and 270° (e.g., top-right vs. top-left) may produce more conflict than others.

Next, consider in more detail the terms which indicate the relational propositions for these terms. These two-place predicates are given lexically by the preposition *over, under, in front, behind.*

X is over the car	*over* (X, car)
X is under the car	*under* (X, car)
X is in front of the car	*in front of* (X, car)
X is behind the car	*behind* (X, car)

Again, these terms must be interpreted in terms of a specified set of H and V axes, and may thus be ambiguous where more than one set of axes can satisfy the proposition. As with the structural propositions, the problem is particularly apparent when these propositions are applied to canonical objects. For the verticality predicates *over* and *under* the conflict is between using object space and environmental space, especially when the relatum is disoriented. For the horizontality predicates *in front* and *behind,* the conflict again is between object space and ego space.

Whereas for the structural propositions discussed for the nouns, *top, bottom, front, back,* adults are expected to use object space as a frame of reference, for the relational propositions built around prepositions, we expect adults to use the environmental space as a framework for vertical relations and ego space for horizontal relations. Consider, for example, *over* and *on top.* An object *over* a canonical object such as a car that was upside down would not ordinarily be assigned to the space adjacent to the intrinsic top. That is, the V axis relevant to the assignment will not be that of the car in its present orientation. Rather, *over* will be the relation specified by the H axis and V axis of the environment. Most adults will agree, however, that *the top* of the car continues to be determined by the roof, even in this bizarre orientation. Note again that the intrinsic top is marked by a noun with the article *the* while the environmental relation is marked by the proposition.

Children, too, change the meaning of the axis according to its use in structural or relational propositions. Again, in the informal study mentioned above, 4-year-old children were tested on the following two items. They were asked to either place a *boat* "on top of" an upside down car, or place an adhesive *dot* "on top of" the upside down car. The first instruction is relational in that it specifies a spatial relation between two toy objects, while the second is structural in that, like a pointing gesture, it merely identifies a part of an object. While all 17 children used the environmental axis to determine the meaning of *on top* for the boat item, only 12 of the children used the environment for the dot item. A similar adjustment was found in comparing *on the top* for the two types of propositions. These data are also shown in Table 5.1.

To summarize, spatial nouns *top, bottom, front,* and *back* are spatial terms which take their properties from the canonical objects. The *top* of a canonical object remains the invariant part across rotation in space.

Spatial prepositions, on the other hand specify relations on the basis of environmental space or ego space or object space and hence do not reflect the orientation of the relation. That is, *over* specifies a relation which ignores the orientation of the objects related.

This distinction is subtle however and most theorists and perhaps most speakers have ignored it. It remains to be seen what children make of it. It is possible for example that young children compute the space for the object more readily than they do for the environment. If so, they will treat the prepositions much like they treat the nouns. The confusion arises because of the ambiguity in the source of the H and V axis to be used in computing the relations *over, under,* and so on. One may use axes specified by the canonical objects or one may use the axes specified by environment and by ego.

On the basis of the discussion presented so far in both this chapter and the previous one, we may summarize the assignment of spatial predicates to objects and events as follows: First, spatial predicates may be assigned to three major classes of relatum: egos, canonical objects (including other observers, and larger canonical environmental spaces like rooms, houses, and the world), and noncanonical objects (including certain frames of reference, such as display frameworks). Second, the interpretation of the relation in every case depends on assigning meaning to the proposition in terms of some axis, or set of axes since we have seen how the specification of an axis is fundamental to each spatial proposition. The axis is based on either the environment, the ego, or the canonical object. Where more than one of these bases may generate the axes, the meaning of the proposition is ambiguous. Resolving the ambiguity requires selecting from the possible axes to arrive at a consistent interpretation for a particular spatial relation. The particular interpretation chosen in each case is expected to be constrained by the extent of invariance offered by each type of axis. Acquiring a concept involves arriving at a consistent interpretation for a particular spatial relation.

The environment provides the most stable reference system because it is common not only to the environment but also to canonical objects and to all persons, hence, axes drawn from that system will be the most invariant; the space generated by canonical objects contain considerable invariance since they are, at least originally, fixed in orientation in space (if they are canonical) and the descriptions are invariant across speakers—an upside-down car is upside-down for both you and me; the ego is the least invariant source of description of relations between objects or parts of objects since spatial structures generated from it change for every person or for each individual in a new spatial location. Thus the order of the invariant properties of the three sources of spatial descriptions are environment (itself a canonical object with an intrinsic vertical axis specified by gravity), canonical objects, and ego.

Let us, then, apply these descriptions to the relatum used in the reported study to determine a basis for assigning meaning. The strategy is to begin with the most invariant interpretation and attempt to apply it to the relatum and to move progressively down the list until we arrive at a meaning for the axis which may be used for that relatum. The hypothesis is that the description will be assigned the most invariant form possible.

Because of the compelling gravitational asymmetry, the normal environment always provides a means for assigning a vertical axis. We would expect, then, that vertical relationships with any of the relatum will be interpreted in terms of the environmental axis. Note, however, since the ego was never disoriented with respect to the environment in the present study, descriptions in terms of ego space or environmental space are indistinguishable. And since the ego initially takes its spatial properties from the environment, we will simply refer to descriptions assigned on the basis of either as "ego-related".

The environment offers no reliable counterpart for describing horizontal axes. The compass point of N-S and E-W are invariant, but they are not accessible to direct perception in a way analogous to gravity. The next option, then, is to use object space. This possibility exists only for canonical objects containing intrinsic fronts and backs. Spatial relationships with these objects, then, were expected to be based on the object-related horizontal parts of the objects, such as spatial relations to the intrinsic front or back of a canonical object.

Finally, horizontal spatial relationships with noncanonical objects must be defined in terms of ego space, since the first two options cannot apply. The horizontal descriptions from ego space are based on the descriptions of the front/back/left/ and right of the body ego. These are not particularly invariant in that they are tied to a particular person and a particular position, hence these relationships should be most difficult to assign and to acquire.

Three hypotheses follow from this analysis. The first predicts the type of description that will be preferred by children for the relatum and various dimensions in terms of these constraints outlined above; the second suggests an ordering in the conformity to these preferred descriptions which corresponds again to the ordering outlined above in terms of their invariance; and the third examines the relative difficulty encountered with those propositions expressed by nouns and those expressed by propositions.

The three types of descriptions and the corresponding relationships are summarized by the following hypothesis:

Hypothesis 1 (H 1):
    a) Vertical ⟶ Ego/Environment-related
    b) Horizontal-canonical ⟶ Object-related
    c) Horizontal-noncanonical ⟶ Ego-related.

This hypothesis predicts that there will be a tendency to interpret vertical relationships in terms of the environmental (or ego) related vertical axis, horizontal relationships with canonical objects to the intrinsic object related features of those objects (the front, the back), and horizontal relationships with noncanonical objects to the ego related designations for front and back.

The second question is to examine the consistency with which these preferences are adopted by children. In general we expect that children will show greater conformity to these choices as a function of their invariance, that is, that the order of consistency will parallel the order of assignment to the various relatum. Accordingly, the second hypothesis predicts that the children will be most consistent in their assignments of vertical descriptions on the basis of the environment, less consistent in their assignment of horizontal relations to canonical objects on the basis of the object space, and even less consistent in their assignment of horizontal relations to noncanonical objects on the basis of the ego space.

When a consistent interpretation has been resolved for a particular proposition, then, the child may be said to have "acquired" the corresponding lexical item. This designation of acquisition is based on the notion that a lexical item is mastered when it has a particular meaning that corresponds to a given situation. Thus, if the child can consistently resolve the inherent ambiguity of "in front" by interpreting the meaning to be derived by the object space if the relatum is canonical and by the ego space if the relatum is noncanonical, then the child has established a meaning for "in front". If, however, the meaning of "in front" is not determined by any rule, even a variable rule which depends on the relatum, then the child has not fully mastered the lexical item. The child's interpretation of "in front" in the latter case would be erratic and unpredictable. Hence the consistency with which the child interprets the proposition in a given situation provides a reflection of the extent to which the child has mastered the corresponding lexical item.

The second hypothesis, then, states that a consistent application of the preferred descriptions outline in Hypothesis 1 will proceed in a given order, and that that order will be the same as the one which determined the assignment of descriptions initially. The most preferred, description, therefore, will also be adopted most consistently. This may be summarized as follows:

Hypothesis 2 (H 2):
Vertical (Ego/Environment Related)   used more consistently than
Horizontal Canonical (Object Related)   used more consistently than
Horizontal Noncanonical (Ego Related)

Therefore, lexically,

V precedes HC precedes HNC.

The lexical specification of this hypothesis is that a consistent use of "top," "bottom", "over", "under" will precede that for "front", "back", "in front", "behind" and that the latter set will be applied to canonical objects before they are applied to noncanonical objects.

Finally, an examination of the propositional form for each relationship in terms of the Principle of Information leads to predictions for a difference between the acquisition of the concepts represented by nouns and those represented by prepositions. The spatial nouns are one place predicates while the prepositions are two place predicates. This increase in information in the representation of the propositional relationships should be reflected in the order of acquisition; specifically, spatial nouns should be acquired before spatial prepositions. This, then, is the third hypothesis:

Hypothesis 3 (H 3): nouns preceed prepositions.

The lexical manifestation of this would be that the nouns "top", "bottom", "front", and "back" should be acquired before the prepositions "over", "under", "in front", and "behind".

Method

To test the hypotheses, an experiment comprised of four tasks involving the memory and description of spatial relations was conducted with 48 children ranging in age from 3.2 to 4.11 years ($\overline{X}$ = 4.1). There were 24 boys ($\overline{X}$ = 4.1 years) and 24 girls (4.1 years).

Each subject was given all four spatial tasks. Three of the tasks tested comprehension and production of linguistic descriptions, that is, the explicit representations of these spatial relations. The fourth task was non-linguistic and provided some access to the entire structural description involved in a spatial relation. Four different orders of presentation were generated such that in no two orders was a particular task preceded or followed by the same task. Six boys and six girls were assigned to each of the four orders.

The relatum used to test the hypotheses varied in their canonicality: one was canonical for both vertical and frontal dimensions; one was canonical for the vertical dimension only; and one was noncanonical on all dimensions. None of the relatum was laterally canonical, so that horizontal was represented only by the frontal dimension.

Hypothesis One was tested by examining the type of interpretation used for each spatial relation for each relatum. Hypotheses Two and Three by examining the number of responses conforming to those designations for each of the spatial relationships. Subjects' responses were therefore, scored in two ways: the type of spatial designation indicated by each response and the number of responses which conformed to the preferred designation for each type of relationship.

Object Placement Task

Materials. The three relatum corresponding to the three degrees of canonicality were as follows. The non-canonical object was a 3.75 cm. wooden cube; the object with intrinsic vertical parts was a bottom 6.50 cm. high that had no marked front or back; and the canonical object with vertical and horizontal parts was a toy car 10 cm. long and 4.5 cm. high. In addition, there was a red wooden star, 3.75 cm. across and a package of self-adhesive red dots.

Procedures. The experimenter (*E*) and subject (*S*) sat side by side at a table. The group of objects was placed in front of *S* and s/he was asked to identify them. A play-like atmosphere was established in which *S* was given a red dot and asked to place the dot in locations indicated by *E*. Beginning with one of the three objects, *S* was instructed to place the dot on "the top", "the bottom", "the front" and "the back" of each of the three objects. The procedure was repeated this time requiring *S* to place the wooden star "over", "under", "in front", and "behind" each of the objects. The order in which objects were presented was counterbalanced across subjects.

Scoring. Responses were scored to calculate the number of responses for each relation which conformed to the interpretation given in Hypothesis One, testing, therefore, only Hypotheses Two and Three. Scores were assigned for each instruction with each of the objects, and could be combined to produce totals for dimensions, relatum, or spatial relations.

Picture Selection Task

Materials.   Three sets of 7 cm. × 10 cm. colour prints were taken of the objects described in the previous task. Set A, Part-Object, showed one of the three objects set in a canonical orientation with one of the six parts indicated in red, such as the car with the front covered in red tape. The top, bottom, front, back and the other two sides were similarly marked, producing six pictures for each object in the set. Set B, Object-Object, showed the star in one of six positions relative to each object set in canonical orientation, for example, star over the block. Set C, Rotated Object-Object, showed the bottle or car rotated in the plane either 90° (on an end) or 180° (upside down). Again the star was placed in one of the six positions relative to each object, producing twelve pictures for each of the bottle and car.

Pictures were displayed on a vertical display board made from a sheet of plywood 30 cm. × 50 cm. with supporting ledges on the midline and at the bottom.

Procedures.   The three parts of the task were always given in the order Set A, Set B, Set C, and are referred to herein as Selection Task A, Selection Task B, and Selection Task C.

S sat behind *E* at a table facing the display board. *S* was told to find the picture that *E* requested.

For Selection Task A, all six pictures for a particular object were on the board arranged in a random order. An instruction, such as, "Point to the picture of the block with the red top" was given, and *S*'s response was recorded. This command was repeated for "top", "bottom", "front", and "back" for each of the three objects.

For Selection Task B, four choices were created for each item, the three incorrect alternatives in each case being selected for the type of error they represented. In this way, the errors could be controlled and analyzed. Subjects were asked to select from the group of four the picture that showed the star "over", "under", "in front of", or "behind" the object relatum.

Selection Task C required subjects to select from among four alternatives the picture with the star "over", "under", "in front", or "behind" the block or bottle when the object was out of its canonical orientation. For each instruction, more than one of the four pictured alternatives provided an acceptable representation of the relationship; for example, when the car is rotated 90°, the description "under the car" may mean near the bottom of the car or at the bottom of the picture. Consequently, when subjects had made their choice, that picture was removed from the board and subjects were asked to find, from those remaining, another picture that fit the description. This was repeated until subjects said no more suitable pictures remained on the board. Responses, therefore, produced a rank ordering of the pictures as representations of each description.

Scoring. The responses from the Selection Task were scored in order to test all three hypotheses. The selections from all three parts of the task were classified for the type of spatial representation involved; that is, ego-related or object-related. If the response indicated neither of these designations, then the type of error committed was described. The type of representation used for each spatial relationship was tested for its congruity with the predictions in Hypothesis One.

The number of responses which conformed to the preferred interpretation for each spatial relation in Selection Tasks A and B was calculated to determine an order of acquisition of consistent meanings for these concepts.

Picture Description Task

Materials. The three sets of pictures from the Selection Task were used for Description A, Description B, and Description C.

Procedures. For each set, the child was shown the pictures one at a time and asked for a description of the pictured relationship. For Description A, the instruction was to describe the part indicated in red, such as "Tell me where the car is red". For Description B, the relationship between the star and the referent object was requested, for example, "Tell me where the star is". Description C showed subjects the twelve (12) pictures used in Selection Task C. Again, subjects were asked, "Tell me where the star is".

Scoring. Each picture in Selection C permitted two descriptions. For example, an upside-down car with a star above the object but near the bottom of the car could take an ego-related description, "The star is *above* the car", or an object-related one, "The car is *below* the car". Responses for Description C were scored by indicating which of the pair of possible descriptions was used by the child. Descriptions which did not fit either alternative for a picture were considered incorrect and not analyzed further. By comparing the observed frequency of use of each description for each type of relationship with the descriptions predicted by the theory, it was possible to test Hypothesis One.

The number of descriptions conforming to the preferred choice given for each spatial relation in Description A and Description B was calculated to test Hypotheses Two and Three.

Memory Task

Materials. The purpose of the memory task was to present complex relationships which had to be encoded in terms of a particular fixed relatum rather than any external environmental cues. To minimize these cues, a box was constructed which created an enclosed black visual field on which the pictured relations were displayed.

The box was approximately 30 cm. cubed. It had five sides, the open side facing down on a sheet of black bristol board. The inside was painted dull black. On one side of the box a 12 cm × 15 mm. rectangle was cut out and tracks placed along the bottom and sides. Thus, a picture could be fitted against the hole from the exterior of the box. On the side of the box opposite the picture space was a "peephole", about 1 inch in diameter and placed so that it would be opposite the center of the picture. The interior of the box was illuminated by two lights attached to a timer.

A set of pictures was also required for this task. Each picture displayed the car (from the previous tasks) in the center of the picture surrounded by three objects, one in each of the three planes—vertical, lateral, and frontal. These three additional objects were a red plane, a blue boat, and a yellow car. Since a particular object was always in the same plane on the recognition trial and varied only in its polar position (that is, "over" versus "under" or "front" versus "back"), it was not necessary for the S to remember *which* object was in a certain position, only that some object was. For example, the S would see the picture and encode that something was *in front* of the car (in terms of object space), *under* the car, and *beside* the car (in terms of object space). The alternative pictures either preserved all three positions (correct response) or violated one of the three. Selecting, for example, the picture in which something was *over* the car instead of *under* it as in the original picture would constitute a vertical error.

Three sets of pictures were created which varied the object assigned to each plane, so that each object appeared in each plane in one of the sets. Subjects were randomly assigned one of these three sets. All possible combinations of the positions produced 8 pictures for each set.

The pictures were taken against a background of black burlap and printed in both 5" × 7" and 3" × 5" formats.

Procedures. The task began with two practice trials. Subjects were told that if they looked into the box, they would see a picture, and that they should look very carefully and try to remember where everything goes in the picture so that they could find it again. The timer started the trial by illuminating the interior lights. Following a 12-second exposure, the lights extinguished and the child was told that she now had to find the picture she just saw in the box.

Four of the 3" × 5" pictures were presented on the display board used in the Picture Selection Task. One was the correct picture, and each of the other three were false on one of the three dimensions. Feedback was provided on the two practice trials, and when the child did not understand, a second look into the box was allowed. The items for the practice trials were two of the pictures from another set.

For the task itself, subjects were shown the pictures of one of the sets in a fixed order. Exposure time for each picture was again 12 seconds, but there was no feedback and no adjustment in exposure time. E recorded which picture subjects chose as being identical to the one they had just seen in the box. The session lasted approximately 15 minutes.

Scoring. Each subject was assigned a score for each of the four categories: correct response, vertical error (over/under), lateral error (beside/near/far), frontal error (front/back), the total of these scores necessarily being 8. The scores also were ranked so that an ordering of these four categories was produced for each subject.

Results

Hypothesis one: Type of representation. The prediction in this hypothesis was that (a) over/under and top/bottom predicates would be ego/environment related, (b) front/back and in front/behind would be object-related for canonical objects, and (c) front/back and in front/behind would be ego-related for noncanonical objects. The data were taken from Selection Task A, Selection Task B, Selection Task C, and Description Task C. Let us examine, first, children's performance on the three picture selection tasks.

The distribution of pictures chosen by subjects in Selection A in which a part of an object was indicated in red are presented in Table 5.2, (Part-Object), for each of the three relatum. The picture based on the predicted designation for each instruction is indicated by an asterisk.

In order to show the correspondence between the fully canonical car and the partially canonical bottle and block, the left and right sides of the latter have been scored as object related front and back in order to contrast those responses with ego related front and back. While these object-related designations for noncanonical objects are assumed to be derived by means of anaology with canonical objects, they are not the product of mere transfer of the parts of the car as they were used by some subjects who had not yet seen the car.

TABLE 5.2
Distribution of Responses for Items in Selection A[1]

(a) BLOCK

			PICTURE			
INSTRUCTION	TOP	BOTTOM	O-REL FRONT	O-REL BACK	E-REL FRONT	E-REL BACK
top	44[2]	0	1	0	1	2
bottom	2	41	2	1	2	0
front	2	1	11	4	27	3
back	1	1	3	8	3	30

(b) BOTTLE

			PICTURE			
INSTRUCTION	TOP	BOTTOM	O-REL FRONT	O-REL BACK	E-REL FRONT	E-REL BACK
top	42	0	3	0	3	0
bottom	1	31	4	2	2	1
front	1	2	10	6	25	4
back	0	0	6	7	5	28

(c) CAR

			PICTURE			
INSTRUCTION	TOP	BOTTOM	O-REL FRONT	O-REL BACK	E-REL FRONT	E-REL BACK
top	45	0	2	1	0	0
bottom	3	29	3	2	7	1
front	5	3	25	4	6	5
back	2	1	1	21	9	13

[1]Cases of 'no response' not included in table.
[2]Note: Underlined figures indicate expected response.

As both ego-related and object-related descriptions for vertical relations coincide for objects in their canonical orientation, it is not possible to choose between them to examine H 1(a). Ego-related and object-related descriptions to diverge however, for horizontal spatial relations, permitting the testing of H 1(b) and H 1(c). Hypothesis 1(b), that object-related horizontal descriptions will be used for canonical objects, may be examined by means of the data obtained using the car as relatum. Given the instruction to "find the car with the red front", children were expected to respond with the object-related front of the car rather than the ego-related front of the car. A comparison of the frequency of ego-related and object-related interpretations showed that the object-related description was, in fact, used significantly more often than the ego-related one (χ^2 = 11.22, $p < .01$).

Hypothesis 1(c) predicted that noncanonical objects will be assigned ego-related descriptions for horizontal parts. A comparison of the designations used for the block and bottle confirmed that the ego-related descriptions were used significantly more often than were object-related ones (χ^2 = 37.51, $p < .01$). Subjects predominately chose the front and back of these objects by reference to the position of the viewers; thus front was the position between the object and the viewer.

Selection B, Object-Object, contributed to the examination of the same hypothesis. These data are presented in Table 5.3. The four alternative responses to each instruction are listed with the spatial designation implied by each. A polar error refers to a picture in which the star is placed on the correct dimension but in the wrong polar position, such as "over" instead of "under". A dimension error refers to a picture in which the dimension of the instruction has been violated, such as "over" instead of "in front". Finally, a perspective error resulted if the child took the picture to be a top view rather than the intended front view. In this case the picture of the star "in front of the block" was sometimes taken by children to be a top view such that the "star" was seen as being "over the block". Since these responses were correct descriptions of the display if taken from another perspective and may in fact have been biased by certain lighting cues, they were designated as perspective errors.

For 1(b), the data for the horizontal instructions with the car were examined. Rather than the predicted predominance of object-related descriptions for the canonical objects, it was found that object-related and ego-related descriptions were used equally often (χ^2 = 0.73, n.s.).

A similar analysis of the responses for the block and bottle showed that, as predicted by H 1(c), ego-related descriptions were used more often than were object-related ones (χ^2 = 70.55, $p < .01$).

Selection Task C, the rotated Object-Object Task, tested all three parts of Hypothesis One in that the alternative representations for vertical relationships become disentangled when objects are positioned in ways other than their canonical orientation. Object-related descriptions would be determined by the location of the nearest relevant part, that is, "over" would be closest to the intrinsic "top"; ego/environment-related ones by the invariant vertical axis, that is, "over" would be in an upward direction corresponding to the top of the picture. (Pictures were always shown upright so the top of the picture pointed to the top of the room and to the top of ego.)

The data for Selection Task C are reported in Table 5.4. For each instruction, the total number of times the picture was chosen as the best represen-

TABLE 5.3
Distribution of Responses for Prepositions in Selection B

INSTRUCTION	DESCRIPTION	FREQ.	INSTRUCTION	DESCRIPTION	FREQ.
(a) BLOCK					
over	ego-related	37[1]	in front	ego-related	33
	polar error	2		polar error	2
	perspective	5		obj.-rel.	13
	dimension	2		dimension	0
under	ego-related	34	behind	ego-related	40
	polar error	2		polar error	0
	perspective	12		obj.-rel.	7
	dimension	0		dimension	1
(b) BOTTLE					
over	ego-related	32	in front	ego-related	36
	polar error	6		polar error	4
	perspective	8		obj.-rel.	8
	dimension	1		dimension	0
under	ego-related	38	behind	ego-related	37
	polar error	1		polar error	0
	perspective	9		obj.-rel.	6
	dimension	0		dimension	3
(c) CAR					
over	ego-related	36	in front	obj.-related	25
	polar error	3		polar error	4
	perspective	4		ego.-rel.	17
	dimension	4		dimension	1
under	ego-related	36	behind	obj.-related	23
	polar error	0		polar error	2
	perspective	2		ego.-rel.	23
	dimension	0		dimension	0

[1]Note: Underlined figures indicate expected response.

tation of a particular spatial description is presented in the column labelled "Total". In addition, the number of times that picture was the first choice selection is presented in the following column. All statistical analyses were performed on this first choice data. The column "E" indicates the expected value of the first choice distribution by chance given the number of pictures representing that alternative for each instruction. Finally, the χ^2 statistic compares the observed first choice distribution to that expected by chance.

The results indicate that three of the four descriptions of vertical relations were ego/environment-related and thus congruent with hypothesis 1(a). In the fourth description "under the car", the object-related and ego-related picture were selected equally often.

TABLE 5.4
Distribution of Responses for Items in Selection Task C
(Rotated Objects)

INSTRUCTION	DESCRIPTION	TOTAL	1st CHOICE	E	X²
(a) BOTTLE					
over	ego-related	64	35	23.5	
	object-related	26	12	23.5	11.26**
under	ego-related	71	35	24	
	object-related	30	13	24	10.08**
in front	ego-related	27	23	15.3	
	object-related	35	23	30.7	5.81**
behind	ego-related	32	32	15.7	
	object-related	24	15	31.3	25.41**
(b) CAR					
over	ego-related	56	32	24	
	object-related	43	16	24	5.33*
under	ego-related	52	23	24	
	object-related	50	25	24	0.08
in front	object-related	53	23	27.3	
	ego-related	24	18	13.7	2.03
behind	object-related	46	20	26.7	
	ego-related	26	20	13.3	5.06*

$*p < .05$
$**p < .01$
$***p < .001$

Hypothesis 1(b) predicted that object-related descriptions will be used for horizontal relation of canonical objects, in this case the car. The results indicate, however, that ego-related designations were used equally often.

The designations used for the noncanonical object, the bottle, were consistent with the prediction in H 1(c). Ego-related designations were assigned more frequently than were those classified as object-related.

Other evidence bearing on Hypothesis One is obtained from Description Task C. Subjects' descriptions of the pictures of the star in relation to disoriented referent objects took predominantly one of two alternative forms. Responses were scored by indicating which of the pair was chosen by each subject for each pictured relationship.

Although each picture permitted two descriptions, there were only three pairs of descriptions that subjects used for all the pictures. These three pairs were as follows:

1) Vertical ego/environment-related (VE)   – Vertical object-related (VO)
2) Vertical ego/environment-related (VE)   –Horizontal object-related (HO)
3) Vertical object-related (VO)   – Horizontal ego-related (HE)

Each pair applied to two pictures for each of the car and the bottle. To illustrate, an upside-down car with the star at the top of the picture represented the first pair: the star could be described as "above" the car (VE) or "at the bottom" of the car (VO). Similarly, if the car is rotated 90° so that it is on its end (pointing down) and the star is again at the top of the picture, the second pair is represented: the star could be "above" the car (VE) or "at the back" of the car (HO). Finally, the car in the same position but with the star at the left of the picture permits the third pair: the star could be "at the top" of the car (VO) or "in front of" the car (HE).

According to the hypothesis (H 1(a)), subjects should use the ego/environment-related vertical (VE) more frequently than the object-related vertical (VO). Accordingly, each subject was assigned a score for each of VE and VO based on the proportion of the responses which designated that particular description. A t-test comparing the observed proportion for VE with the expected proportion of .50 showed that ego-related descriptions were significantly more common for the bottle ($t_{47} = p < .01$) but not for the car ($t_{47} = 0.86$, n.s.).

For horizontal descriptions of the car, H 1(b) predicted that children would use object-related descriptions (HO) more frequently than ego-related descriptions, (HE). Since these two possibilities were never directly compared in a single pair, the frequency with which each was used can be considered independent correlated data. Consequently, a t-test was used to compare the frequencies of HO and HE responses. The results showed that HO descriptions were used more often than HE for pictures with the car as relatum ($t_{47} = 2.36$, $p < .01$).

The prediction was also tested by comparing the frequency with which subjects used object-related descriptions for the car with that for the bottle. The hypothesis was that object-related descriptions would be used primarily for the canonical object, the car. The mean frequency of object-related descriptions was found to be significantly greater for the car than for the bottle ($t_{94} = 2.33$, $p < .01$).

To summarize, the object with a canonical front, the car, received an object-related description more often than an ego-related one and more often than did the object without a canonical front, the bottle. Thus, in line with H 1(b) horizontal relationships for objects with intrinsic fronts elicit object-related descriptions.

The same procedure was used to test H 1(c) that the bottle would be assigned ego-related descriptions. The results, however, indicated an equal probability of using HE and HO descriptions ($t_{47} = 0.32$, n.s.). The second test of this hypothesis was made by comparing the frequency of ego-related description for bottle with that for the car. Again, ego-related descriptions were used no more often for the bottle than for the car ($t_{94} = 0.12$, n.s.).

It is possible from the hypotheses to predict an overall ordering of the tendency to assign the four types of descriptions. The ranking of these descriptions should be different for each of the bottle and car. For the bottle, vertical descriptions should predominate horizontal ones, and so the two V categories should be more frequent than the two H responses. Within V, it has been argued that the ego would be used to define the dimension, so VE should precede VO. Similarly, since a bottle has no intrinsic horizontal parts, HE descriptions should be more common than HO. Thus, the predicted rank order of the four categories is VE > VO > HE > HO.

The actual use of these categories by subjects was calculated by rank ordering them for each subject according to the frequency with which they were used. These observed rankings were tested against the prediction by the method of comparing multiple hypotheses suggested by Page (1963). The results showed a significant effect ($L = 1273$, $p < .001$), thus indicating congruence between the observed and predicted rank orders.

Similarly, a predicted rank order was generated for the car. The difference in this case was that HO descriptions should be chosen over HE ones, because of the existence of intrinsic parts in the car. The predicted order, therefore, was VE > VO > HO > HE. This against the observed rankings made by subjects, the fit was again significant ($L = 1273.5$, $p < .001$).

A summary of the results for Hypothesis One is presented in Table 5.5. The predictions for each type of spatial relation are listed in the column on the left; the representations subjects chose for each referent on each task are

TABLE 5.5
Summary of Results for Hypothesis One

Prediction	Relatum	Selection A	Selection B	Selection C	Description C
a) Vertical ego > obj.	bottle car	N/A	N/A	ego > obj. ego = obj.	ego > obj. ego = obj.
b) Horizontal canonical: obj. > ego	car	obj. > ego	obj. = ego	obj. = ego	obj. > ego
c) Horizontal non-canonical: ego > obj.	block	ego > obj.	ego > obj.	N/A	N/A
	bottle	ego > obj.	ego > obj.	ego > obj.	ego = obj.

presented in the body. Nine of the fourteen tests of Hypothesis One conform to the predictions and five show no significant ordering effect; in no case is the outcome contrary to the prediction. Two considerations help to explain the five somewhat anomalous cells.

It was found that for all items requiring a vertical spatial judgement and in which the disoriented car served as relatum, the object parts defined the relationship as often as did the ego. This was particularly true for the predicate *under* where the bottom of the car proved to be an important feature.

The possibility that children generally assign vertical relationships on the basis of object-related designations is untenable, because, consistent with the prediction, vertical relationships with the bottle were assigned ego-related descriptions. The "top" and "bottom" of the bottle did not bias subjects' responses as they did for the car. Why, then, would such an effect occur for only some objects?

It appears that if an object has particularly salient intrinsic parts, then those parts may be used to order spatial relations even when other designations are generally more appropriate. This is the case with the car, and it may be reinforced by the fact that the car unlike the bottle, is rarely used out of its canonical orientation. Thus the association between the "top of the car" and "over" is more compelling than that between the "top of the bottle" and "over". Notice, however, that even for the car, the object-related designation never exceeds the predicted ego/environmentally related one; it merely occurs equally often.

The second general anomaly in the data is the equal assignment of object-related and ego-related horizontal designations for the car in two of the Selection Tasks. The explanation of this result may lie in the nature of picture selection tasks. It has been noted that such tasks bias the subject towards committing egocentric errors (cf., Huttenlocher & Presson, 1973; Ives, Chapter 7, this volume; Pufall & Shaw, 1973). An egocentric error in the present task would be recorded as an ego-related spatial designation. The results obtained in the present study, therefore, may be considered additional evidence of this egocentric bias in selection tasks and not necessarily contradictory to the general hypothesis regarding the representation of spatial relations.

The overall results permit us provisionally to take Hypothesis One as an appropriate description of the spatial representations assigned to pairs of objects: vertical relations are assigned primarily on the basis of ego's and environment's major vertical axis; horizontal relations involving canonical objects are assigned primarily on the basis of the spatial parts of those objects and horizontal relations involving noncanonical objects are based upon the ego's position relative to those objects. The exceptions, however, suggest that subjects have codes for both ego relations and object relations and they choose between them, but those choices are generally systematic and predictable. Let us now examine the order in which these relations are resolved and assigned a consistent meaning by children. The basis for determining consistency in each case will be the conformity to the form of representation outlined in Hypothesis One.

Hypothesis two: order of acquisition of spatial relationship. Each of the four tasks contributed evidence to the examination of the hypothesis that vertical spatial relations will be used consistently before horizontal ones and that horizontal relations with canonical objects will be used consistently before those involving noncanonical ones. The scores then, considered the number of responses to each type of relation that conformed to the interpretation outlined in Hypothesis One.

Combining the data for the nouns and prepositions in the Placement Task, the mean scores out of 6 were 5.58 for vertical and 3.45 for horizontal instructions ($F(1,40) = 102.76, p < .001$). Thus following an instruction to produce a vertical arrangement of objects was easier to interpret than following one which resulted in a particular horizontal array of the same items.

The difference between canonical and noncanonical objects for horizontal instructions was indicated by the interaction between Relatum and Dimension ($F(2,80) = 9.23, p < .001$) for the nouns. While there was no difference between the three objects for vertical instructions ($F(2,80) = 0.56$, n.s.), the differences for horizontal instructions were significant ($F(2,80) = 17.30, p < .001$). A Scheffé test showed that the mean scores for the block and bottle did not differ from each other, but were both significantly lower than the mean score for the car ($F(2,141) = 17.01, p < .01$). A similar interaction was observed for the prepositions, ($F(2,80) = 4.92, p < .01$). Again, differences were found only with horizontal instructions ($F(2,80) = 12.04, p < .001$). The children were more consistent in representing the relationship with the car as a relatum than they were in representing the same relationship with the bottle or block (Scheffé test: ($F(2,141) = 13.09$, $p < .01$).

The Selection Task likewise showed the predicted differences between performance on vertical and horizontal items; while the mean score out of 6 for vertical instructions was 4.74, that for horizontal ones was only 3.67, ($F(1,40) = 32.41, p < .001$).

In this task, however, horizontal relationships with the car were not found to be easier than those with the bottle. This may be due to the egocentric errors on the picture task that were discussed above.

A comparison of vertical and horizontal items in the Description Task again showed the expected difference. The mean scores out of 3.14, or *pi,* were 2.58 for vertical and 1.74 for horizontal descriptions ($F(1,40) = 73.18$, $p < .001$).

However, the predicted difference between the canonical and non-canonical objects for horizontal spatial relations, was confirmed for the nouns but not the prepositions. There was greater agreement in labelling "the front" of the car as object-related than in labelling "the front" of bottle as ego-related ($F(2,80) = 5.03$, $p < .01$); but on the other hand there was greater agreement in locating something "in front" of the bottle as ego-related than there was in locating something "in front" of the car as object-related ($F(2,80) = 16.52$, $p < .001$).

For the Memory Task, subjects received a score on each of the four categories based on the number of times the alternative representing it was selected. The four categories were: Correct, Vertical error, Frontal error, Lateral error. With 8 trials, the total score was 8.

The distribution of the responses among these categories appears in Table 5.6. Since the categories are not independent, χ^2 analysis is not possible. However, it is possible to compare the observed frequency in each cell with that expected by chance. With four alternatives, the probability of selecting any one by chance is .25. This represents an expected value of 96 for each cell, or a mean of 2.0 choices for each subject. Comparisons of the observed frequencies with the expected values indicated that the correct answer was selected more often than chance ($t_{47} = 6.09$, $p < .001$), vertical errors were committed less often than by chance ($t_{47} = 6.67$, $p < .001$), and horizontal errors were chance responses (lateral: $t_{47} = 0.75$, n.s.; frontal: $t_{47} = 1.25$, n.s.). Hence, the representation given by subjects to the information in the vertical dimension was better formed and better recalled than that for the two horizontal relations.

To further test this ordering, namely that vertical errors would be less frequent than horizontal ones, a rank order analysis of these categories according to the responses of each subject was performed. The expectancy was that the number of correct responses would be greatest, lateral and frontal errors would be next most frequent, and vertical errors would be

TABLE 5.6
Distribution of Responses for Memory Task

	CORRECT	V-ERROR	L-ERROR	F-ERROR
Number Responses	163	48	89	84
Expected Value	(96)	(96)	(96)	(96)
Proportion Responses	.42	.13	.23	.22
Expected Proportion	(.25)	(.25)	(.25)	(.25)

least frequent. No prediction was made about the difference between frontal and lateral information. Applying Page's method, the observed rank ordering agreed with the prediction (L = 1303.75, $p < .001$). This order analysis corroborates the findings presented above.

Hypothesis three: Acquisition of nouns and prepositions. The data from the Placement, Selection, and Description Tasks may be analyzed according to whether the spatial term is a noun, indicating the structural relation between a part of the object and the whole object, or a preposition, describing the relationship between two objects. On the basis of the principle of information it had been predicted that spatial nouns would be acquired before prepositions. That is, because they are simpler, the possible ambiguity in interpretation should be resolved for the nouns before it is resolved for the prepositions.

For the Placement Task, no differences were found in performance according to whether the instruction was a noun or a preposition ($F(1,40)$ = 0.33, n.s.). The mean score out of 6 was 4.51 for the nouns and 4.52 for the prepositions.

The Selection Task produced an effect in the direction opposite to the prediction. The mean score for nouns was 4.02 and that for preposition was 4.39, a difference which was significant ($F(1,40)$ = 4.13, $p < .05$). According to the interaction to instruction by dimension ($F(1,40)$ = 13.14, $p < .001$), however, that difference obtained only for horizontal items ($F(1,40)$ = 15.16, $p < .001$); vertical items were equivalent ($F(1,40)$ = 0.63, n.s.).

Finally, the Description Task again yielded results apparently contrary to the hypothesis. The difference between the mean score for the nouns, 1.87, and the mean score for the prepositions, 2.45, was found to be significant ($F(1,40)$ = 60.61, $p < .001$). These scores are out of 3.14, or *pi*. The interaction with dimension was again significant ($F(1,40)$ = 17.99, $p < .001$), although the effect this time applied to both horizontal ($F(1,40)$ = 12.09, $p < .001$) and vertical items ($F(1,40)$ = 77.95, $p < .001$).

What, then, is involved in the representation of these relationships? The data indicate various effects which seem to contradict each other as well as the experimental hypotheses. To reconcile these differences, let us examine each of the vertical, horizontal canonical, and horizontal noncanonical relationships in turn.

For vertical relationships, the nouns and prepositions were equivalent for the Placement and Selection tasks but different for the Description Task; in the latter case there was less consensus in interpreting the nouns than the prepositions. This difference, however, may be attributed to a single picture which was ambiguous and hence created problems of interpretation. The picture used to represent the "bottom of the car" could be seen as illustrating, instead, the "side of the car", as it was the lower facing side that was indicated in red. In the forced choice paradigm of the Selection Task, subjects were willing to accept this picture as superior to the alternatives as a representation of "bottom"; in a free situation, however, "the side" was often considered the more appropriate description.

The data support this interepretation of the problem. The mean scores out of 3.14 for the four relevant instructions are as follows: "top", 2.75; "bottom", 1.79; "over", 2.96; "under", 3.07. Only the score for "bottom" deviates from the rest of the vertical items. This fact, in conjunction with the lack of difference between nouns and prepositions found in the other two tasks, supports the claim that there is no difference in the order of mastery of nouns and prepositions for vertical relationships for these children.

Second, an examination of the scores for the canonical object only, that is, the car, likewise indicates that there is no difference between the spatial relations with nouns and those with prepositions. Across the three tasks, the proportion of conforming responses for the horizontal instructions with the car are as follows: "front", .60; "back", .66; "in front", .60; "behind", .70. These scores are not significantly different from each other. Similar results were reported by Harris and Strommen (1972). Again, no order of acquisition for nouns and prepositions is indicated for horizontal relationships with canonical objects.

The differences between nouns and prepositions for horizontal relationships which were detected by the analysis of variance are all attributable to relationships with noncanonical objects. The proportion of responses conforming to the ego-related interpretation of tasks for the bottle and block are as follows:

		Block	Bottle
Noun	"front"	.49	.52
	"back"	.51	.49
Preposition	"in front"	.60	.61
	"behind"	.69	.69

Here the difference between the nouns and prepositions is significant, and it appears as though the prepositions are resolved before the nouns.

To understand these results it is necessary to consider what young children do in the face of a difficult problem. One primary strategy is to commit an "egocentric error"; that is, to transform the difficult relationship "in front of the block" to the more comprehensible "in front of me". This strategy was adopted for many of the test items, and children who found an item difficult could be seen to use an egocentric interpretation of the problem. Such a response, however, was distinguished from the alternative interpretations, such as object-related or ego-related, in every case *except* a horizontal relationship to a noncanonical object. Here, the egocentric error coincided with the ego-related description, and the scores for these items were inflated by the inclusion of both interpretations.

For all three types of spatial relationships, then, it appears that the acquisition of the corresponding nouns and prepositions is roughly equivalent. In spite of the prediction generated from the Principle of Information, there is no evidence to support the hypothesis that the nouns are used systematically before the prepositions.

A summary of the data pertaining to the order of systematic use for all the relationships is presented in Table 5.7. The proportion scores are calculated by considering all the instances of that item across tasks and represent the probability of a 4-year-old child adopting that interpretation for that item. The overall difference between the nouns and prepositions is not significant (F(1,22) = 0.87, n.s.). The difference between the six spatial relationships indicated in the table is, however, significant ($F(5,18)$ = 15.08, $p<.001$).

TABLE 5.7
Proportion of Responses for each Spatial Relation across Tasks
Conforming to Preferred Descriptions

	Nouns		Prepositions	
Vertical (ego-environmental related)	eg.	the top .82	eg.	over .89
Horizontal Canonical (object related)	eg.	the front of car .63	eg.	in front of car .65
Horizontal Non-canonical (ego-related)	eg.	the front of block or bottle .50	eg.	in front of block or bottle .65

A Newman-Keuls analysis identified the relevant differences as follows: Vertical nouns and prepositions are easier than horizontal canonical nouns and prepositions, and horizontal noncanonical prepositions ($p<.05$) and horizontal noncanonical nouns are the most difficult ($p<.05$). Stated symbolically, for the nouns: V > HC > HNC, and for the prepositions: V > H, where no differentiation between canonical and noncanonical objects occurs. Thus there are two deviations from the predicted order: first, for the prepositions only, horizontal relations with canonical and noncanonical objects appear equivalent (consider, however, the problem of confounded egocentric errors) and second, that the nouns and prepositions appear to be acquired simultaneously rather than sequentially. For younger children Kuczaj and Maratsos (1975) found that the nouns "the front" were applied successfully before the prepositions "in front".

Structural Descriptions of Spatial Concepts

The three hypotheses together provide a means for examining the nature and complexity of the structural descriptions for spatial concepts. Structural descriptions which are based on a few relatively invariant features were constructed more readily than were those based on more relatively variable features. Spatial concepts emerged from the structural descriptions of objects as a function of the complexity inherent in each of these concepts. If a spatial concept can be described by a relatively simple structural description, such as the invariant designation for vertical relationships, it will be acquired before a concept which commands a more sophisticated designation, such as the ego-related descriptions necessary for horizontal noncanonical relationships.

Some aspects of the structural descriptions of objects and events are preeminently salient and subsequently amenable to explicit representation. In the Memory Task, no lexical representation was provided by the experimenter nor required from the subjects to bias their selection of certain spatial features in the mental representation of the display. Nonetheless, children remembered the vertical relations better than the horizontal ones as was expected on the basis that ego-related and object-related descriptions coincided for vertical relations while they often conflicted for horizontal ones. Further, the order corresponded to that observed for children's competence with the corresponding lexical items.

It may be argued that performance on the Memory Task merely indicated the features for which subjects can assign a lexical representation to facilitate memory of the display. However, subjects' recall of a relationship such as "in front of the car" in this task was at chance level (.23 compared to chance of .25) while the probability of the same subjects providing a correct description "the star is in front of the car" on the Description Task was found to be .75. It seems unlikely then, that the difficulty was simply subjects' inability to formulate the correct lexical description.

The data from all the tasks supports the theory that development of spatial concepts proceeds by extracting invariant predicates from the structural descriptions for objects and events and constructing new meaningful representations for these predicates. The two principles can be used to predict both the organization of the meaning and assigned to these features and the order in which the features will be detached from the objects and assigned meaning.

The product of this endeavor is not comparable to an adult system of spatial concepts. The extraction of features was motivated by considerations of invariance of the feature rather than generalizability of the description. How, then, is this system adapted for adult use?

Adult Descriptions of Space

This eclectic system of spatial representations is probably not widely used by adults. Adults are relatively sophisticated in the assignment of structural descriptions to objects and between objects. As a result they can voluntarily select the form of description to be applied consistently and with greater generalizability. How do adults reconcile the differences between the ego-related descriptions and the object-related ones?

The set of items used in Part C (rotated objects) of the Description Task was shown to 20 adults. Of these, 14 produced descriptions which essentially ignored the orientation or appearance of the referent object. Their responses "above", "below", "to the left", and "to the right" made no reference to the appearance or orientation of the referent object nor of the variable object related to that referent.

Of the remaining six adult subjects, two consistently used object-related descriptions, two used object-related descriptions for the car only, one used a mixed approach, and one used an object-related description *only* for the picture of "under" the upside down car. Notice, that deviations from the majority response were in a direction similar to that used by children, and towards descriptions that were relatively invariant or generalizable.

What is the structure of the spatial representation that served as the basis for adults' responses? First, it is clear that adults rarely used the object-related descriptions which were so common in the children's responses. Whereas children would say, "The star is over the car" adults would simply say that the star was "above". Similarly, whereas children would say, "The star is in front of the car", adults would simply say, "To the left". This ellipsis indicates not only lack of attention to the particular objects or their orientations, but also that the implicit relatum of the description may not have been the pictured object at all. Moreover, for children *"in front"* was determined by where they designated *"the front"* to be; for adults these two descriptions were independent.

Neither are adults basing their responses simply on ego-related representations of space. Descriptions such as above, below, to the left, to the right, based only on their own position could not be used to adequately describe the relationship between two other objects; only the relationship between the star and the speaker would be indicated. In addition, no description for a car would specify the front as "left" and the back as "right" simply by analogy with the viewer's left and right side; some other feature would be required to force that interpretation. If we then exclude both object-related and ego-related descriptions as the basis of the adult responses, what structure is responsible for these descriptions?

It appears that most of the adult subjects consider the picture to generate a spatial framework, and treated that space as a noncanonical object as outlined in Chapter 4. That is, adults assigned the descriptions top, bottom, front, back, left, and right to the spatial properties of the picture so as to coincide with ego space. They then used that picture framework as the relatum for the star. In so doing, the adults found an economical solution to the problem of describing all of the possible relations (in that task) while treating as irrelevant all of the information about the orientation and identity of the objects involved. Adults could do this, we suggest, because they could intentionally and consciously assign whatever spatial framework they thought appropriate and general to the task. Children on the other hand were dominated by the more immediate frameworks of egos and objects.

Two factors impede children's ability to use the picture as a noncanonical relatum. First, since it has been shown that children cannot make the left/right differentiation successfully until approximately 7 years of age (Piaget, 1928) it is unlikely that they could use it as an explicit feature of the framework which adults assign to these spatial relations.

The second is that the generation of this structure in the first place depends on the ability to intentionally plan and assign a particular type of description. The absence of that planful, intentional assignment leaves children subject to an ego-related or object-related basis rather than coordinate them into a general structure.

To summarize, in our view, spatial relations are based on the relation of objects to some relatum, either those specified by ego, the environment, or by some other canonical object. All of these types of descriptions are present from an early age and are constructed out of the same basic spatial predicates. Development may be described in terms of the progressive mastery of increasingly complex spatial relations that require solving ambiguity created by competing sets of axes. More importantly, development consists of learning to use consciously or explicitly these spatial relations for comprehending, describing, and remembering various spatial relations.

As to the order of acquisition and use of spatial terms, we have found that at least for the children in this study who were 4 years of age, the spatial nouns were understood as well as, but no better than, prepositions. Moreover, it is difficult to say when these terms are mastered because they can be applied successfully in some contexts and not in others: *"In front"*, for example, can be handled more consistently for noncanonical objects than for canonical ones, because the latter may be assigned either an object-related description or an ego-related one. Furthermore these data indicate that terms specifying vertical relations *top* and *over* with their negative counterparts *bottom* and *under* are acquired before those specifying horizontal relations *front, back,* and *in front* and *behind.* Most of the variability in the experiment resulted from the fact that while adults assumed a consistent frame of reference for the assignment of these terms, for example, the spatial framework of the picture, children assigned these relations on the basis of either the environmental space, the object space, or ego space. Their chosen interpretation and the consistency with which they applied it depended upon the invariance of the descriptions; for vertical relations, environment, object, and ego all lead to the assignment of the same spatial relationship hence they are readily assigned; for horizontal relations involving canonical objects, object-related and environment-related descriptions frequently come into conflict, and hence they are less readily and consistently assigned; while for noncanonical objects, only ego-related descriptions were relevant, and hence they were relatively easily applied. The ease or difficulty of a spatial relation, then, depends not only upon the predicate of the relation but also upon the structure of the relatum to which a stimulus is related.

Egocentrism

Piaget and Inhelder (1956) emphasize the development from egocentric to decentered space. Although they claim that children initially order all relations in terms of ego, whether or not it is appropriate, the evidence presented here shows that, especially for canonical objects, spatial relations are frequently object-related.

In addition, Pufall and Shaw (1973) have also shown that this egocentrism is not inevitable. What then accounts for the occurrence of egocentric errors? While egocentric spatial relations are perhaps the simplest in some sense, they do not represent a stage of development. Rather both children and adults apply ego-related descriptions to layouts and displays in order to cope practically with those dimensions that are not clearly specified by the environment or other canonical objects. Even adults construct representations of their house or apartment which are in part an ego-related route map: "When you come in the door, on your left is the diningroom, etc." (Norman & Rummelhart, 1975). Even those representations assume some invariant properties of environmental and object space in that you must mention whether you come in the *front* door or the *back* door—an object space factor—and the values for vertical relations as in "*up* the stairs" or "the *top* bunk" are specified by environmental space. Furthermore, such route map descriptions are dependent on knowing the location, direction and orientation of the viewer and hence they are not applicable if the viewer is moved—as for example if she comes in the wrong door—or if the display is rotated. It was for this reason that the more general spatial relations represented by maps and blueprints and the like were invented: They may be "read" from any position and in any order.

But "abstract" systems of spatial representation are somewhat more complex and must be assigned intentionally. For these reasons young children may frequently revert to ego-related descriptions and so produce egocentric errors. Some evidence supports this suggestion. Pufall (1975) constructed a display containing two types of features. A "repeated" feature occurred when each side, or feature, of an object was the same, such as a "tree". In terms of the present theory these are objects lacking intrinsic distinctive spatial sides; they are noncanonical. A "unique" feature appeared in objects which are different on each side, such as a "barn". In terms of the present theory these are canonical objects with intrinsic spatial parts. Subjects were required to place an object next to both of these types of features on displays which had been rotated 90° or 180°. Egocentric errors were far more frequent for placements next to repeated features than next to unique ones. That is, on a perspective task, egocentric errors were more prevalent for relationships with noncanonical objects than with canonical objects.

Hence, it appears that egocentrism is a form of response which occurs only in special circumstances. If, as Piaget and Inhelder suggested, egocentrism is a general response strategy, then the incidence of egocentric errors should have been equal across the various types of spatial relations. It appears, rather, that while subjects construct both ego-related and object-related descriptions, the latter are readily applied only to canonical objects and are invariant across rotations and perspectives; for more difficult problems, such as those with noncanonical objects, children revert to ego-related descriptions and may commit egocentric errors. Adults adopt more general descriptions which are invariant across these changes. We shall see the interplay between these forms of representation in Chapter 12.

By analyzing spatial relations in terms of underlying structural descriptions and by considering children's limited ability in constructing these descriptions, it is possible to account for their ability to handle various spatial relations. As the features of the structural descriptions become consciously available to the child, s/he is able to represent those relationships in language and thought and use them to solve an increasingly wide range of spatial problems.

6 The Development of Strategies for Solving the Perspective Task

with Joanne Rovet
Hospital for Sick Children
Toronto, Canada

Spatial cognition and spatial thinking have been given many descriptions varying from "the ability to move, turn, twist or rotate an object or objects and to recognize a new appearance or position after the prescribed manipulation has been performed" (Guilford, 1947), to "the ability to recognize the identity of an object when it is seen from different angles" (Thurstone, 1950), to "the ability to comprehend imaginary movement of objects in three dimensional space" (French, 1951). Such attempts at definition and measurement were adequate as long as a theory of spatial cognition was concerned only with problems of individual differences—some people are better than other people on certain tasks—or with problems of development—performance is a function of age and experience—and so on.

The problem for cognitive psychology on the other hand is to describe the set of representations and procedures that constitute that ability or set of abilities. By approaching problems of spatial cognition and spatial development with the goal of specifying the mental representations and cognitive operations underlying particular spatial problems, it becomes possible to understand the differences between various spatial problems, and more importantly to determine the relationship between the processes involved in one spatial task, such as the perspective problem, and those involved in apparently different tasks. Consequently, this chapter will examine the problem of comparing different perspectives of a single object, the following one, chapter 7, will deal with perspective problems involving complex arrays, chapters 8 and 9 will include an analysis of rotation problems, and chapters 10 and 11 examine processes in the judgement of spatial orientation. In all cases, our analysis is based on specifying the mental representation and transformational procedures required for the solution to each problem. The perspective task has come to serve as a prototypic measure of spatial cognitive development. The task was first described by Piaget and Inhelder (1956) in their studies of children's spatial cognition. They presented children of different ages with a pasteboard model of three mountains differing in shape, size, and color and asked them to indicate how a wooden doll placed in a number of different locations about the display might see the mountains. Judgements were indicated in three different ways: selecting a view from a set of pictures, reconstructing a view from a set of models, and reconstructing a model from a depicted view. They found that children were unable to determine the alternate perspectives of this display until relatively late in childhood—at about 9 or 10 years of age. Until this time, children often took their own point of view to be that of the observer and so committed what Piaget and Inhelder called an "egocentric error". A series of predictable developmental stages for the solution of these problems at different ages was described by Piaget and Inhelder although no explicit statement was given about the underlying cognitive strategies.

The task has been replicated in many forms, using other types of stimuli and other response means (see Chapter 7, for a discussion of alternate means of response). In all cases, however, the information about the alternate perspective may be retrieved either directly from a representation specifying the relation between observer and display, or if that is not possible, indirectly, through a transformation on a representation based on the child's own point of view. In addition, that representation may contain one or two critical features of the display, or a less explicit but richer description of the display components. It is with these alternative strategies that this study is concerned.

STRATEGIES FOR SOLVING THE PROBLEM

The age at which a child can solve perspective problems appears to vary from as early as 2 years (Benson & Bogartz, 1977; Masangkay, et al., 1974) to as late as 9 or 10 years or older (Dodwell, 1963; Flavell, 1968; Hardwick, McIntyre and Pick, 1976; Huttenlocher and Presson, 1973; Laurendeau & Pinard, 1970; Marmor, 1977 Shantz and Watson, 1970). Some of the parameters which appear to affect age of competence are array type (Borke, 1971, 1975; Coie, Costanzo & Farnill, 1973; Fishbein, Lewis, & Keiffer, 1972; Masangkay, 1974), number of choice items (Borke, 1971; Fishbein et al., 1972) and means of response (Borke, 1975; Fishbein et al., 1972; Harris & Bassett, 1976; Ives, Chapter 7 this volume; Kielgast, 1971).

Several explanations can be offered for this variability. One is that perspective-taking functions are indeed available in thought at a young age but performance is limited by other task constraints. It is possible, for example that the problem encountered by children in the Piaget and Inhelder task was that the complexity of the display they used made it difficult for children to form representations of the alternate views until this late age. Had the identical study been conducted but with a simpler display, Piaget and Inhelder might have found evidence of perspective-taking abilities in younger subjects. Although no other studies have systematically varied codability, several have reported that age of competence may depend on the complexity of the description of a view (Pufall, 1975; Walker & Gallin, 1977).

Alternatively, age differences in perspective taking ability may reflect the developmental emergence of different cognitive strategies appropriate for different versions of the perspective task. Different strategies have been described including the rotation of images (Cox, 1977; Huttenlocher & Presson, 1973), drawing of inferences (Huttenlocher & Presson, 1973), and the development of schemas (Nigl & Fishbein, 1974), although no one has yet succeeded in reducing all of these putative strategies to a single underlying form of representation nor related these representational forms to specifiable features of the perspective or rotation task. The purpose of the present study is to examine whether there are different strategies for solving the perspective problem as a function of the codability of the display. Three factors are examined for their effects on codability: the presence of known features or parts, the relation between the positions of the child and the observer given by the angular separation between the child and viewer, and the initial orientation of the display vis-á-vis the child and/or the observer.

According to the theory outlined in Chapter 3, a spatial display is assigned a structural description which represents or describes the properties and relations of that display either relative to each other or to some other object, whether landmark, viewer, or ego. If the display can be coded in terms of a set or explicit features such as front, back, and so on, then these will be used in the representation (cf. Ives & Rovet, 1979). If such features are not available, then the structural description will include the more detailed implicit features of the display constructed nonetheless from essentially the same set of spatial features or predicates. In the first case, the operations performed on the representations are similar to those involved in a verbal description in that they involve discretely stated relations between features; in the second case, particular spatial features are less likely to be singled out with the result that the operations are more similar to the analogue transformations involving images of the whole object or display.

Thus for the perspective task, if a view of a display has known codable features such as "front", then the representation should exploit those descriptions and the codings could be given propositionally, perhaps lexically; if a display cannot take such a description, as appears to be the case for complex displays such as the three mountain task or for abstract geometric forms, then the representation may involve an implicit structural description similar in form to an image. Alternatively, even complex displays may require the formation of propositional relations between identifiable components and either the observer for the perspective task or to the alternative display for the rotation task.

Furthermore, in order to solve the perspective problem, the child must code the features of the display from a particular point of view. The two possible sources for this perspective are the child, that is ego, and the observer. Thus descriptions such as "The doll's front is in front of me" represents an ego-referent interpretation of the problem while "The doll's back is in front of the observer" is the observer-referent counterpart. If the child constructs the ego-referent representation, then the correct solution requires some transformation of that description to account for the observer's viewpoint. This may be accomplished either rotationally, as in transforming an image of the display as the child imagines moving around it, or notationally, as in exploiting the logical relationships between spatial relations such as front and back. Which of these strategies the child can adopt will depend upon the type of representation that can be assigned to the display.

The critical feature of the representation, then, is whether the display is related to the ego or to the observer; the result is expressed in either an ego or observer-referent relationship. Since the internal structure of the display is never altered, object-referent relationships that hold among the objects or features of the display itself are inadequate for judging the appearance of the display from another viewpoint. Nonetheless, certain types of displays may be more easily encoded in terms of the relation to the ego or to the observer when some information about the object-referent relationships is included in the representation. The difference between types of displays is determined by whether the component objects are canonical or non-canonical.

Consider first the canonical objects with intrinsic spatial properties. If the child simply codes the relation between himself and the display, that is, assigns an ego-referent description, for example:

at the front (ego, x), i.e., I am at the front of the car.

and if he or she is unable to transform or annul this representation to take account of the position of the observer, the child would make an egocentric response. Similarly, if the observer's view happened to coincide with the child's view, as in the O° rotation condition, the codes are identical and the child's view will generate a correct response. Finally, if the two views are not identical, the child may either attempt to translate his ego-related description into the observer-related description, for example:

front (ego, x) ⎯⎯⎯⎯➤ *back* (observer, x)
iff ego and observer are separated by 180°,

or construct an observer-referent description directly. An observer-referent description would interpret the relation between the canonical features of the display in terms of the position of the observer. This would take the form:

back (observer, x), i.e., The observer is at back of the car.

This representation could then be used to pick, for example, a picture of the back of the car, without calling for any spatial transformation of that representation.

The empirical consequences of the use of either the ego-referent or the observer-referent strategy is that there will be no linear relation between the difficulty of the task and the angular distance separating the child and the observer. Rather, problem difficulty will be determined by the relationship between ego or observer and the canonical features of the display. For example, if the child assigns an observer-referent description to the display, then the critical factor will be the simplicity of the code relating observer and object. Since front and back are clearly visually distinguishable for the canonical objects employed in this study, while alternative sides are confusable, observer-referent descriptions will be simple when the observer is either at the front or the rear of the car, and complex when the observer is at one side of the car. Specifically, when the observer is either 0° or 180° separated from the child *and* the object is positioned with either the front or the back towards the child (such that the observer is adjacent to either the front or the back of the canonical object) the task will be easy. Similarly, when the observer is positioned at 90° or 180° from the child and the object is positioned such that one of the sides is toward the child (again such that the observer "sees" the front or the rear of the object) the task will be easy. All other positions and orientations will be more complex. If the child assigns an ego-referent description, he or she will succeed on the tasks in which the observer sees the same display as the child (the 0° problem). Other problems will be easy or difficult depending in part on the simplicity of the code relating ego and object. These descriptions will be simple when ego is at the front or back of the object but complex when ego is at one side of the object. Note that for this procedure to yield a correct solution to the problem, the child would have to develop some procedure for getting from the ego view to the observer's view in the non 0° cases. We shall discuss such procedures in Chapter 8.

Notice that in both cases the solution to the problem requires noting only the relationship between one canonical feature of the display and one viewer, either the ego or the observer. More subtle features of the display are irrelevant to the task.

For noncanonical objects, the problem may be quite different. Firstly, the absence of known, nameable canonical parts makes the formation of the ego-related or observer-related descriptions discussed above more difficult since distinguishable parts would first have to be identified. Consequently, the object-referent relationships that specify the internal structure of the display may be coded as well. One possibility is that this internal structure would consist of an unanalyzed structural description of the display as constructed from the child's point of view. Such representations are what others have called "images". This description of the structure of the display could be constructed from the point of view of the ego and examined for changes as the child imagines moving around the display, to the position of the observer. If these judgments are made on the basis of mental rotations, then the angle of separation between ego and observer should be a critical factor in problem difficulty.

Alternatively, these complex noncanonical objects may be coded in a way similar to canonical objects but with one exception. Subjects may have to construct an object-related description of the object or display only to the extent that they can distinguish and identify critical components of the display which can then be used analogously to the distinctive features of canonical objects. In the first phase, the subject may identify such features as the plane of the figure, the number and disposition of its arms with such labels as: top arm, bottom arm in the plane, bottom arm perpendicular to the plane, and so on, and in the second phase code the relation between one or more of these identifiable features and the position of the ego or the observer.

The empirical implications of these two hypotheses differ. If subjects form an image of the object and mentally rotate their perspective with respect to this image, then the latencies and error rates should show a linear effect of the angular separation between the position of the child and that of the viewer. If subjects assign descriptions to the features of the display and then relate these to the position of the observer, there will not be a linear effect of angular distance but rather evidence for the simplicity of the spatial code relating object and observer as described for the canonical objects above.

These hypotheses were tested by examining error and latency patterns of children at three grade levels who were given four types of displays for the Perspective Task. Two of the tasks involved canonical displays with known, codable spatial properties—fronts, backs, and sides—namely, a girl and a car, and two noncanonical objects with unknown spatial properties, namely, three dimensional replicas of the Shepard-Metzler figures.

Method

Thirty-seven first (N = 11), third (N = 15) and fifth (N = 11) grade children from a Catholic elementary school in a Toronto suburb participated in this study. The mean ages were 6.4, 8.7, and 10.5 years respectively. Each child was seated at a table on which was placed the perspective task materials. One experimenter who administered the test sat across from the child; a second, who recorded both responses and latencies, sat to the child's right. The child was told that they would be playing a game, the object of which was to determine how the objects in front of them would be seen by someone else at various places around the table.

The materials consisted of a two-inch wooden and plastic Fisher-Price doll (the Observer, O), a 12-inch diameter brown wooden disc, five toy objects (the arrays), and twenty tiny replicas of the arrays (the choice items). Four different colored dots were painted 90° apart along the circumference of the disc to indicate the viewpoint locations with the dot either adjacent to the child; the 0° position, to the child's right, the 270° position, to the child's left, the 90° position, and across from the child, the 180° position. (These object orientations are shown in Fig 6.1.)

The five arrays were a 3-inch female doll, an orange car 5 inches in length, a brown plastic horse 4 inches high, and two different shaped cubic

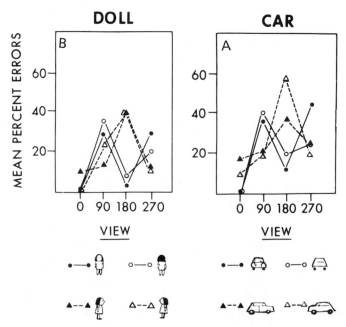

FIG. 6.1   Mean percent errors as a function of viewpoint for canonical displays.

figures each standing 4 inches high. These objects were made to resemble the Shepard-Metzler (1971) figures and were constructed from either red and yellow Leggo blocks (the RY block) or from blue and white Leggo blocks (the BW block). The doll and car served as "canonical" object arrays, the block figures, as "noncanonical". The horse was used for practice trials.

The arrays were placed in the center of the disc with the canonical arrays being oriented in the front, back, right, or left side view with respect to the child. The noncanonical arrays were oriented either with the upper arm toward the child or one of three successive 90° clockwise rotations from the view, called P_1, P_2, P_3, and P_4 respectively. (Those block orientations are shown in Figure 6.2.)

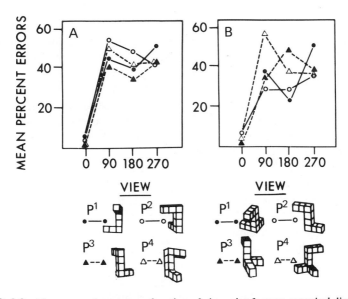

FIG. 6.2   Mean percent errors as a function of viewpoint for non-canonical displays.

The four miniature replicas of each array were affixed to an 11 × 4 inch wooden board. These were shown in four different orientations corresponding to the four views of each array with the order of orientations varying randomly for the five displays. The orientations were coded from A to D.

The procedure included several practice trials with the toy horse array and response alternatives until the child appeared to understand the requirements of the task. The child was told if his response was correct or not during this phase of the testing only. The experimental trials which followed consisted of four sets of 16 trials, one set per array, representing all combinations of viewpoints and orientations for each array, with array order and trial order varying randomly from child to child.

Thus, the basic design included four Arrays (doll, car, and two block figures), four Viewpoints indicating the position of the observer, (0°, 90°, 180°, and 270°, four orientations with respect to the child, (front, back, right side, and left side, or P_1, P_2, P_3, P_4), and three grade levels (one, three, and five; approximate ages of 6, 8, and 10 years respectively). Array was a within subject factor, while Grade level was a between subject factor.

Responses were scored both for accuracy and reaction time latency.

Results

The scores for boys and girls were combined in all analyses after a preliminary analysis revealed no significant sex difference. Error and latency data were handled separately.

Errors. A comparison of canonical and noncanonical object arrays using a 3 × 2 (Grade level × Array) mixed Analysis of Variance indicated a significant Array effect, $F(1,66) = 46.49$, $p < .001$), and a Grade × Array interaction, $F(2,77) = 3.71$, $p < .05$). The main effect of Array is due to more errors for noncanonical (6.26 errors) than canonical (3.82) arrays ($p < .01$). The interaction with grade is due to a decrease in errors with age for canonical but not non-canonical object arrays (Newman Keuls; $p < .01$). These means are given in Table 6.1.

The second set of analyses involved separate comparisons on the data of the four arrays, using a 3 × 4 × 4 (Grade × Viewpoint × Orientation) mixed analyses of variance for each set of data.

For the car array, the significant findings are Viewpoint, $F(3,136) = 13.91$, $p < .01$ and Orientation × Viewpoint, $F(9,408) = 15.74$, $p < .01$; there was no significant Grade effect. The Viewpoint effect is due to a sub-

TABLE 6.1
Percent Errors as a Function of Grade Level for
Canonical and Non-canonical Object-Arrays

	Grade Level		
Array	One	Three	Five
Canonical			
Doll	16.70	27.10	8.40
Car	29.60	28.80	12.90
Total	23.15	27.95	10.65
Non-canonical			
RY Blocks	31.70	44.20	26.30
BW Blocks	34.20	28.80	28.30
Total	32.95	36.50	27.30

stantial increase in errors ($p < .01$) for the 90°, 180°, and 270° positions compared to the 0° position (see Figure 6.1A). Most importantly, the Orientation × Viewpoint interaction reflects a significant increase in errors when O sees a side view of the car (Newman-Keuls; $p < .05$) and a decrease in errors when O sees a front or rear view.

For the doll array, the significant findings are as follows: Grade, $F(2,33)$ = 4.13, $p < .05$; Viewpoint, $F(3,132)$ = 35.00, $p < .001$; Orientation × Viewpoint, $F(9,396)$ = 5.87, $p < .01$ (see Figure 6.1B). The Grade level effect is due to the significantly better performance of fifth grade children (1.53 errors) than first (4.00 errors) or third (3.00 errors) grade children (Newman-Keuls; $p < .01$). The Viewpoint effect as found for the car, is due to a significant increase in errors for the three non-0° positions compared to the 0° rotation. Similarly, the Orientation × Viewpoint interaction results from the fact that the conditions in which O is at the 90° or 270° viewpoints and the array is oriented frontwards or backwards and those in which O is at the 180° viewpoint and the array is oriented sideways are more difficult. In all these difficult cases, it may be recalled, the observer "sees" a side view of the doll.

For the RY block display, the only significant effect is due to the Viewpoint of the Observer ($F(3,32)$ = 59.10, $p < .01$, (see Figure 6.2A). A Newman-Keuls test revealed that the simplest condition was that in which O was at the 0° position (.21 errors); the next level of difficulty when O was at 180° (2.07 errors); the most difficult when O was at 90° (2.40 errors) and 270° (2.15 errors) ($p < .05$). These viewpoint differences, however, must be interpreted in the light of the effects of orientation of the display which shows up more clearly in the latency data.

For the BW block figure, Viewpoint and Orientation both contribute significant main effects, ($F(3,126)$ = 110.5, $p < .01$ and $F(3,136)$ = 2.92, $p < .05$, respectively, (see Figure 6.2B). The Viewpoint effect is again due to fewest errors for the condition in which O is at the 0° rotation position (.19 errors), the next fewest errors occur when O is at the 180° location (1.73 errors); and the most when O is at the 90° (2.12 errors) or 270° (2.05 errors) locations (Newman-Keuls); $p < .05$). The Orientation effect can be accounted for by significantly fewer errors when the display is shown in the P_1 or P_3 orientations (top arms facing front or back) (Newman-Keuls; $p < .05$). Both the effects of orientation and viewpoint will be explained when we examine the latency data.

Some patterns in the error data are worth summarizing. First, the canonical displays are substantially easier than the noncanonical ones. Indeed, there is little indication of improvement with the noncanonical items over the age range studied. Secondly, there is a clear observer by orientation interaction for the canonical objects indicating that the relations between the critical features of the display and the position of the observer was the primary determinant of the ease or difficulty of the item. The nature of this code will be spelled out in more detail in the analysis of the latency data. For the noncanonical items, the error data suggests the use of a propositional rather than an imaginal coding, although the exact nature of the representation used remains to be seen. A strategy based on the formation of images would have produced a linear relation between the error scores and the angular separation of the viewers. Instead the only clear pattern was that, overall, observer positions congruent with the child (0° separation) and those opposite to the child (180°) seemed somewhat simpler than those in which the observer was to either side of the child (the 90° and 180° separation conditions). As we shall see in the analysis of the latency data, however, there is yet another possible strategy for encoding these relationships which is based on the relation between the orientation of the display and the viewpoint of the observer.

Latencies. Four reaction time protocols were obtained for each child, one for each array, but only those protocols from relatively errorless performances were included in these analyses. This criterion was placed at a maximum of one error per Orientation or Viewpoint condition, that is, four errors per protocol. This constraint was satisfied by 20 protocols for the doll array, 16 for the car array, 11 for the RY block figure array and 14 for the BW block figure array from the original set of 37 protocols per array. Six children supplied four protocols, six children three protocols, five children two protocols, and nine children one protocol. Table 6.2 presents the proportions of children in each grade level producing these errorless protocols.

Only reaction time values of correct responses were considered for the analyses. Missing entries and exceedingly high latencies (more than double the value of the next highest latency) were replaced by the procedure recommended by Winer (1962, p. 281). About 10% of the values were replaced by this method.

For the car array, Viewpoint × Orientation is significant ($F(9,114) = 316$, $p<01$). As the error data indicated, the problem was easier, that is, solved faster, when the O "saw" a front or back view than when O "saw" a side view of the car (Newman-Keuls; $p<05$). The mean latency scores are plotted in Figure 6.3A.

TABLE 6.2
Propostion of Children Obtaining Errorless
Protocols as a Function of Grade Level

Array	Grade Level		
	One	Three	Five
Canonical	.41	.37	.73
Non-canonical	.23	.40	.36

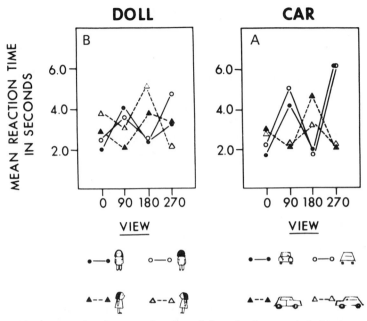

FIG. 6.3   Mean reaction times as a function of viewpoint for canonical object arrays.

For the doll array, the Viewpoint effect was significant ($F(3,44) = 3.34$, $p < .05$) and results from significantly longer latencies in the conditions where O's position differed from the child's ($p < .01$). The Grade × Orientation × Viewpoint Interaction was significant ($F(18,104) = 2.91$, $p < .01$) since the Orientation by Viewpoint Interaction which was obtained for the car, was significant only for the fifth grade subjects. Some evidence of this interaction was observed for the third grade subjects, but not for the first grade students. Recall that the first and third grade subjects found the doll items difficult and made many more errors than did the fifth grade subjects and hence the latency data is based on few subjects.

The mean latencies across grade for the doll display are shown in Figure 6.3B. For the doll, as was the case with the car, the latencies are significantly shorter when the O "sees" a front or back view of the display (O at 0° or 180° when the orientation is front or back *or* O at 90° or 270°, when the orientation is to the left or right side). The latencies observed when O "saw" the side of the display however were more systematic across all grades for the car than they were for the doll.

For the RY block display, the results indicate significant Grade × Viewpoint ($F(6,24) = 5.59$, $p < .01$) and Orientation × Viewpoint ($F(9,68) = 2.05$, $p < .05$) interactions. The Grade × Viewpoint interaction indicates that there are different effects of angular distance for children at the three grade levels. Specifically, for first graders there is no relation between angular separation and item difficulty while third and fifth graders found 180° and 90° items more difficult than the 0° items. As will be seen, this difference reflects the code subjects used in solving these problems.

Figure 6.4A presents the mean RTs as a function of the viewpoint of the observer, O, and the orientation of the display (designated as views P_1, P_2, P_3, P_4 in Figures 2 and 4) The response latencies were significantly longer for three conditions: O at 90° and the display in the P_3 orientation; O at 180° and the display in the P_4 orientation; and O at 270° and the display in the P_1 orientation (Newman-Keuls; $p < .05$).

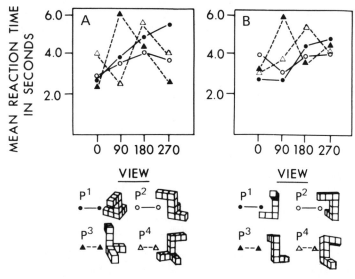

FIG. 6.4   Mean reaction times as a function of viewpoint for noncanonical block figure arrays.

Clearly, counter to expectation, the angular separation between the child's view (Ego) and observer view was not a primary factor in determining the difficulty of those items in which Ego and Observer perspectives differed. Although the four displays are identical, the orientations of the display determines the ease of calculating the perspective from a particular viewpoint in a way that is similar to that found with canonical objects.

Let us try to reconstruct the mental codes that could produce this pattern of difficulties. The key to the code comes from the observation that the display has three distinctive arms: the top arm, (a); the bottom arm in the plane of the top arm, (b); and the bottom arm perpendicular to the plane of the other two arms, (c). Further each of these distinctive arms points towards three of the four possible viewpoints. Suppose then that the code relating the display to the viewpoint was based on these relations having the general form:

front (arm X, Observer).

Applying this general form to the specific orientations and viewpoints we find that each orientation of the block specifies three relations, one to each of the arms, while the fourth, having no identifiable arm, would be unspecifiable. Consider the block in orientation P_4 represented by the open triangles in Figure 6.4A. If O is at 90°, the representation would be:

front (arm b, O)

if at 270°:

front (arm a, O)

if at 0°:

front (arm c, O)

but if at 180° there is no arm which points toward O hence no code is readily constructed.

front (?, x).

Clearly in this case, the 180° item should be most difficult as indeed, Figure 6.4A clearly shows.

Similarly for the blocks in orientation P_1 and P_3 the display for which the code (front (arm X, O)) cannot be constructed are, as the model suggests, significantly more difficult.

The same analysis shows why orientation P_2 is both easiest and shows no interaction with Viewpoint in either the error and latency data. For P_2, one arm points towards each of the three viewpoints other than ego; hence all three are relatively easy. The potentially difficult item in which no distinctive arm points towards the observer is the 0° viewpoint item. But this item is easy in any case as the viewpoint of ego and observer coincide and the choice can be based on a simple ego-related description. Further refinements in the model could be based on the relative codability of the various arms but the level of analysis goes beyond the precision of the available data.

For the BW display, the significant results are Grade ($F(2,11) = 4.28$, $p < .05$), Viewpoint ($F(3,33) = 9.56$, $p < .05$) and Orientation × Viewpoint ($F(9,94) = 5.19$, $p < .01$). The Grade level effect reflects a steady decline in RT with age ($F_{lin} (1,11) = 7.50$, $p < .05$); the mean RTs across grade levels are 4.89, 3.74, 3.47 seconds respectively. The Viewpoint effect reflects the fact that the latencies are shortest for O at 0° (3.31 seconds); next shortest for O at 90° (3.86 seconds); and longest for O at 180° and 270° (4.45 and 4.52 seconds respectively) ($p < .05$). Again, however, collapsing the data in terms of angular separation masks the important effects of the Viewpoint × Orientation interaction.

The Viewpoint × Orientation interaction, which is displayed in Figure 6.4B, results from the difficulty associated with three particular orientations: for P_1, the latencies are longer at 180° and 270° than 0° and 90°; for P_3 they are longest at 90°, next longest at 270° and shortest at 0° and 180°; for P_4 latencies are longest at 180°, next longest at 90° and 270° and shortest at 0° ($p < .05$). There is no significant difference between viewpoint conditions for the P_2 orientation.

Let us apply the same account to these data. First, unlike the RY displays, these displays have only two distinctive arms, an upper arm, (a); and a lower arm, (b). Assuming that the spatial relations are of the form:

front (arm X, *O*)

choice of viewpoint will be easy when one of the distinctive arms points toward the location of *O*. In P_1 this predicts greater difficulty for 180° and 270° positions as follows:

at 0°:
        front (display, ego)
90°:
        front (arm b, *O*)
180°:
        front (?, *O*)
270°:
        front (?, *O*)

This is precisely the pattern reported in the data above.

Notice, too, that if the code were constructed from the point of view of the child, that is, the ego-referent relationship, and then transformed into the view of the observer through logical relationships such as "opposite", then the 180° condition for this item would be easy while the 90° condition would be difficult. The pattern of results obtained not only reject that hypothesis but also support the claim that codings are based on distinctive features which are coded directly from the point of view of the observer.

For P_2, the 270° viewpoint could be expected to be more difficult but in fact no differences were significant. For P_3, 90° viewpoint could be expected to be most difficult as indeed it is. For P_4 both 90° and 180° viewpoints could be expected to be difficult; that for 180° is significantly so. On the whole then, this form of representation successfully accounts for most of the data. Experimental subjects code the relation between a distinctive property of the display and the location of the viewer and then rely on this representation to select the correct alternative model.

Discussion

It seems clear then that although there are substantial differences in difficulty between the well-known canonical displays, the car and the doll, and the "abstract" non-canonical block patterns used in this experiment, the strategies applied are much the same. In both cases, children identify distinctive properties of the display such as front, back, top arm, and the like, and then specify the spatial relation between that component of the display and the location or viewpoint of the observer by means of a spatial proposition of the form:

front (feature of display, *O*)

The major determinant of difficulty of the items then is the presence/absence of a distinctive feature of the display which may be directly related to the position of *O* by means of a spatial predicate. That rule accounts successfully for all of the orientations of the canonical objects and for 6 of the 8 non-canonical object orientations.

The difference in difficulty between the canonical and non-canonical objects may be explained by reference to the ease of identification of distinguishable parts. In the case of canonical objects, the distinctive parts that entered the spatial propositional representations already possessed distinctive names; for the non-canonical displays, subjects had to determine these distinctive parts for themselves, a task at which first grade children were extremely limited. This is a skill that develops markedly over the age range from 6 to 12 years and beyond.

There was no indication in the response patterns of subjects at any age for the formation and rotation of mental images. All of the analyses pointed towards (if one may be excused a spatial metaphor) the formation of a spatial proposition relating a distinguishable feature of the display and the position of the viewer by means of a spatial predicate such as *front,* or perhaps *adjacent to.* A more detailed description of this strategy is offered in Chapter 8. The use of this strategy presumably reflects the nature of the task used in this experiment. Subjects' task was to identify the view from some perspective. As the location of the viewer was specified by means of the dot, Subjects could use those positions as landmarks to which the property of the display could be related. Indeed, it seems unlikely that the children even determined if the blocks in the various orientations were in fact identical to one another. The judgment of identity of displays presented in various orientations is the concern of Chapter 8.

Two other points bear mention. First, were the subjects using a verbal code to specify the spatial relations? There is no evidence that subjects could verbally express the relations involved in their decisions; indeed, adults have difficulty providing verbal descriptions of complex arrays. Yet the evidence presented suggests that these codes were explicit propositional codes which related the observer to particular features of the display for all except perhaps the 0° rotation items. Yet that is not to say that Subject formulated a verbal statement of that proposition. The representation is based upon an analytical structure of components and relations which must have been separated out as a belief or an intention whether or not that proposition was actually expressed as an utterance. Indeed, it would seem to be a serious error to confuse the proposition with its explicit expression; yet, in this account, the two have the same meaning.

Finally, a word on the ego-related representation. The item on which the Observer and the child viewed the display from the same point of view was always easiest, a general finding which has been often described as egocentrism. The erroneous extension of egocentrism is the tendency to assume that the observer's perspective on a display is the same as that of the ego. In this study we saw little indication of egocentrism. However, we have not explained why 0° rotation problems are the easiest. In one way, the ease of this item is obvious; the child need not construct an alternative for the viewer. But what does the child construct as a perceptual representation of their own point of view? The child's perception of the display involves the automatic assignment of a relation between ego and display in terms of such predicates as in front, to the right, to the left, behind, under and the like, but unlike the *voluntarily* constructed representations required for the items on which ego and Observer do not share the same perspective, perceptual predicates are assigned automatically as part of an implicit structural description. That is, this item may be solved by perceptual recognition. Such problems are described more fully in Chapters 10 and 11. The other items require that the properties and relations assigned automatically from the ego point of view are *intentionally* and consciously assigned to the observer-display relations to solve the non-0° rotation problems. This form of representation, as we shall see in Chapter 8, is inadequate to handle the rotation problems.

7 The Development of Strategies for Coordinating Spatial Perspectives of an Array

with William Ives
*Harvard University Project Zero
and Wheelock College, Boston, Mass.*

In the previous chapter we examined children's use of two possible strategies for solving spatial problems which involve a transformation in the perspective on an object. Specifically, we proposed that an object containing identifiable canonical features, such as top, bottom, left, right, would be represented in terms of those features and judgements of appearance from alternative perspectives would be based on the spatial relation between these features and an observer. Evidence for this strategy would be reflected in systematic differences in problem difficulty attributable to the codability of features of the display. Thus, in purely linguistic and logical terms, if a child sees the "front" of the doll, then a viewer separated from the children by 180° must necessarily see the "back" of that doll. It is also possible, that objects which are less amenable to such featural descriptions, such as abstract arrangements of blocks, may be coded in a different manner. The structural description constructed for the representation of these objects may rely not on the distinct explicit features of the display which are represented lexically by front, back, etc., but may include a richer variety of implicit features yielding a representation more analogous to an "image". Evidence for this strategy would be reflected in an increase in reaction time as a function of the angle of separation between the child and viewer since some type of rotation of the image would be implicated. The results of the study, however, indicated that even for these complex abstract objects, representations are based on the distinctive features which are coded simply in terms of the position of the observer. These problems, nonetheless, are more difficult than are their counterparts using featured objects since the features must first be identified and distinctively represented.

The question now arises as to whether or not some similar representations and procedures may be used to solve a complex perspective task such as Piaget and Inhelder's three mountain task. In their task, the display was complicated in two ways. First, the items themselves, that is, the mountains, were unfeatured objects, that is they have no canonical front, back and so on, and as we have seen in the previous chapter, the problem is more difficult for unfeatured than for featured objects. Second, the display contained not a single object, as in the preceding chapter, but an array of objects, in this case, three mountains.

The present chapter has two general aims. The first is to examine the two strategies outlined in the previous chapter for their use in solving perspective problems when the display is composed of an array of unfeatured objects. While the abstract objects used in the previous chapter failed to introduce adequate complexity to bias subjects towards a more complete image-like coding of the display, it is possible that the need to represent an array rather than a single object would have this effect. Moreover, arrays comprised of unfeatured objects may be especially difficult to encode in explicit propositional form and so a richer coding of the display may be recruited in solving problems based on these displays. Hence, in the present study, strategies for solving the perspective problem are examined for both single featured objects and an array of unfeatured objects.

Second, it is possible that the response mode interacts with the coding assigned on the basis of these two strategies to determine problem difficulty. That is, it is possible that verbal questions such as "What is in front?" map directly into propositional representations while picture selection tasks map more directly into some unanalyzed image.

Let us review briefly the two possible perspective strategies to see how they might relate to the two display types used in the present study. In one strategy, the child is assumed to use some form of continuous, anticipatory imagery as has been generally assumed in the literature (De Lisi, Locker, & Youniss, 1976; Harris & Basset, 1976; Huttenlocher & Presson, 1973; Nigl & Fishbein, 1974). In the other strategy the child makes use of an explicit, categorical description corresponding to the perspective of the other viewer such as "the front of the car" is in front of the "viewer".

Two sets of predictions, each concerning an aspect of problem difficulty follow from each of these strategies. First, as argued in the preceding chapter, an image-like representation based on a detailed set of perceptual features of the display would produce an ordering of problem difficulty which reflects the angular separation between the child and the observer. Therefore, perspective taking scores should improve as the rotational distance separating the child's view from the other's view is decreased. This would, after all, be the finding if the task were physically executed. Similarly, if the representation is unanalyzed and remains "image-like", responding to an alternative perspective task would be through the selection of a picture which indeed preserves the spatial information.

However, if children construct explicit propositional representations of the target perspective using such predicates as those described in Chapter 6, scores should reflect not the rotational distance but rather the complexity of the appropriate spatial representations. In this account the "side" or "back" of a car, for example, should be easier to represent than the front corner which requires a more complex representation. Furthermore, canonical referent objects, that is, objects having an inherent "side" or "back" such as a car should be easier to represent than those lacking distinct invariant features. Spatial relations among three mountains which have no inherent, canonical form representations[1] would need to be described in terms of the relationship between objects, e.g., "the red mountain is in front of the yellow mountain" and therefore be more complex. In addition this second account would postulate that a linguistic rather than pictorial response mode would improve scores, since it more directly maps onto the explicit form representations postulated to underlie the solution of the task.

In the previous chapter, we examined the effect of the codability of single objects using a pictorial means of response; in the present chapter we examine the effect of codability by introducing an array of unfeatured objects and single canonical objects which take more or less complex descriptions (front vs. front corner), and examine each under two response conditions, a verbal question and picture selection task.

Method

Subjects. One hundred and twenty children attending the Corvette Junior Public School in Scarborough, Ontario, were tested. There were 40 children in each of three grade levels. The kindergarten children had a mean age of 5.5 years; the grade two children had a mean age of 7.4 years, and the grade four children had a mean age of 9.8 years. The children were randomly selected from several classrooms and the specific grades were chosen on the basis of pilot testing.

Materials. Four canonical toy objects with inherent explicit representational features (car, man, house, horse) and a three mountain display adapted from Laurendeau and Pinard (1970) consisting of a red, yellow, and blue mountain of varying sizes placed on a green board were used as the referents in the task. In each case a toy boat was also used as a referent in a practice trial. In the picture selection condition, a separate pictorial display was used with each object. The displays for the canonical objects (those

---

[1]Except, of course, top and bottom of the mountains which are not relevant to this task.

with inherent explicit representational features) consisted of five black and white photographs representing the front, side, back, front corner, and back corner views of the specific object mounted in a random order on a display panel. The choices for the three mountain display was similar to those for the canonical objects except that the pictures were colored drawings since color was the most salient distinguishing feature among the mountains (see Figure 7.1). A black 35 mm. camera mounted on a tripod was used to mark the "other" viewpont in all instances.

Procedure.   Each child was escorted into a small room containing a chair placed in front of a small empty table with a slightly larger table behind, on top of which was the toy boat. The camera was placed at the side of the taller table and focused on the boat (see Figure 7.2). The child was invited to look through the camera and was asked what he saw. If the child simply named the object, the experimenter asked what part of the boat was seen. If the child then failed to mention an orientation, the experimenter asked if the child saw the front (side, back) of the boat. Next, the camera was moved to a new position and the child was allowed to note that the view through the camera had changed. Then the object itself was turned and the child was again allowed to note that the view of the boat had changed.

Picture Selection Condition.   Next the child was asked to sit in the chair and the array of boat pictures was placed in front of the child on the smaller table (see Figure 7.2). The child was asked to look over all the photographs and was allowed to note that they each represented different views of the same boat.[2] After identifying the appropriate pictures, the child was told that he was going to play a game and pretend he was a photographer. In the game the child had to tell the experimenter what picture the camera would take from different positions but the child had to remain seated while answering the questions.

The practice trial then began and the child was asked to point to the picture which the camera would take from its present position. The experimenter stood behind the camera and paraphrased the question to ask the child what view the experimenter would see from his present position behind the camera. If the child answered correctly, he was told he had been correct and the camera was moved to a new position or the object was turned to a new orientation or both. Then the questioning was repeated. If the child was incorrect, he was asked to come and look through the camera and then the questioning was repeated when he returned to his seat.

The child was given five practice trials with different orientations of the boat presented in a random order which allowed for the camera to be placed

---

[2]The child had to indicate by pointing which picture showed each of the five orientations of the boat represented in the array as a criterion for admission to the study. Only four Kindergarten children failed to reach criteria and four additional children were tested.

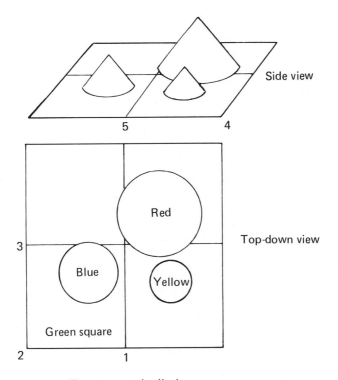

Side view

5   4

Red

Top-down view

3

Blue

Yellow

Green square

2   1

Three mountain display

Perspectives:
1. = Yellow in Front of Red
2. = Blue in Front of Red
3. = Blue in Front of Yellow (and Red)

4. = Red in Front of Blue
5. = Red in Front of Yellow

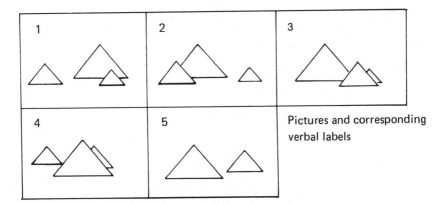

Pictures and corresponding verbal labels

FIG. 7.1   Materials for the perspective task using the three mountain display based on the materials used by Laurendeau and Pinard (1970).

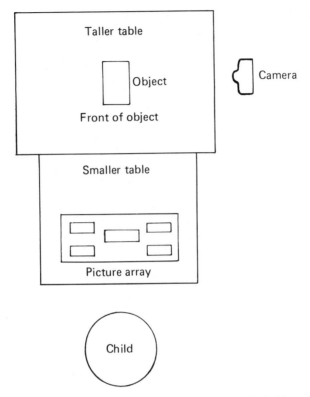

FIG. 7.2   Top-down view of the perspective task using canonical objects illustrating orientation 8 (see Figure 7.3) and the picture selection condition.

in positions of 45°, 90°, and 180° from the child's position. This random order also allowed for each of the five linguistic descriptions of the spatial features of the canonical object (front, back, side, front corner, back corner) to be the basis for the correct response.

After the practice trial was completed, one of the canonical objects or the three mountain display and appropriate pictures were placed on the tables. The boat and boat pictures were removed at the same time. The child was then tested using the same procedure as in the practice trial except that he remained seated at all times and was not told whether he was right or wrong.

Presentation order for the five canonical objects and the three mountain display was randomized between subjects. Each child was shown five of the ten possible combinations of randomly selected object orientations and camera placements (hereafter called orientation) for each display receiving either the odd or even orientations as represented in Figure 7.3. This allowed for twenty responses per child for the canonical objects with two

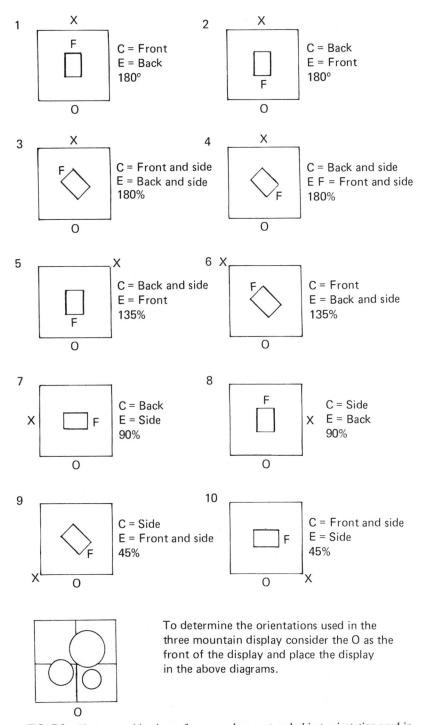

1. X
   F
   C = Front
   E = Back
   180°
   O

2. X
   F
   C = Back
   E = Front
   180°
   O

3. X
   F
   C = Front and side
   E = Back and side
   180%
   O

4. X
   F
   C = Back and side
   E F = Front and side
   180%
   O

5. X
   F
   C = Back and side
   E = Front
   135%
   O

6. X
   F
   C = Front
   E = Back and side
   135%
   O

7. X   F
   C = Back
   E = Side
   90%
   O

8. F
   X
   C = Side
   E = Back
   90%
   O

9. F
   X   O
   C = Side
   E = Front and side
   45%

10. F
    C = Front and side
    E = Side
    45%
    O   X

To determine the orientations used in the three mountain display consider the O as the front of the display and place the display in the above diagrams.

O

FIG. 7.3   The ten combinations of camera placement and object orientation used in the perspective tasks. X refers to the camera's position, O refers to the child's position, C = the correct response, E = the egocentric response and 180° refers to the number of degrees between the camera's view and the child's view.

responses per orientation for each child. The ten combinations of object orientation and camera placement in Figure 7.3 were chosen to allow the camera to be placed in positions of 45°, 90°, and 180° from the child's position and to also allow the correct linguistic response to be the front, back, side, front corner, and back corner orientations of the object an equal number of times. The camera placement and the orientation of the object were manipulated independently. In addition, each child saw either the five even or five odd orientations of the three mountain display as shown in Figure 7.1. This allowed for ten responses per orientation for each age group within both the picture selection and verbal response conditions.

Verbal Response Condition.   In the verbal response condition, different children were tested, but they followed the same procedures as the picture selection condition except that the child described the camera's perspective verbally rather than by pointing to a picture. Therefore, in place of using an array of pictures in the practice trial, the experimenter spoke the names of the five orientations. The verbal labels used were: "front," "back," "side," "front and side" (front corner), and "back and side" (back corner). As in the picture selection condition, the child had to be able to identify the five orientations of the boat, this time using the names provided. Again, only four kindergarten children failed to reach criterion and four additional children were tested.

The verbal labels for the three mountain display were: "red in front of yellow," "yellow in front of red," "red in front of blue," "blue in front of red," and "blue in front of yellow (and red)" (see Figures 7.1 and 7.3).

Results

The Three Mountain Task.   Data from the three mountain condition were initially analyzed separately from the canonical object condition. Children's responses were categorized as being either a correct response, an egocentric error, or a non-egocentric error. Each category was analyzed using separate 3 (Age) × 2 (Response Condition) × 10 (Orientation) non-independent analyses of variance. A summary of the findings is presented in Table 7.1 along with the relevant results from Laurendeau and Pinard's (1970) perspective task which used picture selection as a response means. Although the trends are comparable, the results of the picture selection condition in this present study are considerably better than those in the Laurendeau and Pinard study, possibly because of such factors as the practice trial and more explicit instructions in our study.

A comparison between the picture selection and verbal response conditions of the present experiment reveals that the picture selection responses are correct on 38% of the trials across all grade levels, while the verbal responses were on 79% of the trials ($F_{(1,18)} = 120.93, p < .001$).

TABLE 7.1
Results of the Perspective Task Using the Three Mountain Display
and the Related Results of Laurendeau and Pinard (1970)

Grade and Condition	Responses[a]		Non-Egocentric Errors
	Correct	Egocentric	
Kindergarten: (5.5)[b]			
Picture Selection	25	36	39
Verbal Response	64	13	23
Laurendeau and Pinard			
Age 5	09	20	71
Age 6	07	39	54
Grade Two: (7.4)			
Picture Selection	35	32	33
Verbal Response	83	12	06
Laurendeau and Pinard			
Age 7	17	53	30
Age 8	17	57	26
Grade Four: (9.8)			
Picture Selection	55	29	16
Verbal Response	92	05	03
Laurendeau and Pinard			
Age 9	35	42	23
Age 10	36	45	19
Overall Totals			
Picture Selection	38	32	29
Verbal Response	79	10	11

[a]Scores are percentages of total responses and chance for correct and egocentric responses is .20 and .60 for non-egocentric errors.
[b]Mean age for the grade level.

More important, however, is the distribution of errors between the categories "egocentric" and "non-egocentric". There is a 32% egocentric response rate across grade levels in the picture selection condition but only a 10% egocentric rate in the verbal condition, ($F_{(1,18)} = 75.28$, $p < .001$), with the difference accounting for 36% of the total variance in the analysis of egocentric errors. This difference is particularly compelling when interpreted in terms of the probability values for chance response: probability for egocentric response is .20 and for non-egocentric response, .60; the observed values for egocentric errors are above chance on the picture selection task and below chance on the verbal task. The tendency for a greater than chance occurrence of egocentric errors is also indicated in the

Laurendeau and Pinard data which reflects the fact that their response measure was pictorial.

As Table 7.1 indicates, in both response conditions, performance improved across grade level ($F_{(2,18)}$ = 20.18, $p < .001$) in a significant trend ($F_{lin (1,18)}$ = 40.33, $p < .001$) and grade level accounts for 20% of the variance. The orientation main effect for correct responses is not significant ($p < .10$) since the number of correct responses does not vary as the result of a change in the rotational distance between the child's view and the camera's view (see Figure 7.4). Nor is there any significant variation as a result of a change in the particular description of the other's view (e.g., yellow in front of red, red in front of yellow). Note, however, that the three mountain task was constructed so that there is no variation in the linguistic complexity of each correct description as the preceeding examples illustrate (see Figure 7.1).

The Canonical Object Task. Children's responses to canonical objects, that is those objects with distinctive fronts, backs, and sides, were categorized either as correct, as an egocentric error, or as a non-egocentric error. These scores are presented in Table 7.2. The results were then analyzed separately for each of these three categories in a 3 (Grade Level) × 2 (Response Condition) × 4 (Object) × 10 (Orientation) non-independent analysis of variance. The object effect is non-significant in all analyses ($p < .10$) so all generalizations may be made across the four canonical objects. There is a significant main effect for Grade Level and Response Condition. The main effect for Grade Level ($F_{(2,54)}$ = 132.76, $p < .001$) primarily reflects a linear increase of correct scores with increasing Grade Level ($F_{lin (1,54)}$ = 264.53, $p < .001$). The response conditions, picture selection versus verbal description, are significantly different both for the number of correct responses and for the number of egocentric errors. In the verbal response condition 83% of the total responses are correct while in the picture selection responses only 47% are correct ($F_{(1,54)}$ = 594.12, $p < .001$). Symetrically, only 3% of the verbal responses are egocentric while 40% of the picture selections are egocentric ($F_{(1,54)}$ = 721.46, $p < .001$). These two patterns replicate the findings obtained for the three mountain display.

Discussion

The graph in Figure 7.5 assesses the contribution to problem difficulty of three factors: rotational distance, propositional complexity of the relationship, and response mode. Of these, rotational distance is the only factor unrelated to performance; in fact, the error rate is actually the reverse of one which would be expected by a rotational strategy in that the smallest distances are generally the most difficult problems. Let us, then, examine the effect of response mode, propositional complexity, and their interaction, to arrive at a description of the strategies children develop to solve these perspective problems.

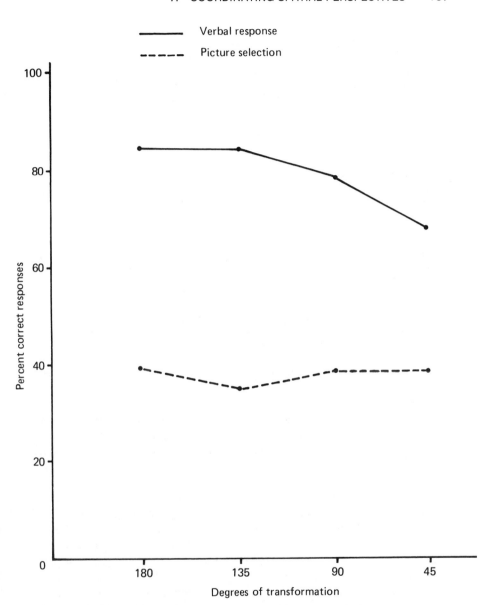

FIG. 7.4   Percentage of correct responses on the perspective task using the three mountain display by degrees of transformation from the child's view to the camera's view.

1. Effect of Response Mode

For both the three mountain and the canonical displays, performance was better in the verbal response condition than in the picture selection condi-

TABLE 7.2
Results of the Perspective Task Using Canonical Objects

Grade and Condition	Responses[a] Correct			Egocentric			Non-Egocentric Errors		
Kindergarten (5.5)[b]	C[c]	S	T	C	S	T	C	S	T
Picture Selection	23	46	31	53	47	49	25	13	21
Verbal Response	43	86	69	08	04	05	50	12	26
Grade Two (7.4)									
Picture Selection	34	54	46	50	35	41	17	11	13
Verbal Response	82	89	86	03	05	04	15	07	10
Grade Four (9.8)									
Picture Selection	50	74	64	38	19	27	11	08	09
Verbal Response	90	98	94	01	01	01	10	02	05
Overall Totals									
Picture Selection	36	58	47	47	34	39	18	12	14
Verbal Response	72	91	83	04	03	03	25	07	14

[a]Scores are percentages of total responses and chance for correct and egocentric responses is .20 and .60 for non-egocentric errors.
[b]Mean age for the grade level.
[c]C = responses requiring complex predicates (i.e. "front and side"), S = responses requiring simple predicates (i.e. "front"), T = the total of C and S.

tion. Since we interpret better performance as reflecting a match between the response alternative and the representation assigned to the display, it appears that children were constructing equivalent representations for both types of displays and that those representations took the form of specifying distinct propositional relationships. Thus, even in solving the three mountain task, children code the display in terms of explicit propositions which are constructed to distinguish the viewpoints in terms of their critical features, e.g., red in front, yellow in back, and so on. On this basis, the verbal response mode is beneficial for two reasons. First, because it is congruent with the explicit representations assigned to the display, and second, because it serves to guide the child in the initial assignment of those representations. The question itself, that is, does the camera see red in front, or yellow in back, and so on, signals to the child that those are the critical aspects of the display for which a spatial relation needs to be constructed. The pictorial conditions offers no direction regarding the relative significance of the various features of the display, and the child, presumably, is lead to look generally at all of them.

The second way the response mode showed up in the results is that egocentric responses occurred frequently in the pictorial mode and

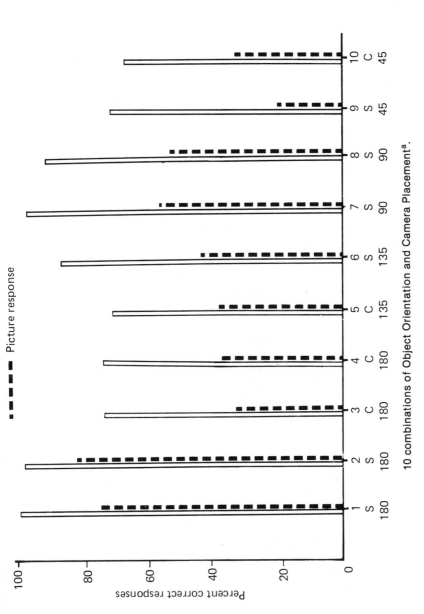

FIG. 7.5 Percentage of Correct Responses by Orientation and Means of Response on the Perspective Task Using Canonical Objects.

[a]S = simple verbal label for correct response, C = complex verbal label for correct response, 180° = the degree of transformation from the child's position to the camera's position.

negligibly in the verbal mode. We shall return to this finding in the third section which deals with the interaction between response mode and display complexity.

Both findings regarding response mode, namely the relative difficulty of the picture mode and the abundance of egocentric errors for that condition only, are consistent with the results of a study by Huttenlocher and Presson (1979) in which children's ability to solve perspective problems was tested by two types of questions, appearance question and item question. Although in their study both question types were based on pictures, the item questions were analogous to verbal mode in this study in that the picture isolated a critical feature of the display. A discussion of their study is presented in Chapter 8.

2. Effect of Propositional Complexity

The complexity of the proposition required to represent the spatial relations between display and the observer was examined in two ways. First are there differences in difficulty between the simple and complex views of the canonical objects? Second are there differences between canonical and non-canonical displays? We will consider both of these aspects of complexity.

For the canonical objects, we hypothesized that the relations requiring simple linguistic descriptions (front, back, or side) would result in fewer errors than the relations requiring more complex linguistic descriptions (front-corner, back-corner). This is in fact the case. For simple descriptions 73% of the responses are correct with 18% egocentric errors and 9% non-egocentric errors, while for complex descriptions only 54% are correct with 26% egocentric errors and 21% non-egocentric errors. A planned comparison indicates that this difference is significant for correct responses ($F_{\text{simple vs. complex }(1,54)}$ = 194.85, $p < .001$). These differences are also significant for the other response categories.

Second, considering only the simple descriptions, we may order them as well for complexity. Kuczaj and Maratsos (1975) in their study of language acquisition found that children acquired "front" and "back" about the same time and both were acquired before "side". If order of acquisition is taken as an index of complexity we can predict that children will respond correctly to front and back more often than side. This, too, is the case in our data. When rotational distance is held constant (orientation 7 vs. 8 in Figure 7.3) there are more correct responses (77% vs. 72%) on the orientation requiring "back" than on the orientation requiring "side" ($F_{7 \text{ vs. } 8 (1,54)}$ = 5.24, $p < .05$). However, orientations with the same rotational distance which require "front" and "back" (orientation 1 vs. 2 in Figure 7.3) responses are not significantly different, $p < .10$).

The comparison between performance with single canonical objects and the noncanonical array reveals the same role for complexity. The overall performance shows that 65% of the responses are correct for the canonical objects with no difference between the objects, 59% of the responses are correct for the noncanonical array ($F_{\text{three mountain vs. canonical }(1,72)}$ = 12.35, p < .001).

This comparison becomes more revealing, however, when the canonical objects are divided according to simple versus complex descriptions and the noncanonical display compared with each of these separately. Thus, for simple canonical representations, the child would encode the relation by means of a single embedded proposition of the form:

front ((front) car, camera) i.e., The front of the car is in
front of the camera,

while a complex viewpoint would require a complex representation consisting of two predicates of the form:

front ((front and right) car, camera) or *front* ((front) car, camera) and
front ((right (car), camera), i.e., The front right corner of the
car is in front of the camera.

Similarly, the noncanonical array would require a complex representation consisting of two predicates of the form:

front (blue, camera) and back (yellow, camera) or
front ((front (blue, yellow)) camera), i.e., The blue mountain
is in front of the camera and the yellow mountain is at the back.

Note that the front/back dimension laid out in object space, assigns front to the area adjacent to ego/viewer and back to the area away from ego/viewer as we would in describing the front of the desk and the back of a desk.

If we compare the percentage of correct responses to each of these three types of problems (see Tables 7.1 and 7.2) we find that performance for all subjects and in both response modes is virtually identical for complex canonical objects and noncanonical arrays, and that both of these are poorer than performances for simple canonical objects. This congruity between the results of the complex canonical objects and noncanonical arrays suggests that much the same procedure is used in solving both these problems. All three problems require the identification of critical feature(s) of the display and the assignment of a spatial predicate relating that feature to the location of the observer located at some position around that display (see Chapter 6 for a discussion of ego-related versus observer-related descriptions). In addition, the two latter problems are more difficult because they require two embedded predicates while the first problems require only one.

This explanation of the effects in the ease of identifying and coding of display features is consistent with results from other perspective studies. Fishbein, Lewis, and Keiffer (1972), for example, found a high degree of accuracy in a perspective task which used canonical objects with explicit spatial features. Furthermore, their pretraining procedures explicitly identified the front, back, and side of the objects for the subjects, thereby drawing attention to the relevant features. In a study by Huttenlocher and Presson (1973), however, the displays did not have obvious canonical forms and performance was much poorer. In addition, there were a large number of egocentric responses in their study, a finding we would now predict from the fact that responses were signalled pictorially and no clue was given as to the critical features of the display or the spatial predicates that were critical to the picture choice. This point is considered more fully in the following section.

3. Interaction between Response Mode and Complexity

Finally, the interaction of response mode and display complexity was examined through an analysis of the error patterns. The complexity of the propositional description influences the type of error and each mode of response has its own characteristic error pattern. This is particularly evident in the kindergarten responses presented in Table 7.2. In both verbal and picture conditions, orientations with complex propositional descriptions result in more errors. However, picture selections result in more egocentric errors (53% vs. 8%), and verbal responses in more non-egocentric errors (50% vs. 25%).

The egocentric errors in perspective tasks appear, then, to be related to the pictorial mode of response rather than to a general characteristic of pre-operational thought as suggested by Piaget and Inhelder. Similar evidence has been offered by Elliott and Dayton (1976). Egocentric errors are most likely caused by an interaction of the visual array and the pictorial response mode which encourages the child to focus on the unanalyzed representation rather than on the discrete formal qualities of the display. Therefore, a perspective strategy is not evoked, but rather the child matches the pictures with a remembered visual array to produce an egocentric error. Hardwick, McIntyre, and Pick (1976) reported similar results in research using a triangulation task to study the cognitive maps of children and adults. They found that children made more egocentric errors on a perspective task (imagine yourself in another position) when the stimulus (a room) was visible than when it was obscured. That is, children have difficulty extracting an explicit form representation and making their response on the basis of it when they are faced with an image of the whole display whether real or pictured. This may be complicated as well by the child's inability to consider two complex representations of the same display, one that he knows to be true of his own view, and one that would be true of the observer's view. Being unable to accept two contradictory descriptions as true, and being unable or unwilling to suspend his own view, the child chooses his own view, thereby committing an egocentric error.

The non-egocentric errors displayed a different pattern. When the correct orientation requires a two-part linguistic description (e.g., "front and side" which was the term used for the front corner) kindergarten children tended to leave off one component of this description. For example, instead of saying "front and side" the child would simply respond with "front" or "side" and this type of error accounts for 96% of the non-egocentric kindergarten errors in the verbal condition seen in Table 7.2.

Note what this suggests about the nature and uses of "images" generally. Recall that the angular separation between the child and the observer did not contribute to the item difficulty from which we inferred that no image had been rotated. Now we note that if children attempted to use such an image, or what we have called an unanalyzed structural description in the picture selection task, they fail. The image led to the selection of a picture not of another perspective, but of one displaying their own point of view. Apparently, the image could not be rotated; what could be constructed to represent the view from another perspective was not an image but an explicit set of propositions which relate distinctive constituents of the display to the spatial properties of the viewer.

Development of Perspective-Taking Ability

The results of this study suggest a model of development which is based on two factors: an increasing ability to code complex displays by means of compound predicates as evidenced by the difference between the simple canonical task and the complex canonical and three mountain tasks; and an increasing ability to isolate and activate the spatial predicates critical to the task as shown by the superiority of the verbal response mode.

Kindergarten children have little difficulty with problems for which a simple spatial proposition is sufficient, and they are particularly competent when the response is signalled verbally. By grade two, the children could handle complex spatial propositions as well, namely those appropriate to the complex objects and the three mountain array, provided that the response mode was still verbal. At this age, there is about a 50% success rate in solving the simple canonical object task using the picture selection technique. Finally, for grade four, the children are extremely good with all problems using verbal response and have improved considerably in their competence with the picture response, particularly for simple canonical objects.

It appears, then, that an adequate theory for solving perspective problems, would consist of two main principles: the identification and or assignment of critical features and relating these critical features to an observer by means of simple or complex spatial predicates. Development would involve the maturation of these two skills so that they can be applied to situations of increasing complexity. The problems examined in both this and the previous chapter, however, could be solved strictly on the basis of relating one feature to the observer by a single spatial predicate, namely what is in front of the observer. A more complete model must include the ability to generate an entire representation of the space seen from the observer's point of view. Once knowing what is "in front" of the observer, for example, to what extent can the child specify the rest of the object or array laid out in front of the observer so as to predict in addition what would be in back of the observer, or to his right? It is this third aspect of the problem, namely the generation of a complete spatial framework from another point of view, that is primarily responsible for the relative difficulty of the picture response mode in the present study and which will be pursued in the following chapter.

8 On the Representations and Operations Involved in Spatial Transformations

The previous chapter demonstrated that children solved the perspective problem, that of selecting the perspective seen from another person's point of view, by identifying distinguishing features of the display and labelling, by means of spatial predicates, the relation between that feature and the observer. These spatial relations have in other chapters been described as observer-referent descriptions. The concern in this chapter is with generalizing that theory to include an account of the form of the spatial relation recruited for the solution to rotation problems. In these problems, a display is rotated, or imagined to rotate, and the child either judges whether two depictions are the same object in different orientations, or predicts a correct depiction of a given display after a particular rotation.

By far the most popular of the theories advanced to explain adult performance on the rotation problem is that of Shepard and his colleagues (see Shepard, 1978 for a review). In their classic studies, Shepard and Metzler, (1971) and Metzler and Shepard (1974), Cooper (1976) observed that when adult college students determined whether line drawings of pairs of differently oriented geometric figures represent the same three-dimension objects, their reaction times were linearly related to the angular distance separating the displays. They interpreted these relationships as evidence that subjects perform a mental rotation of a mental image in a way that corresponds to the physical rotation of an object in space. This pattern of results was observed for a variety of different stimuli and task conditions. In fact, Cooper and Shepard (1973a) have shown that subjects can even "prepare" a mental image for later comparison with another stimulus in a successive presentation paradigm by mentally rotating it a specified distance until its orientation matches that of the stimulus to be presented.

However compelling the theory of mental images, it is not adopted here for two reasons. Firstly, "images" are themselves in need of explanation (see Chapter 2) and secondly, a theory of images fails to specify how truth judgments are made. This issue was first made central in the philosophy of Bradley (1922) and Frege (1952) in which the theory of ideas was criticized and replaced by a theory of propositions. Bradley's way of putting the problem was to claim that the idea of an object may be thought of as having an image of that object, but to say what an image *is* is different from saying what that image (or idea) *means*. What it *means* is the way that the idea refers to objects so as to permit judgments of truth or falsity. Frege's way of putting the problem was to say that the units of thought are not concepts, but propositions which may be true or false. The trouble with images, simply, is that they may be useful as a theory of ideas but not for a theory of judgments. And it is judgments of truth or falsity which these and most psychological tasks require. Image theory says merely, that if the images of the two objects are congruent, the displays represented by the images are congruent. But it is not clear what it means for two images to be congruent. If specified, it would presumably reduce to the two displays "taking" the same propositional description. If such propositions are necessary for judgments, we may as well construct such propositions in the representational phase of the task.

How are rotation tasks solved? Just and Carpenter (1976) proposed a model for solving rotation problems based on the use of propositional descriptions of the display and their transformations. By naming the primary arms in the block display as "open", "closed", and "central", the relationship between features may be described in terms of vectors which are represented in the form:

$$(\text{OPEN } (r,\ \theta,\ \phi))$$

where r is the length of the arm and θ and ϕ are two angles defining its relationship to other display components.

Just and Carpenter further identify three stages in the comparison process involved in the solution of the problem: initial search for comparable components in the two displays, transformation of one component into congruity with the corresponding component in the second display, and confirmation by checking the relationship of other display components. The traditional time-dependent effect of angular separation reported for rotation problems is attributed to the longer search times required at all three stages of this process when there is greater spatial displacements between the compared displays.

Such a strategy would both produce correct responses and be consistent with the reaction time data reported for these problems, although the underlying representation suggested by their model may be more abstract than necessary. It is possible that subjects may adopt the basic strategy they describe but simplify the representation by coding the object-referent description of the display not in terms of the absolute orientation of the display, as suggested by Just and Carpenter, but in terms of the perspective of the viewer. That is, the codings would be structurally equivalent to those proposed in the previous chapter for solving the perspective task. These representations would still be object-referent relationships, since all the information is expressed with respect to other display constituents, but they would be constructed from a particular point of view. This use of the perspective of the viewer imports features of ego-referent relationships to the scheme, and hence may simplify the representation problem. This hybrid we call ego-related object-referent relationships. It differs from that suggested by Just and Carpenter primarily in the first stage, namely the coding of the original object *O*. Rather than assign a representation to the display in terms of its absolute orientation, we suggest that the subject assign an object-referent description to the object much as we described in our analysis of the perspective problem. In locating the primary comparable components of the display, we suggest that the display is assigned properties *as if* it were a canonical object with an intrinsic top, front, right, and left sides. These assigned spatial properties are determined by the perspective of a viewer. We may clarify the various uses of these forms of representation by an appeal to some simpler "object rotation" tasks.

Upon comparison of figure *a* with figure *b* (See Figure 8.1) a viewer would first find or assign spatial properties to *a*, such as top, front, left and

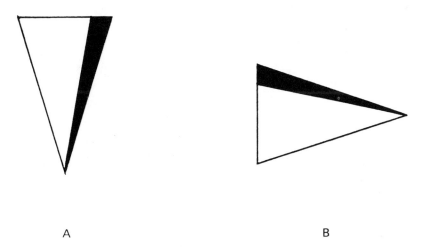

A   B

FIG. 8.1   Noncanonical figures may be temporarily assigned intrinsic spatial features to facilitate the coding and comparison operations.

right, on the basis of the properties of ego space. That is, the ego's right becomes the right side of the triangle. In *a* then, the bar is on the right side and the mental coding would be:

right (bar, *a*), that is, the bar is on the right of *a*.

Similarly, the designation for the top of the triangle, is supplied on the basis of ego; the ego's top becomes the triangle's top.

In comparing *a* with *b*, the viewer cannot simply apply ego-related descriptions to *b* for in that case the bar would be on the top:

top (bar, *b*), that is, the bar is on the top.

and the two triangles would be judged as different. Rather, to make the comparison, these assigned spatial parts must be treated as invariant, thereby creating canonical objects with a top and bottom and a left and right which have been determined by ego-space. The viewer can then search *b* for the corresponding top and only then assign a spatial predicate relating the location of the bar to the triangle *b*, thus:

right (bar, *b*), that is, the bar is on the right of *b*.

As the two representations match, the triangles are judged as the same. We shall return presently to consider the effects of the angular separation, *r,* between the two displays.

Alternatively, viewers could, as Ghent (1961) has shown, take the pointed end of the triangle to be the top and then assign the spatial predicates that the triangle would have if it were rotated into the ego space in which the top of the triangle corresponds to the top of the ego and the sides are assigned the predicates they would have in their new position. That is, if the pointed end is the top of *a* then the bar is on the left, thus:

left (bar, *a*).

Comparison with *b* would consist again, of finding the top and then assigning a parallel description, thus:

left (bar, *b*).

Again, the two descriptions match and the triangles would be judged the same.

Now we come to the problem of the rotation. The ease or difficulty of "finding the top" of the second object would be a function of the angular separation, r^1, between the tops of the to-be-compared objects or displays. Although this angle seems to be of minor significance in comparing the above triangles, it is indeed an extremely important part of the spatial comparison process especially when one is dealing with complex transformations and complex displays. For the task described above, the subject must scan the direction and distance of r in finding the comparable constituents. But while searching that angle, the subject may not actually compute a value for r. On the other hand, a subject could actually compute and operate upon that angle (thereby giving phenomenological reality to the rotation aspect of the problem). The angular separation, r, between distinguishable components of the triangle, the pointed ends for example, could be computed ($r = 90°$ counterclockwise) and that value could then be applied to the bars and the resulting propositions again compared. Alternatively, the whole display could be treated as an object and the subject's task would be that of finding an r which would relate those whole objects. This last strategy, however, is dependent upon the display being a cohesive object with distinguishable parts, and is, hence, identical to the first strategies described. In complex tasks the value r may be repeatedly applied to the comparable constituents of a display greatly exaggerating the effects of angular separation. However, it is important to note that the value of r is synonymous with the value through which the object had to be rotated to coincide with a second object. Hence, in a "rotation" strategy, a viewer computes r by rotating objects into congruity, in a "non-rotation" strategy the viewer computes r by comparing the end points of the rotation. There are, then, three ways of coping with r: one through simply scanning through the distance r, one through specifying an angle separating the analogous constituents, and one through transforming one display into the orientation of the other through successive stepwise movements of the objects. This last is in fact, the procedure suggested by Just and Carpenter (1976). Moreover, they argued that the stepwise increment is 50°, a distance which corresponds well to the propositional coding for 45°, "central oblique". Bryden (1973), Cooper and Podgorny (1974), Cooper (1975) and Tapley and Bryden (1977) found subjects who habitually employed one or more of such strategies. However, while these different options may account for the different strategies used by subjects on such spatial tasks, some recognition of r is essential for the solution.

In addition then to assigning distinguishing properties to the to-be-compared objects, subjects must have some means of computing the spatial predicates relating the analogous constituents. We have simply called this spatial predicate r, the transformational relation between corresponding constituents:

$$r \text{ (arm a, arm a}').$$

---

[1] r is a categorical or discontinuous rather than a metric or quantitative value.

That is, *r* is the spatial predicate relating the corresponding constituents of object A and A′. However, to see specifically how *r* is represented it is necessary to look in detail at the type, direction, and extent of the rotations that make up *r*.

Just as there are three dimensions in terms of which features of objects can be specified: top/bottom, front/back, left/right; so too there are three *axes* around which rotations can occur. Furthermore, rotations can occur in one of the two *directions* for a certain *distance*. Any rotational transformation, *r*, must then, be specified in terms of values for each of these 3 variables. The axes are the familiar Cartesian x-axis, y-axis, and z-axis, but the axes are assigned, we suggest, on the basis of ego space with top, front and sides. The x-axis involves rotations in depth around a Horizontal axis; rotation can be either top towards or top away from viewer; and it can go any distance. The y-axis rotation involves depth rotation around a Vertical axis again in one of two directions, either right towards (counterclockwise) or right away from (clockwise) the viewer, and again any distance. The z-axis involves rotations in a plane around a frontal axis either top to the right (clockwise) or top to the left (counterclockwise) for a particular distance. These rotations we may call lateral axis rotations, vertical axis rotation and frontal axis rotation respectively. Any rotation keeps the values in one dimension invariant while allowing the other two to vary. These characteristics may be summarized as shown in Table 8.1.

TABLE 8.1

Type	Characteristics	Axis	Invariant dimension	Variable dimensions
lateral	depth around Horizontal axis	x	left/right	top bottom
vertical	depth around Vertical axis	y	top/bottom	front/back left/right
frontal	plane rotation	z	front/back	top/bottom left/right

It may be recalled from Chapter 4 that dimensions could be ordered for difficulty from top/bottom to front/back to left/right. On this basis, we may predict an order of difficulty for these three types of transformations on the basis of which dimensions each specifies as variable. Specifically, we would predict that vertical axis rotations are the most difficult of the three; frontal axis rotations the next most difficult, and lateral are the easiest for subjects to manage.

In this context it is worth noting that the Piagetian rotation and perspective tasks involve the most difficult transformation, those around the vertical axis which require left/right as well as front/back transformations. Rotation tasks such as those described by Shepard and Metzler and those in the present study, involved both lateral and frontal rotations. And, as predicted above, rotations in depth, that is, lateral rotations, were easier than in the plane rotations, that is frontal rotations.

We have available then the two components of our representations which are required to make judgments of equivalence in spatial rotation tasks. The first has to do with the detection of distinctive constituents of the object or display assigned on the basis of ego space. The second has to do with the relational predicate, r, relating comparable constituents of the to-be-compared displays. Let us now apply these representational components to a series of experimental tasks that have been used to test spatial cognition.

Experimental problems involve two types of displays: *arrays,* which involve unrelated constituents and *objects,* which involve related constituents or features. This distinction is one that was examined more fully in Chapter 1. It will be recalled that the spatial structures in arrays and objects are essentially equivalent, the only difference being that they are more or less automatically assigned to and taken as invariant for objects while they are more consciously and intentionally assigned to arrays because they are usually taken as having variable spatial relations. In the experimental tasks discussed here, however, the two are essentially equivalent in that the constituents of arrays are empirically controlled such that their internal structure is invariant, and hence they are structurally equivalent to objects.

Secondly, experimental tasks involve two forms of movement. Either the viewer moves (or pretends to move) relative to the display or else the display moves (or is taken to move) relative to the viewer. The first are typified by Piaget and Inhelder's (1956) perspective problems and the second by Shepard and Metzler's (1971) rotation problems. Since some perspective problems were considered in the previous chapters, they will be discussed here only as they relate to our development of a general explanation for solving problems in spatial transformations.

The combination of these two factors, type of array and type of transformation, yields four types of problems of spatial transformations. (See Table 8.2).

1. Viewer Transformation Relative to an Object Display

This problem which was examined in the preceding chapter, requires viewers to judge what a single object would look like from various perspectives. Essentially, the difficulty of the tasks could be explained on the basis of the assignment of distinguishing constituents of the objects and positioning them relative to ego space—front, back, left, right. Furthermore,

TABLE 8.2

| | | DISPLAY | |
		Object	Array
TRANSFORMATION	Viewer	Chapter 6	Piaget & Inhelder
		Flavell	Huttenlocher & Presson
	Display	Shepard & Metzler	Huttenlocher & Presson

the question "What would it look like to an observer (*O*)?" requires determining only what would be in front of *O*, as we argued in the previous chapter, by retrieving the appropriate distinguishing feature.

2. Viewer Transformation Relative to an Array

This is Piaget and Inhelder's classic three-mountain problem. It involves a fixed complex array of constituents having no obvious internal spatial structure, such as fronts or backs. The task is to select a picture correctly representing the view from various positions around the display. The complexity of the task has been shown to diminish when the display has internal distinguishing spatial properties (Pufall & Shaw, 1973). The identification of such features in effect reduces the problem to that stated in the task above, namely, viewer transformation relative to an object. Huttenlocher and Presson (1979) have studied this problem in a unique way which makes it easier to isolate the critical cognitive operations, hence we shall analyze this cell in terms of their problem in the following section.

3. Array Transformation Relative to a Fixed Viewer

Since most display rotation studies have involved single objects, this task is somewhat unusual. It has, however, been studied extensively by Huttenlocher and Presson (1973, 1979). An array of objects is rotated through various distances relative to a viewer who is then required to select a picture showing what the transformed array would look like. These array and viewer transformations may best be discussed together in terms of the study by Huttenlocher and Presson in which arrays consisting of some discrete objects were moved relative to a viewer or a viewer was moved relative to the array. We shall return to the fourth cell, that is, object transformations relative to a fixed viewer, after our discussion of the study by Huttenlocher and Presson.

As mentioned in a study by Huttenlocher and Presson (1979) these two cells were examined with a group of third-grade children. Since their study involved only arrays, the only feature distinguishing these tasks, was whether the display moved relative to the viewer or the viewer moved relative to the display. In addition, they introduced a variable reflecting two question types. In the "item question" condition, children responded to four questions for each of the four positions around the display, and each of which required the child to select from a set of four objects the one that would be in that position after the transformation. In the "appearance question" condition, children responded by selecting a picture of the entire display of four objects that would be an accurate representation of the display after the rotation to each of the four positions. Left-right confusions were minimized by applying green and red stickers to the child's left and right hands respectively.

The percentage of errors committed on each of these problem types in their study are summarized as follows:

	Appearance	*Item*
Array Rotation	15	32
Viewer Rotation	56	20

In addition, Huttenlocher and Presson report that there was no significant occurrence of egocentric errors in the Array Rotation problem, and for the Viewer Rotation problem 80% of the Appearance question errors were egocentric while 49% of the Item question errors were egocentric. Further, the egocentric errors in the Item questions were virtually confined to left-right confusions at 180° transformations.

Huttenlocher and Presson's account of these data rests on two assumptions. First, with respect to coding, they insist that the coding used ties the units of the display to some feature in the external framework, although they leave unspecified the precise nature of that coding. While they acknowledge that the viewer may serve as such an external reference feature, they attribute only limited value to such a coding and do not pursue it further.

Second, they argue that subjects interpret the task instructions literally, that is, they mentally transform either the display or their own position depending on the instruction. Thus the mental operations underlying each of these transformations would necessarily be different.

Array Rotation. The Array Rotation, then, is solved by rotating each of the four display constituents with respect to the external coding it is assigned. Since the item questions ask what would be in each of the four positions, each item must be transformed into its new position and all four transformations must indeed be carried out. The appearance questions, however, permit the child to arrive at the correct answer by rotating only one of the four display components into the new location since the internal structure of those components is never violated by the distractors. Hence, appearance questions are relatively easy compared to item questions.

Because displays are coded with respect to external frameworks and not to the child's own positions, two steps are required for the solution to the Viewer Rotation problems. The child must code the relationship between the viewer and the framework, and then recode the display with respect to that new viewer position. Although it is not very difficult to imagine the viewer moving with respect to the framework, hence the simplicity of item questions, it is very difficult, they argue, to imagine the second step, namely the reordering of the display with respect to that new position. They claim that "while the subject has reoriented the viewer vis-á-vis the *array and room,* picture selection requires reorienting the *array* vis-á-vis the *room*" (p. 390). Failure of this step not only produces the incorrect answer but typically produces the description that would be true of the child's current position, that is, the egocentric error.

While the system proposed by Huttenlocher and Presson succeeds in accounting for the data in each of their four experimental cells and also in explaining the particular occurrences of egocentric errors, we believe that the explanation is piecemeal. That is, it may be possible, to account for performance on all problems by posing only one form of spatial coding and one form of mental operation to represent the transformation. In addition, while Huttenlocher and Presson do not describe the means by which the transformation is achieved and instead use descriptions like "rotate the display", "imagine moving the viewer to a new position", and the like, we argue that the structure of those transformations can, and indeed must, be expressed in terms of the formal codings used to make the judgments.

The simplest coding which provides the necessary information for all transformations is that which individually links each display component to the child's own initial position with respect to that display. There is no need to implicate other external features of the environment, nor is there any need to relate display components to each other. This ego space is adequate for representing all the critical aspects of the original display. The displays, locations, and transformation involved in the two tests are shown in Figure 8.2. The coding that subjects assign to the display and then operate on would be the following:

front	(A)
green	(B)
back	(C)
red	(D)

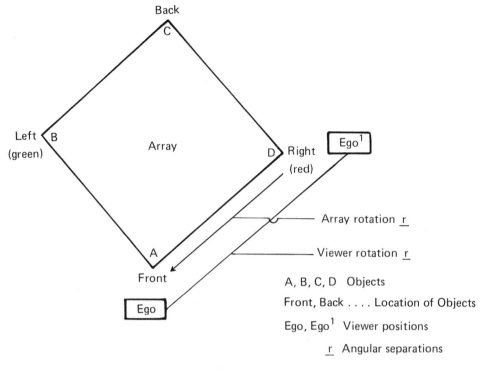

FIG. 8.2 Objects, locations, viewpoints and transformations included in the array rotation and viewer rotation tasks.

Second, the transformation relating ego to a new location (ego[1]) or a display constituent A to a new location (D) may be represented propositionally by means of *r* having the components described in a previous section, namely:

$$r \text{ (type, direction, degree).}$$

When this transformation is applied to the predicate of any of those codings, the argument reflecting the correct description after the transformation may be directly retrieved.

Consider an example for an Array Rotation problem. In the display depicted in Figure 8.2, the child would code the four propositions as stated above. The child is then told that the display is moved so that the green side is now in front of the child. The value for *r* describing that transformation is computed as type = vertical; direction = front to the right, or counterclockwise; degree = 90 or quarter turn. Note that the child need not have an elaborate lexical system for representing these moves. The propositions need not have any explicit verbal form. They can, nonetheless be given rather straightforward verbal expression as they are mostly binary, that is front to the right vs. front to the left, and so on. We would expect, in fact, that as the lexicon becomes more differentiated in these ways, the problems would become easier only because the storage and recall of these transformations is easier. Their propositional structure, we would argue, is identical with or without explicit verbal formulation (see Chapter 1).

The transformation r is then applied to the predicate of the relevant proposition. For example,

$$green + r \longrightarrow front.$$

But green is **(B)**
Hence, after the transformation,

$$front \textbf{ (B)}$$

That is, the new argument for front is the original value for green. Similarly, the child can easily compute the location of the other three constituents for any given transformation thus:

$$
\begin{aligned}
back \ (C) \ and \ back + r &\longrightarrow green, &\therefore \quad green \ (C) \\
red \ (D) \ and \ red + r &\longrightarrow back, &\therefore \quad back \ (D) \\
front \ (A) \ and \ front + r &\longrightarrow red, &\therefore \quad red \quad (A)
\end{aligned}
$$

For item questions all of these values would have to be computed. For appearance questions, as Huttenlocher and Presson pointed out, only one of these transformations is required to select the correct alternative for each of the four questions and hence the item questions are more difficult than the appearance questions. But in both cases, then, we have a coding of the four constituents in terms of the locations specified by ego space, plus a derived transformation relating the initial and end points of the rotation. Together these specify the correct solution for all of the questions. They differ only in the number of constituents to which the spatial transformation need be applied.

Viewer rotation.   When the Viewer moves relative to the display, as in the Viewer-Rotation problem, the mental operations are composed of the same basic constituents as in the Array Rotation problem, items coded in terms of location specified by ego space and an angle of rotation, r, separating the two points of view. But in this case it is not objects which change locations but the ego-related framework which must be changed. For this reason, as Huttenlocher and Presson point out, these problems tend to be more difficult.

First, however, it is important to notice that logically, subjects could solve viewer rotation problems in much the same way that they solve array rotation problems. Suppose that subjects specified the locations of the objects shown in Figure 8.2 in the way that they do for the array rotation tasks, namely:

front   (A)
green   (B)
back   (C)
red   (D)

Secondly, suppose that the viewer coded the change in position of ego to that of the observer by means of a value for r specifying that transformation, thus:

$$\text{front (Ego)} + r \longrightarrow \text{green (Ego)}$$

and the value for r in that transformation would be $90°$ (in a particular direction around a particular axis). If the subject realized that the value for the movement of Ego was the movement of each spatial position, he or she could now simply take the value for r and apply it to each location in ego space to determine the spatial location from the new point of view, i.e. the observer space. The object in that new position is the same object that occupied the corresponding position as it was described by ego space. For example,

front $+ r \longrightarrow$ green, and green was B, therefore, front is now B
green $+ r \longrightarrow$ back, and back was C, therefore, green is now C
back $+ r \longrightarrow$ red, and red was D, therefore, back is now D
red $+ r \longrightarrow$ front, and front was A, therefore, red is now A

And so on for each value of r in each rotation of the Viewer.

However, there is no indication that subjects realized the logical equivalence of the viewer rotation and the array rotation tasks. That is they do not notice that for Ego to move $90°$ to the right is equivalent to object B moving $90°$ in the opposite direction from the right to the front of Ego. Their failure to note this equivalence is understandable, for to do so would involve an Einsteinian concept of the relativity of motion. Furthermore, Huttenlocher and Presson's data suggest that indeed the subjects took the instructions seriously and attempted to imagine that the viewer was at new location, relative to a fixed display. What representation and operations would make that attempt possible?

In the Viewer Rotation problem, the problem may be solved solely on the basis of ego space and the knowledge that the display components themselves do not move. The child constructs an ego space representation of the display, as we have shown in Figure 8.2. Again, the coding locates each display object with respect to one of the ego space positions front, back, red, green. The child is then told that the new position for the observer is at a certain point which had previously been coded as for example, green, in her ego space. As we have seen in the previous chapter, the child is easily able to construct a description of the relationship between the O and the object or feature immediately in front of O providing that the object is distinctive. This operation would have the form:

front (B, O), that is, B is in front of the observer.

When asked what is in front of O, the subject simply reads off the value B. Note, however, that even in making this judgment of the observer space, the child preserves her own ego space and the object locations specified in it, including that, in ego space B is at the green side, thus:

green (B)

In a simple case, such as the perspective problems discussed in the previous chapter, this value for "front" in the observer space provided an adequate solution to the problem and the procedure could end at this point. In a study by Presson (1980), a model of a room with distinctive features served a similar purpose in helping the child identify a front. Fewer egocentric errors occurred in this condition. More complex problems, however, require that the child construct a more complete description of this observer space, including back, left, and right.

In the next step, then, the child projects a dimension from front to back from the fact that B is at the front. But the endpoint of this new dimension coincides with the position red in her current ego space, and she knows that D is at red; hence, she may conclude that in the observer space, D is at the back. Specifically:

1. Derived front projects a front/back dimension yields a new location, back.
2. But from ego space, subject knows that location is red.
3. And she knows that object D is at red.
4. Hence, she can conclude that D is at the back (in the observer space).

The rules for handling the assignment of the left-right axis are slightly more complicated. The value r represents the angle separating the front-back axis in ego space from the same axis in the observer space. In the above example this value would be 90° (in a particular direction around a particular axis). This value calculated on the basis of the front-back axis can then be applied to the left-right axis to complete the observer space. In other words, the transformation involving r is applied to axes rather than to locations. These relations are spelled out as follows:

1. ego left/right axis + r yields observer left/right axis.
2. the right end of this axis specifies a new location for right (red) in this observer space.
3. But from ego space, she knows that that location is front.
4. and she knows that object A is at the front.
5. Hence, she can conclude that A is at the derived red side.

By the same procedure, the derived location and the object located there may be determined. In both cases the subject derives the observer space that provides the locations for the objects. The objects to be found at each of those locations is derived from the ego space structure given by her actual position. The task essentially, then is one of integrating values for ego space with values for the observer space.

Some evidence for this procedure of constructing spatial descriptions is taken from a study by Harris and Bassett (1976). They found that when children were asked to construct an array of blocks that would reflect the appearance from another point of view, they began their reconstruction with the block most prominent to the other viewer, in our terms, the value for *front* (block, O). They proceeded by supplying blocks to the other position in terms of this initial placeholder.

As Piaget has demonstrated for many tasks, it is difficult for the child to simultaneously consider two descriptions of the same event. In the viewer rotation problem, the child must simultaneously consider her present ego space description which is used to preserve the locations of the objects and the observer space description which she is calculating in order to solve the problem. Since it is difficult to entertain both viewpoints, the more compelling one, namely that which is visibly given from her actual position, may be retained at the expense of the other. Hence, when the problem becomes difficult, the child chooses the view which preserves the structure of her current ego space. However, as Huttenlocher and Presson have demonstrated, if the child is allowed to move to the new position, the problem becomes easy, even if she is not allowed to see the display. This is because the ego space projected on the display is congruent with the observer space required to solve the problem and so the child needs consider only one spatial description of the display.

The solution to the Viewer Rotation problem, therefore, requires two mental operations. First, the child must notice the adjacency relationship which determines the proposition for "front" from the point of view of the observer. Second, this position is used as the basis for projecting two axes to describe the observer space of the display. Each of the endpoints of these new axes coincides with one of the positions in the original ego space, and the object which occupies that position is then assigned a new location in observer space.

On this basis, we may explain why the appearance questions are so difficult while the item questions are so easy. The item questions facilitate this mental process by requiring the child to construct the observer space one position at a time, since each question focuses on one of these positions. The questions suggest the solution in that they inform and guide the child in treating the rotation as four separate problems each of which may be solved on the basis of the above rules. The problem is readily solved in that the child is essentially told to specify each position and relate it to what she knows about the array. The appearance question, on the other hand, gives no such directions. The child knows that the spatial structure must be different from the one describing her current ego space, but has difficulty both in constructing this new structure and in dealing simultaneously with that new structure and with her current ego space. Again, as we mentioned above, the complexity of this problem sometimes leads her to choose the structure which is currently true of the display, namely, the egocentric response. Thus the difference between the item questions and the appearance questions is in the extent to which the questions point to the underlying mental operations required for the solution to the problem.

Nonetheless, it is important to notice that the spatial structure recruited for the solution to the Viewer Rotation problem is identical to that used to solve the Array Rotation problem. In both cases, the display components are each given an absolute coding in a position specified by ego space. In both cases, too, a displacement is noted which is represented by r, although the value of r is explicitly required for the solution to the array rotation but only implicitly or indirectly relevant for the solution to the viewer rotation problem. Finally, the problem becomes difficult when the initial ego space is no longer appropriate for the solution to the problem, as in the viewer rotation task, and especially problematic when there is no indication provided as to how to reconstruct an appropriate observer space, as in the appearance questions.

4. Object Rotation Relative to a Fixed Viewer

In these problems, subjects are typically presented with two schematic displays of a complex object and asked to judge whether the two displays represent the same object in different orientations, or whether the displays represent two different objects. Although such tasks have long been used to measure "spatial ability", much of the more analytical research with such tasks has been conducted by Shepard and his colleagues who studied the mental procedures used by adult subjects in solving the problem. The development of skill in solving these problems has been conducted by Rovet and will be reported in the next chapter.

Again we will consider the solution to these problems in terms of the particular constituents and their locations in the two displays and the computation and value for r used to represent the transformation between comparable constituents. As we whall see, the spatial codings and their relations have the same form as those used to solve the spatial problems described in the other three cells. Indeed, the object rotation tasks are structurally identical to the array rotation tasks.

Consider the displays in Figure 8.3 taken from Rovet (1974). The problem is to determine in each case if the two objects pictured in each display are in fact the same. The codings involve the isolation of distinctive

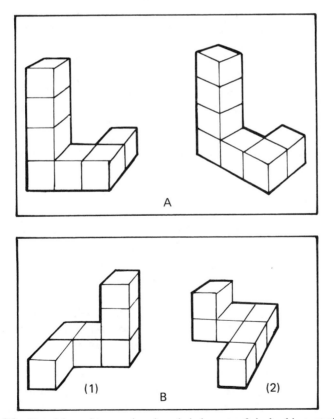

FIG. 8.3   Materials used to examine viewer's judgments of single object rotations.

features, the specification of their locations in terms of particular positions in ego space, and then the computation of r, the angular separation between the comparable constituents. Let us consider in detail objects 1 and 2 in display B of Figure 8.3. The first problem is to locate the identifiable comparable features of the two displays. Having selected them, a particular feature of object 1, such as the long arm, is assigned a spatial coding in terms of ego space, such as: *at the top* (long arm 1), that is, the long arm is at the top of object 1. In comparing object 1 to object 2 the viewer searches for the analogous constituent, the long arm, and codes its location as before: *front* (long arm, 2), that is, the long arm is at the front of object 2. Next the viewer computes the value for r which represents the difference between the two locations: r (long arm (1), long arm (2)) where r = lateral, top towards ego, 90°.

Having computed this predicate r, a second major constituent may be identified in the first object. For example, short arm is towards ego: *front* (short arm), (1), that is the short arm is at the front of 1. Again, the second object is searched for the comparable constituent. Two logically equivalent strategies are available at this point. In one, the comparable constituent is assigned a spatial predicate and the value of r relating the two locations is again computed. If this value is the same as that derived for the long arm, the objects may be tentatively taken as the same. Comparisons of other constituents are continued until all the factors selected above have been checked. If the two values for r are different, for any constituent then the two objects are judged to be non-equivalent and processing may end.

Alternatively, the subject may apply the value of r calculated on the basis of the angular separation separating the long arms of object 1 and object 2 to the location of the short arm in 1 in order to predict its location in object 2. If the appropriate arm of 2 is in the expected location, then, again, the figures may be judged the same. If the arm is not in the location specified by r, the figures are judged to be different. The distance searched for analogous constituents plus the number of times that the value r must be applied would account for the latency effects associated with increasing angular separation. Again, the process would continue until all of the constituents had been compared or until one discrepancy had been found.

Indeed Metzler and Shepard's suggestion is quite similar to the one outlined above. First, they suggest that the internal representations of two presented objects must not be coded in terms of an intrinsic and rotationally invariant structure, what we would have called an object-related description, as then the two structures could be compared directly and no comparisons would be more difficult than any other. Secondly, they conclude that "the internal representation of an external object captures its three-dimensional structure—not as that structure exists in the object absolutely—but only as it appears relative to a particular angle of regard" (Metzler & Shepard, 1974, p. 196).

This strategy outlined above not only yields correct solutions to rotations problems, but also posits concrete and specifiable features for the mental representation, and accounts for the well known effects of angular separation. Finally, it utilizes the same forms of mental representation of space that we have used to explain performance in the other three problems of spatial transformation.

9 The Education of Spatial Transformations

with Joanne Rovet
Hospital for Sick Children
Toronto, Canada

> *The picture makes a genuine contribution to knowledge.*
>
> Goodman

In the preceding chapter, an account of the cognitive processes involved in carrying out a mental rotation of either an array or a single object was advanced in some detail. Those processes involved the isolation of distinctive properties or features of the displays, their spatial location in ego space, and the computation of a value specifying the angular separation of the to-be-compared constituents. While these representations consist of specific propositions built around spatial predicates, propositions are not necessarily given explicit verbal form.

The non-verbal, yet propositional nature of these representations of spatial relations raises some questions about the development and education of spatial cognition. Can such operations be taught and if so, how? The primary concern of the present chapter is the extent to which these spatial processes can be developed through some forms of instruction.

Clearly, subjects improve with age and practice on any mental task. Some of that improvement may be the consequence of "explication" of spatial cognition as discussed in Chapter 2. An equally important part of development may result from the increasing fluency in the assignment of the spatial predicates to the locations of various constituents of a display or to the spatial relations between constituents, without those representations ever achieving an explicit verbal form. Finally, it is possible that the voluntary assignment of these spatial predicates depends on the mastery of an appropriate symbolic form.

Several theories have been offered as to how spatial skills are "educated". Piaget and Inhelder maintained that a child acquires his spatial abilities primarily from his own active involvement with real objects in the environment. A child acquires knowledge about the trajectories of falling objects by throwing and observing objects fall, learns about the changes in the shapes of objects by actually bending, and folding objects, and learns about the changes in the appearances of rotating objects by actually turning and manipulating objects in space. In fact, they argue that active manipulation of objects is *absolutely* necessary to develop the skills required for solving complex spatial problems because only active experience with real objects teaches the child both about the changes that occur to objects or groups of objects and about the coordination of the actions that produce these changes.

But such a description accounts only for the normal occasions of acquisition and use of spatial representations discussed herein; it overlooks entirely the internal structure of those skills and the fact that many alternative forms of activity may implicate and thereby develop that internal structure. If the analysis of the process is adequate, children could be taught the system explicitly as a set of formal relations; if the process involved is not known, one may encourage their development through practice, demonstration, depictions, and the like.

Consider, briefly, the consequences of verbal explication of these spatial structures in the viewer rotation task. In Chapter 7 Ives showed that by making the spatial relations explicit, even young subjects could be led to solve a simplified perspective task. Furthermore, the Huttenlocher and Presson findings that subjects were superior on the item questions than the appearance questions in the viewer rotations tasks (perspective task) may be interpreted in just this way. When the adult interlocutor asked the child a specific series of questions as to what was in *front* of the viewer, the *back* of the viewer, the *left,* the *right,* subjects performed significantly better than when the child had to construct that representation for himself as in the appearance task. That is, a spatial problem of this sort may be facilitated by explicitly stating for the child the spatial predicates relevant to his construction of the viewer's perspective. Although these predicates are generally assigned automatically to ego space, when they must be constructed or reconstructed for a viewer's space there is every possibility that the child does so through the conscious, sometimes verbal, isolation of these critical spatial relations. This line of argument suggests that if these same questions had been asked of children in the "appearance" items, their performance would have improved.

Because Piaget attributes children's spatial development primarily to physical experience, he insists that one cannot acquire these skills "mediately", that is via instructional means as ordinary language or such visual media as film since they do not provide for direct active experience (Piaget, 1971). He expressly states that media are "totally inadequate" for developing an understanding of space because media only supply learners with "representations...of objects or the events or the results of possible operations...without leading to any effective realization of these operations themselves." He says further, that "a pedagogy based on the image, even when enriched by the film remains inadequate for the training of operational constructivism since the intelligence cannot be reduced to the images of a film (but requires) the primacy of spontaneous activity and of personal or autonomous investigation" (1970, p. 72-75).

Nevertheless recent research on the educational potential of instructional media has indicated that children do acquire new concepts and sometimes new skills from exposure to media. As we have seen, verbal instruction teaches by specifying the critical elements and relations relevant to a problem (cf. Vygotsky, 1962; Olson, 1970, 1974). Less is known about how, precisely, children develop non-verbal mental skills through education generally or through visual media such as film or television in particular.

Salomon (1979) has proposed that media develop mental skills when the form of mental representation is isomorphic to the form of expression of a symbol system. For Salomon, film is a good instructional medium for spatial cognition because it can depict continuous spatial transformations and the mind performs continuous spatial transformations. However, as we have argued in the previous chapters, these transformations are carried out by means of assigning and operating upon spatial, relational propositions hence it is not clear that a film is any more or less isomorphic to those mental processes than any other medium. That is not to deny that film may have some instructional effect, but it may have that effect quite independently of the actual representations and operations subjects use in solving the problem.

Wood (1980) has taken the problem of tutoring one step fruther by suggesting that instruction, whether through demonstration, talk, or film, has an effect by playing upon the discrepancy between what children can understand and what they can actually do—what is sometimes referred to as the gap between perception and production. If children can understand a demonstration, description or depiction, they construct a mental model of that demonstration, description or depiction—that, in fact is what comprehension is—and they then use that model to guide their subsequent attempt to achieve the previously understood goal. If the tutoring was not understood, of course, it would have no relevant effect on a child's subsequent performances. In his experiments, Wood has shown that if children have a goal clearly in mind and if they understand that the demonstration illustrates a means to the achievement of that goal, that demonstration begins to influence their attempts at performance, in this case the assembly of a wooden toy. Repeated attempts bring more and more of the features of the demonstration to bear on a child's actual performance on that task. Tutoring had an effect even if it was not known how, precisely, that knowledge was represented by the children.

To summarize, contrary to Piaget's claim, there is some evidence that cognitive skills may be effectively trained through particular forms of instruction. Furthermore, instruction may be effective even in the absence of detailed knowledge of the cognitive processes involved in that skill. Consequently, a variety of instructional procedures may be appropriate for the recruitment and practice of a set of underlying cognitive processes.

The purpose of the present experiment is to determine whether the ability to solve rotation problems is amenable to "mediated" film instruction, as opposed to practice in the physical manipulation of concrete objects.

Specifically, the purpose of this experiment is to examine the effects of two types of instruction, a film animation and actual practice in the physical manipulation of concrete objects, on the development of spatial rotational skill. To examine that problem, groups of grade three children were presented with one of three versions of the filmed animation or with a Block manipulation task involving the same set of spatial rotations and the effects of these forms of instruction were assessed by means of a number of spatial tasks.

Subjects and Design. One hundred and twenty-eight grade three children with a median age of 9 years, drawn from five schools of the Catholic school board of York County, Ontario participated in the study. The five different treatment conditions consisted of three variations of the same filmed demonstrations, an active manipulation condition, and a no treatment-control condition. The stimulus figures used in the films were similar to those used by Shepard and Metzler and were constructed by gluing red wooden blocks end-to-end to form figures each of which possessed a central stem and two arms which projected in different directions from the top and bottom of the stem (see Figure 9.1).

The three colorful, lively, animated, professional-quality films were produced by editing versions of the same basic film[1]. The first film, called Complete Rotations served as the basic film. The second and third films, called Partial Rotations and No Rotations were edited versions of the first film. The latter two films were created by editing out either part or all of the rotation sequence shown on the Complete Rotation Film. A single constant image in the form of a question mark was substituted for the edited film frames to keep the overall length of the film and the coherence of the sound track intact.

The Complete Rotations film consisted of the presentation of 16 problems with an accompanying narration which required a viewer to determine whether pairs of objects shown in different orientations would match if they were rotated into the same orientation. The first five problems, serv-

---

[1]We are indebted to Richard Pierce and Joe Barr of the OISE film-production unit for their assistance in the production of these films.

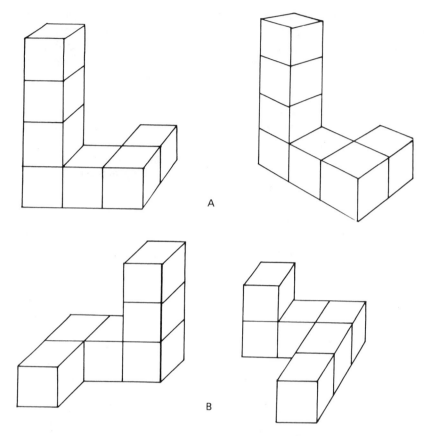

FIG. 9.1   Pairs of images to be rotated into congruence. Those in A are congruent while those in B are not.

ing as warm-up items, showed two-dimensional stimulus shapes in different orientations in the picture plane accompanied by the narrator's words "Are these two pictures of the same object?" The final eleven instructional problems presented pairs of three-dimensional block-like figures shown in different orientations, half of which were identical and therefore could be rotated into congruity and half of which were different and therefore could not. After each problem pair was presented on the screen, the child was asked "Are these the same?" following which a superimposed copy or "shadow" of one of the objects moved off the original to a space between the original objects and then rotated slowly around a fixed axis in time with the musical sound track, until its orientation was the same as the other object. It moved over slowly until it was superimposed on the second object. The original pair of objects remained static and visible throughout. The superimposition showed clearly whether or not the two objects were in fact identical. The animation sequence was filmed with overexposure to create the effect of a ghost rotating on the film, leaving the original pair visible throughout. If the pair of objects were indeed identical, then the ghost vanished when it moved into congruence with the second object; if the original pair differed, then the differing feature of the ghost remained visible on the screen. In each case it was the object on the left of the screen which rotated into congruence with the object on the right of the screen. The actions of the moving object were always accompanied by a lively musical jingle, which played the role of "thinking music" as familiarly used on television quiz programs. In addition a narrator served to introduce the film, each of the problems, and the conclusion as to the identity or non-identity of the two objects after the rotation and superimposition sequences were complete. This film lasted about 6 minutes.

The two edited films were identical to this film in all respects except that each had part *or* all of the rotation sequence removed by editing, and replaced by a constant shot of a question mark flanked on both sides by the stimulus figures. Thus each film showed the ghost move from the left to the center of the screen and after a delay showed the rotated object moved from the center position to be superimposed on the picture on the right. These edited films did not, however, show the entire rotation.

In the Block Rotation Training or "Manipulation" condition, children were shown how to solve the same kinds of problems as the film, by actively manipulating real objects in different spatial orientations. Children who were assigned to this condition were seen on an individual basis. A child was seated at a small table on which was placed in succession pairs of objects, resembling the stimuli and orientations, shown in the Complete Rotation film. These objects were presented as problems and the child was required to state whether the pair was same or not, without touching the original pair. Instead the child was given a third object, identical to one of the objects on the table and in the same orientation as that object, and was shown that this object could be used to solve the problem by rotating it from a position similar to the first block into congruence with the position of the other block to determine if they matched. If so, the child was to infer that the original pair matched.

Subjects in the three film conditions and in the Block Manipulation condition had three training sessions in successive school periods. Each session lasted about 6 minutes. Pilot testing had indicated that three training sessions were optimal. The fifth group, which served as a control condition received no special attention during this phase of the study.

The basic paradigm consisted of a Pretest phase, a Training phase, and a Posttest phase. There were two posttest sessions, one given immediately after completion of the training procedures and one given 2 weeks later. The

Pretest consisted of pairs of photographs of the objects set in various orientations that were used in the films. The Subject's task was to decide if the two pictures were pictures of the same object. In addition, children were given the verbal battery of the Canadian Lorge Thorndike Intelligence Test. The first posttest included an alternate and a more difficult form of the Rotation pretest and four additional spatial tests which served to assess the generalizability of the effects of the various forms of training. A third Rotation test was given at the second posttest session.

The Rotation pretest consisted of a simplified version of the Shepard-Metzler task presented on 35 mm slides. Each slide showed two of the stimuli, set in different spatial orientations. The child's task was to decide whether or not the stimuli on the slide represented the same or a different figure. The test consisted of a set of 33 slides, 3 of which were used for the purpose of instruction and practice. Fifteen of the slides showed pairs of figures, which if spatially rotated could be seen to represent identical objects while the other fifteen showed pairs which could not be rotated into congruence; the two figures differed in that one object was reflected in the opposite direction from the corresponding arm of the other object. The objects of each pair were separated by angular displacements of 30°, 60°, or 90° in depth (backwards or forwards) or about the objects' axes of symmetry (clockwise or counterclockwise).

Each child's performance on this task served both as a basis for inferring spatial mental representation and for assignment to the five treatment groups. The five children obtaining the five highest scores were assigned randomly one to each of the five groups, the children with the next five highest scores assigned randomly one to each of the five groups, and so forth. This procedure resulted in five experimental groups each with an N of 25, equivalent in pretested spatial skills.

There were four transfer tests in the posttest phase. The first two consisted of items of the Primary Mental Abilities (PMA) Spatial Relations sub-test, presented in a group administered test booklet. Thirteen items (PMA-1) required subjects to select a shape from a series of rotated figures to fit into a space to complete a square, much like a two-item puzzle. Fifteen items (PMA-2) required them to select a shape to match a standard from a set of mirror-image variants shown in different orientations. The other transfer tasks were the Array Rotation and Viewer Perspective tasks adopted from Huttenlocher and Presson (1973) and described in the preceeding chapter. The Array Rotations tasks required the subject to imagine how an array appeared after a rotation occurred whereas the Perspective task required the subject to imagine how an observer saw the same array from a different vantage point. Sixteen trials representing all possible Viewer Location combinations were given for each of these two tasks. These tasks were administered to the children on an individual basis with the order of the two being counterbalanced.

Results and Discussion. Consider first children's performance on the Rotation Task pretests and posttests. The dependent variable for these tasks is $p(\overline{A})$, a non-parametric estimate of signal detectability (McNicol, 1972) which takes into account false alarms or the effects of guessing. The data for the three Rotation Tasks were analyzed by three separate factorial-design analyses of variance with Means of Instruction, Angular Separation, and Sex being the three factors. Let us consider these data in two parts, first to determine the effects of instructions and secondly to examine the forms of representation involved.

The effect of instruction. Prior to training, overall performance on the five experimental groups was very similar. After training, however, significant differences were found between the training groups on the Rotation Task both immediately after training and after the 2-week delay. Analyses of variance indicated that Means of Instruction was a significant factor both on the immediate posttest ($F(4,113)$ = 3.91, $p<.05$) and on the delayed posttest ($F(4,113)$ = 2.57, $p<.05$). These results are presented in Figures 9.2 and 9.3.

Individual contrasts between means using the Newman-Keuls procedure showed that the differences between instructional means on both posttests were as follows: Complete Rotations film and Block Rotation training were superior to the Partial film condition ($p<.05$) and this condition was superior to the No Rotation film and Control conditions ($p<.05$).

These results on the Rotation Task permit us to draw free conclusions about the role of instruction in the development of spatial cognition. First, an appropriate form of instruction can contribute to the acquisition of a mental skill. In fact, on the basis of norms calculated from the pretesting given children of various ages, it appears that 12 minutes of instruction was roughly equivalent to 3 years of untutored development on these rather specific tests.

Secondly, the effectiveness of the Complete Rotation condition relative to the Block rotation condition contradicts Piaget's claim that the only means to the development of mental skills is through direct physical experience. In this study at least, both were appropriate means, one symbolic and one practical, for the development of this spatial skill.

Thirdly, from the fact that the performance of the children in the No-Rotation Film condition, that is those children who viewed the films presenting the problems and subsequently their solutions, was no better than the untutored control subjects, it may be inferred that there is little benefit of presenting problems and solutions if the means of solution is not indicated as well. That the partial rotation film fell half way in between the full film and the no-rotation film suggests that the films had a single effect which varied as a function of the degree to which the instructional means recruited the relevant cognitive processes.

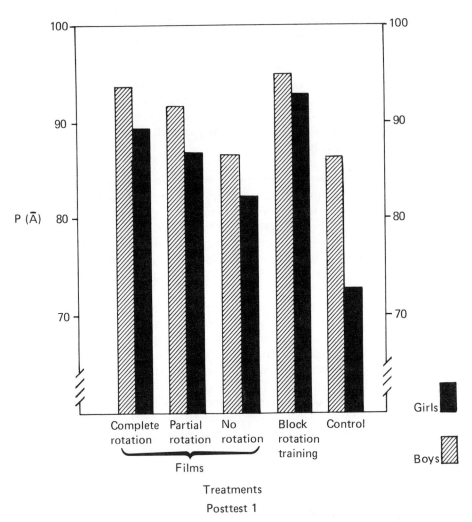

FIG. 9.2   Children's performance on the immediate posttest.

Finally, it may be noticed that there were consistent sex differences in all conditions; specifically, boys performed better than girls. These differences, however, did not interact with any of the instructional conditions in this study, nor were they detected for any of the other tasks reported in this volume. Thus, there is no reason to assume that the girls in this study were using different procedures for solving the problems than were the boys. Furthermore, with the additional practice provided by repeated testing, the differences largely disappeared. However, as we shall see in Chapter 12, in ambiguous situations there may be some tendency for females to relate features to more immediate frames of reference than to more geographic frames of reference.

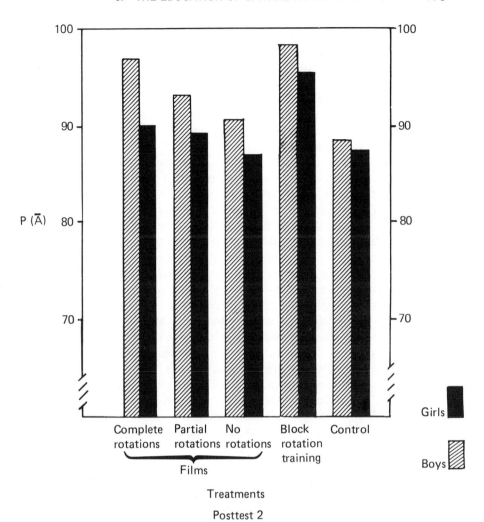

FIG. 9.3   Children's performance on the delayed posttest.

The tests for the generalizability of the effects of the training conditions are less revealing. As is well known the more similar the posttest to the training conditions, the greater the effect of that training on that posttest. This appears to be the case in the present study. The PMA-1 test in which a jig-saw like piece had to be mentally rotated to fit into a pattern, yielded a pattern of results similar to that found on the Rotations test. As revealed by a Newman-Keuls analysis, children who had viewed the Complete and Partial Rotation films along with children who received the Block Rotation training obtained significantly higher scores on this task ($p < .05$) than did children who saw the No Rotation film and children in the control condition.

There were no differences between the treatment groups on the other three tests of transfer. Hence, even if the training effects are substantial, they appear to have somewhat limited generalizability.

Processing strategies. Although the experiment did not permit the detailed analysis of representations and operations such as those discussed in the two preceding chapters, three findings in the current study indicate the nature of these processes. First, the nature of the spatial transformations relating the two views of the object determined the ease or difficulty of the comparisons. This value, which we have called r (see p. 155) is the rotation specified in terms of an axis, a direction, and a distance. In the present study two of these factors were examined, the axes around which the rotation occurs and the distance in space through which the rotation goes. Assuming that the axes of rotation are derived from ego space, it may be argued that rotations in depth, involving front-back transformations, are simpler than rotations in the plane which involve left-right transformations. And secondly, the greater the distance of r, that is the greater the angular separation of the displays, the more difficult the problem.

The effects of the direction and distance of rotations were examined on the basis of the rotation problems presented in the pretest, the posttest, and the delayed posttest. For all three tests combined, items involving objects separated by a rotation in depth were less difficult (3.72 errors for the three angles of separation combined) than those items involving objects separated by a rotation in the picture plane (7.10 errors for the three angles of separation combined). Shepard and Metzler made a similar observation. These findings suggest that subjects are indeed using axes constructed in terms of ego space and that, in that space, front-back transformations are less difficult than left-right ones.

The effects of angular separation between the displays provides further evidence for the form of representation. The analysis for both the in-the-place rotations and the in-depth rotations showed such an effect with the 90° rotation being significantly more difficult than either the 30° or the 60° rotation. As performance on the "Same" items provides a better basis for the comparison of coding strategies—different items do not require that subjects compare all of the major constituents—only the "Same" items will be analyzed in detail to determine the effects of angular separation (A full analysis of these results appears in Rovet, 1974). Because of the smaller number of items involved when the three sizes of angular separation were considered, statistical analyses were carried out only for the combined Plane and Depth rotations. A three factor Analysis of Variance with Repeated Measures on two factors indicated that test session, degree of separation, and a session by degree of separation interaction were all significant sources of variation. The significant sessions factors reflects the gradual improvement in performance on the Rotation Tasks from prettest (2.44 errors) to the first posttest (.89 errors) across all treatment conditions. The effect of angular separation is due to the significantly larger number of errors on the 90° items (2.88 errors) than either the 60° (.87 errors) or the 30° (.71 errors) separation items. The interaction with sessions, however, indicates a decrease in the relative difficulty of the 90° items across sessions when compared to the other two items. These differences are shown graphically in Figure 9.4.

These findings, namely that the distance and direction of the transformation relating to-be-compared displays influences the relative difficulty of spatial rotation problems, suggests that one important aspect of the process involved in solving such problems in the computation of a spatial predicate, r, representing the spatial relations between analogous constituents of the displays and that this value is constructed in terms of spatial properties, locations, and axes laid out in ego space.

The importance of ego space in assigning locations and axes becomes clear if one notices that in-depth and in-the-plane rotations are descriptions which assume a certain position of the viewer. If the viewer were to move around the displays 90° to the left or to the right, what before had been an in-depth rotation would now be an in-the-plane rotation and the relative difficulties of the particular problems would reverse. Hence, rotations in space utilize axes specified by ego-space.

Finally, the pattern of correlations between children's performance on these object rotation tasks, and various other spatial and verbal tasks employed in the study, give some indication of the processes involved in spatial cognition. In the preceding chapter, it was argued that object rotation and array rotation tasks are isomorphic, both requiring the location of distinguishing constituents in ego space and then computing a relational predicate r, relating analogous constituents of the to-be-compared displays. In the present study, the object rotations test was given three times while the array rotation and viewer rotation tasks were given only once. Performance on the object rotation pretest correlated significantly ($r = .19, p < .05$) with performance on the array rotation task. After training on the former, the correlation decreased to .10 and .17 on the prottest and delayed posttest respectively. The viewer rotation test, on the other hand, showed no correlation whatsoever with the object rotations test, the values ranging from .04 with the pretest to $-.06$ with the delayed posttest (Rovet, 1974, p. 240). Hence, there is some evidence that the performance on the object rotation tasks discussed in this chapter are more related to the array rotation tasks than to the viewer rotation tasks. (See Chapter 8, Table 8.2.)

Similarly, verbal abilities showed only small and nonsignificant correlations with performance on the spatial rotations tasks ($r = .11$) for all five experimental groups combined. After training, these correlations became

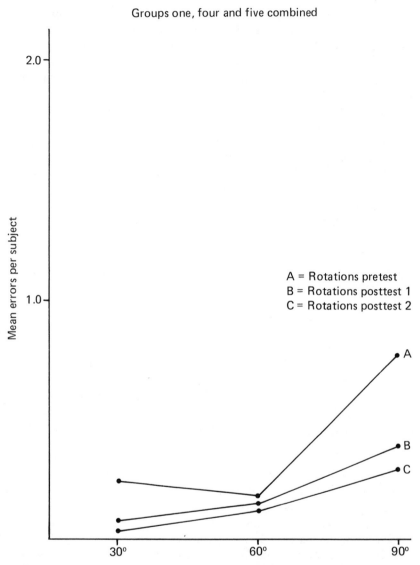

FIG. 9.4   Angular Separation in Degrees (In-the-plane and In-depth items combined).

significant ($r = .19$, $p < .05$), but these correlations vary somewhat depending upon the treatment conditions involved and will be discussed presently.

Patterns of correlations between verbal and spatial tests and subject performance after training may be understood in terms of aptitude by treatment interactions discussed by Cronbach and Snow (1977). Using the Verbal IQ test as a measure of verbal ability and the Rotation pretest as a measure of spatial ability, one can ask whether a child's initial level of competence determines the effects of any particular form of instruction. Alternative forms of instruction may make either different or fewer assumptions about the prior knowledge of the learner than do other forms of instruction. It may be, for example, that the Block manipulation condition makes fewer assumptions about prior spatial abilities than does a mediated, filmed form of instruction.

The data bearing on these hypotheses were analyzed by a regression analysis using the procedure recommended by Bottenberg and Ward (1963) to test for interactions. The relationship between the pretested rotational abilities and those assessed after the filmed training sessions are clear and comprehensible. There were significant differences among the five groups in the immediate posttest ($F(4,121)$ = 2.43, $p<.05$) and they approached significance in the delayed posttest ($F(4,121)$ = 2.09, $p<.09$). These aptitude-treatment interactions are depicted in Figure 9.5 . There is a strong positive relationship between initial skill mastery and subsequent performance for the control group and this relation is attenuated to varying degrees, in the predicted order, by the four instructional treatments as follows: Performance was least dependent on initial skills for the Block Rotation training conditions; next least dependent for the Complete Rotation film, followed by the two edited versions of the film. In other words, the greatest benefit of the Block Rotation training and the Complete Rotation film was for students with the lowest levels of initial spatial ability. Indeed, these most effective forms of instruction had the effect of removing the differences in ability between the most and least skilled subjects on the spatial pretests. Thus, these results indicate that the more explicit the form of instruction, that is instruction which provides the learner with more information about the relevant activity whether through a visual depiction as in the film or through practical action as in the block manipulation condition, the less dependent learning is upon prior levels of skill. For the less explicit form of instruction, the partial rotation film which had a less marked effect on the performance of the group as a whole, the effect of instruction depended more upon the prior competencies of the learners. These findings are congruent with Salomon's (1979) suggestion that explicit instructional films, which he calls "supplantation", make fewer demands upon initial competencies than do less explicit films, which he calls "short-circuiting". Alternatively, it may simply be that, in this case, all of the benefits of instruction fall to the less able subjects and their benefits are directly related to the quality or informativeness of the instructional film.

Although the verbal IQ test scores had only low correlations with the spatial test scores, there was a significant interaction between verbal ability and the effects of instruction for the delayed posttest (see Figure 9.6). Since

178

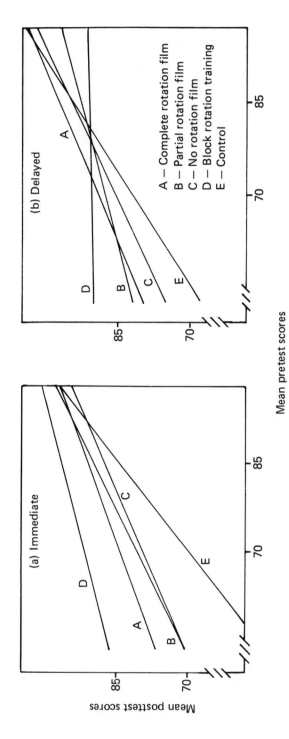

FIG. 9.5 Aptitude treatment interaction of Spatial Rotation Pretest scores and performance on (a) the posttest and (b) the Delayed posttest after different forms of instruction.

the interaction was not significant in the immediate posttest, these results are only suggestive.

The interesting relation shown in Figure 9.6 is that there are significant differences among the interactions between verbal abilities and each of the training conditions. Specifically, the two incomplete film conditions tended to be positively correlated with verbal abilities while the block manipulation was negatively correlated. The full film and control conditions showed little effect of prior verbal ability on performance.

It may be that benefiting from the instructional films, particularly the edited versions of those films, depends upon subjects' ability to comply with the verbal directives accompanying the film (c.f. Imagine the block rotating in space until it just lines up with the other block). It is more difficult to imagine how verbal abilities could correlate negatively with performance of subjects in the block manipulation condition. Perhaps the most important point is that, like for the pretested spatial abilities, verbal pre-test abilities are less important to the acquisition of a skill from an explicit form

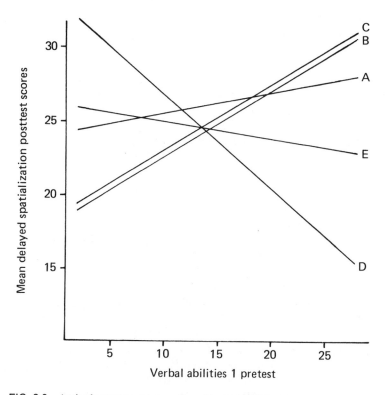

FIG. 9.6   Aptitude treatment interaction of verbal abilities Test 1 as predictor of delayed spatialization posttest.

of instruction than they may be for a more elliptical one. In both cases, then, this study provides some indication that not only are some forms of instruction equivalent to practical action, but also that the more powerful forms of instruction make fewer assumptions about the initial competencies of the learners than do less powerful forms.

Although it is not surprising that there is such a low correlation between verbal and the spatial rotation skills studied in this experiment, it may be that a verbal abilities test based on children's spatial concepts and their knowledge of the spatial lexicon, would be much more closely related to spatial cognition generally than is a verbal IQ test. Such tests generally measure verbal concepts from a quite different semantic domain.

GENERAL DISCUSSION

This study has shown that cognitive operations underlying object rotations are indeed educable and that they can be developed through both the mediated, symbolic form of film and through the direct manipulation of physical objects. The critical aspect of the instruction was the observation of the transformation that occurs when an object is rotated in space—editing out that critical section of the film destroyed its educative effect since these films did not encourage the calculation of r. The observation of this transformation enabled the child to subsequently perform such transformations more readily on the posttest. Note too, that the effect could not be attributed to simple practice with items on the rotation tasks as the No Rotation film provided just that and produced no effect. Rather, what was required was a portrayal of the transformation of an object which linked two static images of the object.

What mental operation would be recruited by such a procedure? We suggest, that it is the computation and application of a value for r, the spatial predicate specifying the axis, direction, and distance of the rotation relating the analagous constituents of the displays. But, as we pointed out in the preceding chapter, the computation of r depends upon the detection of distinguishing constituents or properties of the objects or arrays, and specifying the locations of those constituents both before and after the transformation in order to compute relation between them.

A final word on the generalizability of these operations to the transfer tasks. In retrospect, it becomes clear that the lack of transfer may reflect a general limitation of visual depictions, including film in the development of spatial cognition and in instruction generally. In viewing a film, the appropriate representation and operations are elicited by the display along with others which are not relevant to the solution of the problem. The subject is not in a position to select, nor does the firm select for him or her, as would an explicit verbal statement, the particular aspects of the spatial and visual representation which are critical to this particular task and, hence, general to all related tasks. A verbal training procedure in which just those critical spatial relations were specified and integrated into a decision procedure would not only have facilitated performance on the rotations task but also would have provided a basis for the transfer to superficially different problems to which the same set of representations and operations apply.

Within the bounds of comprehensibility, it seems not to matter much what form of instruction is employed. Forms of instruction, however, may vary in their presuppositions and hence in their comprehensibility. Within those limits, the present study has shown that appropriate instruction is a powerful alternative to direct experience in the development of a spatial skill.

10 On Children's Mental Representation of Oblique Orientation

with Anat Scher
Department of Educational Psychology
University of Calgary

In the preceding chapters it has been argued that spatial relations are mentally represented in terms of sets of predicates, that is relationships between the object in question and various referents including the ego, other objects, and other more general frames of reference. Although the theory presented in the first three chapters argued that the same spatial predicates may occur both in perception and in the more conceptual and linguistic forms of representation, the studies presented up to this point have focused attention particularly upon linguistic and conceptual structures. In this chapter, attention is returned to the mental representation of perceptual relations, the coding, discrimination, and recognition of obliquely oriented lines.

Lines and objects in an oblique orientation have come under study for many reasons. In terms of neurophysiological analyses, the visual cortex of cats has been found to possess more elongated visual fields attuned to the perception of horizontal and vertical lines than to oblique ones; in terms of human visual acuity, adults have been found to be more sensitive to fine graded lines in vertical and horizontal orientation than those in an oblique orientation; in terms of comparative psychology, lower vertebrates have been found to discriminate vertical and horizontal lines but to be unable to discriminate oblique ones; and finally, developmentally, many psychologists have found that children have difficulty discriminating, recognizing, and reconstructing oblique lines and patterns. (For a review see Appelle, 1972, and Olson, 1970a). Typical of the last case is the well-known intelligence test item requiring the copying of a square and a diamond. While squares can ordinarily be copied by 5 year olds, diamonds cannot ordinarily be copied until 7 years of age. It is also a matter of some general interest (see Figure 10.1).

'Good news, Mr. Healey. We've stopped the pound falling!'

FIG. 10.1   The Globe and Mail, Oct. 9, 1976.

Because of the difficulties associated with oblique orientation for young children, a difficulty that apparently disappears with age (see Chapter 11), the mental representation of obliquely oriented lines serves as an ideal task both for examining the structure of perceptual spatial relations and for examining the nature of the development of spatial cognition.

Before we present hypotheses regarding the nature of mental representation of space in terms of the ego-related, object-related, and reference-related descriptions described earlier, it may be useful to describe three well-known theories that bear upon this problem. Piaget and Inhelder (1956) argued that the child's representation of space relies on systems of reference which are networks composed of order and position relations. The systems of reference are, at first, limited and contextually bound and only gradually become more extensive and abstract (Piaget & Inhelder, 1956). Regarding the issue of vertical-horizontal systems of reference, they state that young children do not judge the tilt of oblique lines with reference to such a framework. Only when spatial relationships develop conceptually, through concrete operations, can the vertical-horizontal frame of reference be exploited in judging oblique orientation. The pre-operational child judges orientation on the basis of partial reference systems which do not take all factors into account. Although these partial systems are adequate for the representation of vertical and horizontal lines in certain situations, they do not adequately represent oblique orientations. In terms of the theory advanced herein, it would be argued that while children assign both ego-related and object-related descriptions, they have difficulty with framework-related descriptions and it is the latter which are required for the discrimination of oblique orientation.

Arnheim (1974) offered a similar developmental perspective. He pointed out that during the development of spontaneous drawing, children first master the relations between horizontal and vertical and then proceed to oblique relations; that is they attain the representational concepts needed to handle increasingly complex shapes and shape relations.

Olson (1970a) attempted to account for the difficulty children have with oblique patterns in terms of the spatial mental representations which were required. He found, as Piaget had suggested, that the child codes a visual pattern in terms of reference cues such as proximity, edgedness, and parallelisms with sides and major axes. These features provide enough information to select the oblique line in some contexts and to reconstruct it in others. It is only when these simple features are relevant and adequate to the recognition and reconstruction tasks that the child succeeds. For example, when an oblique line is constructed on a checkerboard in which the diagonal holes are closer than the horizontal and vertical holes (proximity feature), children have no difficulty with the reconstruction. However, this simple topological cue is not adequate to most oblique reconstructions, since ordinarily diagonal holes are further apart than horizontal rows or vertical columns.

What then permits the eventual successful reconstruction of an oblique pattern? Olson argued that it resulted from the progressive explication of the structural components of the display. These structural components involved such propositional relations as "up to the right" and the like, but they were not described in detail. We may note, however, that such descriptions are relative to some spatial framework involving horizontal and vertical axes. Young children on the other hand simply located the checkers relative to each other, an object related description, by means of such features as adjacency, top, and the like, and so failed in most reconstruction tasks.

In a series of studies, Bryant (1969, 1974) demonstrated several factors that enter into young children's discrimination and recognition of oblique orientations. For one thing, young children succeed in matching orientation of lines if they are simultaneously presented but fail if they are sequentially presented—that is, they have difficulty when they must work exclusively from a remembered mental representation. Secondly, he has demonstrated that orientation of lines is represented by means of relating that line or line segment to the features of the square display in which they are displayed—using such features as the reference lines of the display. Thirdly, Ibbotson and Bryant (1976) have shown that when children are required to copy two-line figures consisting of a line set at some angular relation to a given base, their responses were biased towards two important structural features or "markers"—the vertical axes of the display and the right-angular relation between the lines. These markers reflect both the external framework of the horizontal-vertical environment and the internal postural sense of verticality. In terms of the present theory, one feature, right angular relation, would be described as an object-related description while the vertical orientation would be described as a generalized framework-related description. The child's response would be a compromise between these two sets of descriptions.

A THEORY OF REPRESENTATION OF OBLIQUELY ORIENTED LINES

Next let us consider possible structural descriptions involved in the perception and reconstruction of obliquely oriented lines. Firstly, we may expect to find ego-related descriptions of the relation of the line to the viewer. These ego-related descriptions will involve either or both of the orientation and the position as described in terms of the major vertical and horizontal axes and values of those axes, involving, presumably such spatial predicates as:

above (x, H-midline)	i.e. The line segment x is above the Horizontal midline
right (x, V-midline)	i.e. The line segment x is to the right of Vertical midline

These ego-related descriptions could be applied to both the orientation of the line and the position in which it occurred.

The position of the line may be simply represented in terms of these predicates in that the values for the argument H-midline, V-midline may be calculated only once, since the display is always directly in front of the viewer, and the values for the predicates, above, below, left, right are specified directly on the basis of the display relative to ego.

The orientation of the line is more complex in that while any line may be represented in terms of the same set of predicates, for example, (/) could be coded as "up to the right", (above (x, H-midline), right (x, Y-midline)) but the values for the H-midline and V-midline would have to be calculated independently on each trial and applied to the oblique line. Thus a "right oblique" would take the description "up to the right" even if it occurred in the lower left corner of the display. These variable ego-related frameworks we refer to as "framework-related". The difference between position and orientation in the assignment of horizontal midlines and vertical midlines is shown in Figure 10.2. However, as we shall see, children do not use this framework-related representation in any case, hence we shall describe it more fully in the next chapter.

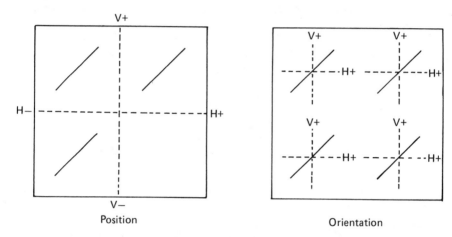

Position   Orientation

FIG. 10.2   While *one* set of vertical and horizontal axes may be used for describing all four positions, four different sets of vertical and horizontal axes are required to describe the orientation.

Secondly, we may expect to find object related descriptions of the relation between the oblique line and parts of the square in which it is presented. Although a large number of such relations could be constructed, only a small set of these are relevant to the set of alternatives involved in the present experiment. For example, the relation between the line and the display as a whole could be represented:

in (line, square), i.e., The line is in the square.

However, as all of the lines in this experiment were in the square, that representation is irrelevant.

Rather, what is decisive in the present experiment is the relation between the line segment and the proper parts of the square, its lines, its corners, and its major axes. Let us adopt Miller and Johnson-Laird's (1976) convention of calling the square frame the relatum y and its proper parts (Ppt y) the four sides, the four corners, and perhaps the two diagonal axes. The relations between the variable line x and these proper parts of the relatum are as follows:

on (x, Ppt y) i.e., The line segment x is on a proper part of square.

Again, however, none of the oblique lines fell on any of the four sides of the square. The only proper parts of the square that the line segments fell *on* were the major diagonals of the square. But can the major diagonals be considered as proper parts of a square when they are not explicitly shown? Both Palmer (1975) and Arnheim (1974) have proposed just that. Arnheim had earlier argued that the axes of a symmetrical figure were important parts of the structure of a visual pattern. The structural pattern is distinguished from the stimulus per se in that it has additional properties which establish its "hidden" structure (Figure 10.3, taken from Arnheim, 1974, p. 13). According to Arnheim, the hidden structure of a square, consists of the cross-shaped vertical and horizontal axes and the two diagonal axes. The center, which is the key source of the psychological structure, is established by the intersection of the axes.

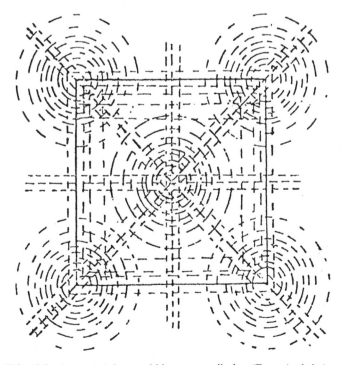

FIG. 10.3   Perceptual forces within a square display. (From Arnheim)

If this analysis is correct we have a second relatum to which a line presented in a square may be related. This set is particularly important to the oblique lines involved in this experiment in that the oblique line either falls on or off the major diagonals of the square as shown in Figure 10.4. If the major diagonals serve as relatum for the line stimulus we would have the following representations:

> *on* (x, Ppt y) i.e., The line segment x is on the major
> diagonal of the square y.

A similar analysis may be proposed for relating the position of the line segment to the corners of the square. Thus, if each of the corners of the

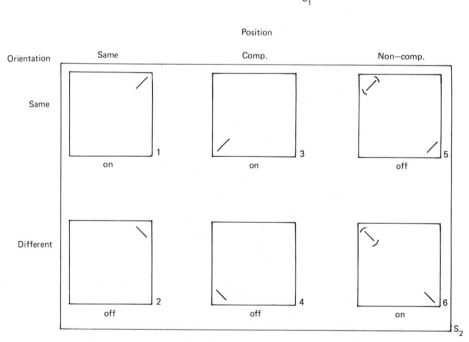

FIG. 10.4   The standard shown as S_1 is compared to the alternatives shown as S_2 which differ in their position, orientation and in relation to the axis of the display (on/off).

square is taken to be a proper part of the square y, the line may be related to these proper parts thus:

at (x, Ppt y) i.e., The line is at a particular corner of the square y.

Whatever the structural description assigned to the line segment, subjects' judgment as same or different of a second line segment will depend upon the correspondence between their structural descriptions. As was suggested in Chapter 1, two displays which take the same structural description will be judged to be same or similar, those which take different structural descriptions will be judged as different. Specifically, if two line segments take the descriptions:

on (x, Ppt y) and *at* (x, Ppt y)

they will be judged as the same. Note however, that few lines satisfy both of those descriptions. If subjects used both of these representations they would be correct on only 25% of the line pairs which in fact have the same orientation. They would reject all of the lines in different positions from the stimulus line as different. If however, they continue to use both of these descriptions but relax their application so as to allow not only identical displays but also similar ones, they will say same to many more pairs of items but in either case the reliance upon these structural descriptions will result in many incorrect judgments. In fact, orientation judgments based upon the relation between the line parts and the intrinsic parts of the square will inevitably result in incorrect judgments. Correct judgments of the orientation of oblique lines in a square frame require the assignment of framework-related descriptions as we discussed above and to which we shall return in the next chapter.

There is some existing evidence which is compatible with the view presented above, namely, the children's mental representations of visual displays are frequently object-related, that is, representations are assigned to lines (and other objects) on the basis of the relation between that line and the other objects or parts of objects in the display. Both Olson (1970a) and Bryant (1974) have shown that the orientation of a line is coded relative to some reference line or reference axis such as the top of the display or a midline.

Similarly, there is some evidence that children code the position of a stimulus relative to other stimuli in the array. Zeaman and House (1965) showed that the easiest discrimination learning task for a young child is a position discrimination but it is not clear if it is easy because the child is using an object-related code or because the object-related code and the ego-related ones are congruent. Bryant (1974) conducted a set of experiments on the child's ability to make position judgments. They did so, he claimed, by coding the position in terms of an in-line/out-of-line cue, that is, they remember the position of an individual object simply by noting those features of the background with which it is lined up. In our terms, these children were using an object-related code, that is, they relate the stimulus display to visible aspects of the background by means of spatial predicates. Finally, as a preceding chapter (Chapter 6) indicated, children decide on the viewer perspective in simple tasks by specifying a spatial relation between viewer and a part of the display, for example: *front* (long (arm), viewer).

In another study of the effect of position on children's judgments of the orientation of lines, on which the present study is based, Bryant (1969) presented a standard line in either an oblique, horizontal or vertical orientation in one of the four quadrants of a square display card. The standard was then removed and subjects had to judge which of two subsequently displayed cards bore a line with the same orientation as the standard. When the standard was an oblique, the comparison cards bore the two opposite obliques; when the standard was a horizontal or vertical, the comparison cards bore horizontal and vertical lines.

The effect of position was studied by either having both the standard and the comparison lines in the same quadrant or the standard in one quadrant and the comparison lines in a different quadrant. When the position of the comparison lines was the same as the standard, the choice was easy, even for oblique items. When the position of the standard and comparison lines differed, however, the oblique orientation judgments fell to chance while the horizontal and vertical judgments were unaffected. Bryant concluded that the lines were coded in terms of the horizontal and vertical reference lines of the display and in terms of the position of the oblique in the display. Since horizontal and vertical lines fall parallel to a reference line, they were successfully recognized; since oblique lines did not fall on or parallel to a reference line, subjects had only the misleading position cue to go on and hence responded at chance.

However, if as Bryant suggested, the child notes only whether the line is parallel to a predominant reference axis and that it falls in a certain position, then recognition of oblique orientation should be good when the second stimulus is presented in the same position as the standard, as indeed it was, *and equally poor in all different positions.* If, on the other hand, as we have argued above, the major diagonals of the square serve as a set of reference axes, then performance will be better on some of the different positions than on others. When both the standard and the correct choice stimulus fall on an axis even if their position differs, performance will be better; when the standard falls on an axis while the correct choice stimulus does not, performance will be worse. In other words, when position has changed, recognition of oblique orientation will not always be at chance but will be easier on some items than on others depending upon the coincidence of the codes set out above. The present was designed to choose between these alternatives.

A second concern of this study was with the processes involved in arriving at the identity decision. Although considerable research has been done on the representation and comparison processes involved in comparing sentences with pictures and with other sentences (Carpenter & Just, 1975; Clark & Chase, 1972; Olson & Filby, 1972; Trabasso, Rollin, & Shaughnessy, 1971) no analogous studies have been done in which perceptual representation is compared, that is, which involves the comparison of perceptual predicates as opposed to conceptual predicates (cf. Miller & Johnson-Laird, 1976). The primary difference, between perceptual predicates and conceptual ones, or as we phrased it in Chapter 3, between implicit and explicit representations, is that the former cannot be articulated or decomposed into separate elements for purposes of judgment while the latter may be treated on conceptual elements and retrieved, compared, and operated on independently and sequentially. If perceptual predicates are unanalyzed in this sense, we may not find the sequential retrieval and comparison operations that characterize the use of conceptual predicates. Rather, we may find the perceptual compared "in parallel" with the degree of congruity in the predicates reflected in an overall judgment of perceptual similarity.

Two studies are presented. The first examines the mental representations assigned to oblique lines and the processes involved in comparing them. The second is an independent assessment of the role of implicit reference axes in the judging of the length of those line segments.

EXPERIMENT 1

The purpose of this experiment was to test two hypotheses about children's judgment of orientation. The first hypothesis is in regard to the nature of the structural descriptions assigned to such displays for the purpose of comparing the line segments. It is hypothesized that those structural descriptions are object-related rather than ego- or framework-related and that they are based on relations between the proper parts of the square framework, namely its references lines, axes, and corners.

The second hypothesis is in regard to the comparison processes themselves. It is well known that conceptual predicates are compared by means of a series of retrieval and comparison operations, the results of which are preserved by means of a binary logical "truth index". However, as we argued in Chapter 3, perceptual predicates cannot be voluntarily articulated into separate constituents, hence they cannot be sequentially compared and the output of these comparisons combined by means of a binary "truth index". Rather, perceptual predicates may be compared in parallel, their outputs being coordinated *not* by means of a truth index, but simply summed by a response rule: Match → Same, Mismatch → Different.

Method

Subjects.   Twenty second-grade children, 7.4 to 8.4 years of age (mean age 7.8), drawn from a school in a suburban, lower middle-class neighborhood, participated in the study.

Apparatus.   Orientation judgment task consisted of 64 cards, each 27 × 20 cm. An internal square frame, 17 × 17 cm., was drawn on each card, inside of which a ±45° oblique line was drawn. The line, 6.5 cm. long, was centered in one of the quadrants of the square, either along the diagonal axis of the square or bisected by it (see Figure 10.4). The cards were assembled in a booklet of 64 cards divided into 32 pairs, each consisting of a card bearing standard line (S_1) and a to-be-judged card bearing comparison line (S_2). The stimuli varied along two dimensions, position and axis.

Position. The standard line segment (S_1) was presented in one of the four quadrants of the reference square. The comparison line (S_2) could then fall in either the Same position as S_1 or a Different position. However, the Different positions could be further differentiated as follows: Complementary positions (COM) were those in which the S_1 and S_2 fell in the opposite corners, along the same diagonal axis. Non-Complementary (NON-COM) positions were ones in which the standard and comparison lines were located in two adjacent corners, that is along different axes of the square. Each square contains two NON-COM positions. (These alternative positions are shown in Figure 10.4.)

Axis. Each oblique line was presented either on the diagonal axis or off the axis (i.e., perpendicular to it). Hence, the standard and comparison lines either had the same relationship to an axis, that is, both were on or both were off the axis, or they differed in their relationship to the axis, that is, one was on an axis while the other was off it.

In addition, two further variables were taken into account. The first was the Orientation of the lines, i.e., Right (/) or Left (\ ) oblique. The second variable was the Orientation-Similarity, that is, whether the two successive lines called for a "Same" or a "Different" judgment. Both variables were counter-balanced.

The combination of the Axis and the Position factors produced eight types of stimuli. For each of these types there were eight possible S_1–S_2

pairs. Since the pilot test showed that absolute position was not a significant variable, this factor was not fully exhausted, but was counter-balanced producing 32 experimental pairs.

The order of presentation of the 32 selected pairs was randomized and the booklet was prepared according to this order. Two blank sheets were inserted between the stimuli of each pair to ensure that at no time was the child able to see both line segments simultaneously.

Procedure.   Since the line segments varied both with respect to orientation and position, and since this was a test of orientation perception, it was essential to ensure that the children were fully aware of how they were to judge the lines. To this end, each child participated in a pretest session. First, the subject saw two small rods being manipulated both in a location and orientation. The experimenter placed them on the table saying "one rod is here and the other there, but both point in the same direction", or alternatively, "this one points in this direction and the other one in a different direction" etc. Then, two demonstration trials were introduced. In the demonstration, unlike the experiment, both the standard and the comparison cards were presented simultaneously. The child was asked if both lines were in the same direction and made this judgment in the presence of both stimuli. In the first demonstration, the position of the two lines was kept the same while the orientation differed. This was reversed for the second demonstration in that the two obliques had the same orientation but different positions. Only subjects who could make the simultaneous discrimination were included in the experiment.

After the subjects had succeeded in the discrimination, they were told that they were going to see two lines, *one at a time*, and that they would have to remember the direction of the first one and then judge whether the second line had the same direction as the first one. One warm-up trial was given, followed by 32 trials. The first oblique was presented for 5 seconds, at which time the experimenter said: "This is the first one." Then the two separating sheets were turned over, one at a time so as to reveal the comparision stimulus S_2 approximately 5 seconds later. The subjects then responded "Yes" or "No" depending on whether or not they thought the second line had the same orientation as the first. An additional interval of 5 seconds separated the trials. The experimenter recorded all responses.

Results

Errors were first analyzed to determine whether one oblique (e.g., Right oblique) was easier than its mirror image. Trials in which the first stimulus was the Right oblique were compared with those in which the first stimulus was the Left oblique. The ANOVA yielded no significant difference between the two orientations ($F(1,19) = 0.32$, n.s.).

Three variables were defined for further analysis of the error data: (1) Position (SAME, COMplementary, NON-COMplementary), (2) Axis (on-axis/off-axis) and (3) Orientation Similarity (Same/Different).

The 32 trials were grouped into 12 cells defined by the above factors and were analyzed by means of ANOVA for repeated measures. The dependent variable was percent errors, therefore subjects having fewer than 2 errors (5 out of 20) were eliminated from the analysis. The cells were tested for homogeneity of variance. The assumption of homogeneity was upheld F_{max} $(12,14) = 5.97$, $p > .05$).

The ANOVA revealed the following significant results:

1. *Position, $F(2/28) = 8.65$, $p < .01$);*
2. *Axis, $F(1/14) = 10.84$, $p < .01$);*
3. *Position by Orientation-Similarity, $F(2/28) = 8.05$, $p < .01$).*

The effect of position must be interpreted in terms of the Position by Orientation-Similarity interaction. Figure 10.5 shows that for Same Orien-

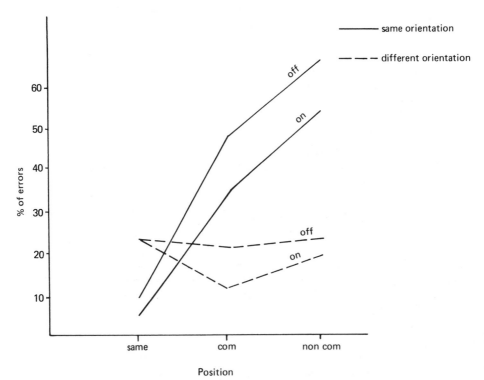

FIG. 10.5   Mean percentage of errors for same and different orientation in various positions on and off the axis.

tation, lines in the SAME position were easier than those in COM and NON-COM positions (Newman Keuls, $p < .01$ and $p < .001$, respectively). COM positions were easier than NON-COM positions (Newman Keuls, $p < .05$). For Different Orientation, all positions were of equal difficulty.

Comparisons of the means for the Axis effect indicated that lines falling on the axis were significantly easier than lines falling off the axis. Although there was no significant interaction of Axis by Position, the data suggest (see Figure 10.5) that the effect of the axis is particularly pronounced for the COM and NON-COM POSITIONS.

In summary, then, items differed in difficulty according to their relationships to the axis and to the interactive pattern between the position of the line and the required response. Four components, however, may be identified to describe differences between the items: Position, Axis, Position by Orientation-Similarity interaction, and a fourth component which is Orientation Similarity per se. This latter variable though not statistically significant accounts for a large proportion of the variance. ANOVA on the 12 means represented in Figure 10.5 showed that the four suggested components account for 98.2% of the experimental variance: Position × Orientation Similarity 45.1%, Position 32.2%, Orientation-Similarity 17.4% and Axis 3.5% (for method, see H.H. Clark, 1973b). These four components will figure in our processing model.

EXPERIMENT 2

The purpose of this experiment was to evaluate the effect of the axis as a factor in the mental representation of length. It was hypothesized that if the axis is a proper part of a configuration it will serve as a relatum not only for the mental representation of orientation but also for the perception of the length of those line segments. Following Arnheim (1974), this may be reflected in a tendency to overestimate the length of a line which falls on the axis of the background pattern or relatum.

Method

Subjects. Sixteen first graders (mean age 6.6), attending the same school as above participated in the study.

Apparatus and procedure. An L shaped figure, each arm 4.5 cm in length, was presented inside a circular frame with a 18 cm diameter. The figure was shown in several different positions as described below. For each figure one of the arms was on an axis (i.e., a diameter of the circular frame) and the other was perpendicular to that axis (see Figure 10.6).

A total of six positions were used in such a way that the effect of other

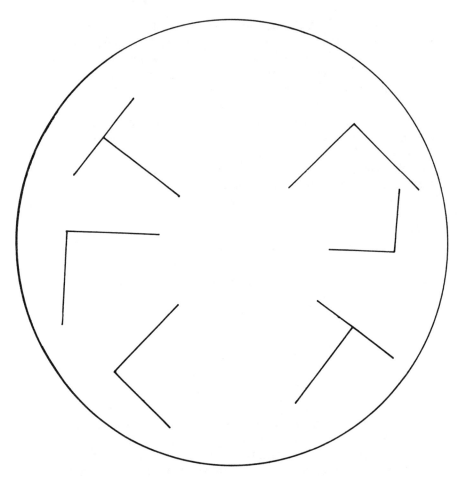

FIG. 10.6   Examples of the 6 Length Comparisons in the Illusion Task.

known illusions, such as the Vertical-Horizontal illusion (Kunnapas, 1955), that is, the tendency to assign greater length to vertical lines, and the T-illusion, that is, the tendency to judge as shorter the bisected lines, were not confounded with the predicted "axis illusion." Thus, the North and South positions in the circle were eliminated, since in these instances the line which falls on the axis is also the vertical line. Six positions were therefore selected (NE, E, SE, SW, W, and NW). For two of these positions, E and W, the on-axis line was horizontal and the off-axis arm was vertical; for the remaining four positions, both arms of the figure were oriented oblique-ly, one on the axis and the other perpendicular to it.

Each of the six positions were used twice giving a total of 12 trials, which were presented in a fixed random order. The children, who were tested in-dividually, were asked to point to the arm of the figure which looked longer. The children were given as much time as they required to make this response, but in all cases, they responded very quickly.

Results

The data were collapsed across subjects and positions to yield the mean number of lines that were judged as being longer, relative to their location, on or off the axis.

For 64% of the trials (i.e., 7.68 out of 12 comparisons), subjects decided that the on-axis line was longer. On only 36% of the trials did they judge that the off-axis line was longer. The Wilcoxon matched-pairs signed ranks test (Ferguson, 1966, p. 360) yielded a significant difference with $p < .01$ ($T = < .20$).

Discussion of Experiments 1 and 2

Features. The findings of Experiment 1 support the hypothesis that children use frames of reference in order to code the orientation of oblique lines. The prediction that comparisons would differ in difficulty as a function of position and axis cues and thus would follow a characteristic error-pattern was confirmed by the data. Observed differences in difficulty of judging orientation of line segments suggest that line segments are assigned object-related descriptions including such features of the relatum as position and axis. Let us consider these features in more detail.

Position. The data indicate that in judging the orientation of a line, its position becomes a powerful cue which interacts with the response. Generally, it was found that when the position within the frame is identical for both lines children fail to judge the orientation only in 17% of the cases. When the position of the lines differ they make twice as many errors (34%). These errors, however, are primarily attributable to cases in which the orientation of the line remains the same although the position has changed. That is, it is difficult to judge that lines in different positions have a common orientation (61.6% and 43.3% vs. 8.3%). When the orientation of the lines differ, however, the position in which they appear is not significant (26.6%, 18.3% and 23.3% for SAME, COM and NON-COM positions).

The position effect found in this experiment supports earlier findings (Bryant, 1969, 1974) and provides additional evidence for the hypothesis that a line segment is mentally represented in terms of its relation to the proper parts of the reference square, in this case its corners of quadrants. A plausible form, as suggested above is:

At (x, Ppt y) i.e., The line segment is at a proper part, a corner, of the relatum y.

<u>Axis</u>. The results of both Experiments 1 and 2 support the hypothesis that the axis of the display is an important component of the reference pattern, or relatum in terms of which a line segment is mentally represented. In Experiment 1, it was found that orientation judgments were facilitated when the line was on the axis of the display; errors increase from 27% for on-axis lines to 34% for off-axis lines. More important is the congruity between the codes for the lines being compared, but this congruity effect cannot be isolated with this type of analysis. We return to it presently.

The importance of the axis of the relatum was further demonstrated in Experiment 2. In making a perceptual judgment about the relative length of two lines, children tended to describe the on-axis line as longer than the off-axis line, even though both lines were, in fact, of equal length. This tendency to assign greater length to an axis line suggests, again, that the axis of a form is a part of the relatum in terms of which the referent line is encoded (Arnheim, 1974).

Hence, both experiments indicate that the axis of a figure, even if not explicit, may serve as a relatum for the encoding of a line segment. How may the axis be used in the orientation judgment experiment? One plausible form, as suggested above, is:

On (x, Ppt y) i.e., The line segment x is on a proper part, an axis, of the relatum y.

The evidence suggests that position and axis of a square serve as the relatum for the mental representation of the orientation of line segments. The next step, then, is to explain how this information is processed in making orientation judgments. First we shall consider a theoretical model which is based on the sequential application of binary logical operations to the two proposed codes. It will be argued that the child's response is not adequately represented by this method. Rather, we propose that the output of the comparison of the two codes is simply summed rather than related by means of a binary logic.

A binary logical model. A consideration of position and axis information could yield accurate orientation judgments if subjects adopted the following binary or two-valued logical model for relating the output from these two comparison processes: match the position of the two lines, match the axis values, and relate the output from the two matching operations by means of the following decision procedure. First, compare the axis. If the outcome of the axis-matching operation is positive compare the positions. If position is SAME or COM, the orientation is the same; if position is NON-COM, orientation is different. If the outcome of the axis-matching operation is negative, the role of a position match is reversed. This sequence of operation may be summarized as follows:

position match (SAME or COM) + axis match   → Same
position match (SAME or COM) + axis mismatch   → Different
position mismatch (NON − COM) + axis match   → Different
position mismatch (NON − COM) + axis mismatch → Same

Orientation judgments which rely on processes such as those described above, require a full mastery of binary logic. That is, the outcome of the first test determines how the outcome for the second test is to be interpreted. The high frequency of errors indicates that this system is not yet acquired by the 7-year-old children who participated in this experiment. Thus children may fail to judge orientation correctly because they lack the ability to coordinate sequentially the information which they have extracted. To this point, then, it seems clear that children are employing a code similar to the one described above but that they are unable to combine the output of the code-comparison process by means of a binary logic (cf. Olson & Nickerson, 1977). What decision processes were they then using? Let us examine their performance in another way.

Signal Detection Analysis

Our analysis of the referent object or relatum in terms of which the line segment is encoded is a necessary but not a sufficient account of how the child arrives at a response decision. Other factors such as the criterion for making a decision should be also considered (Vurpillot, 1976).

In an attempt to evaluate the characteristics of the decision-making strategies, a signal detection method was employed. Signal detection theory was developed to describe the relationship between a variety of signals and noise to specify conditions under which ideal detection performance will take place (Swets, 1973). This technique isolates the effects of the observer's response bias, or decision criterion, and provides a relatively pure measure of the capacity to discriminate. This method seems to be most adequate for the evaluation of the operating characteristics in our experiment (e.g., position, axis, response tendency). However, due to the difficulties in collecting from young children the type of data suitable to the requirements of a signal detection analysis (large number of trials for each type of comparison), the results should be regarded as suggestive only.

Table 10.1 shows the d' and β values for the various positions.

Differences in d' indicate encoding differences, while β differences indicate response differences. The analysis revealed both types of differences. The *perception* of the two lines as well as the *response* associated with it changed according to the positional relationship of the two lines. The tendency was to respond "Same" when the position was the same, and "Different" when the position differed. Thus, three different values were obtained for the d' parameter, as a function of the relatedness of the three

TABLE 10.1
Signal Detection Analysis for Position

	POSITION		
	SAME	COM	NON COM
d'	2.01	1.09	0.40
β	4.99	1.49	1.22

positions (SAME position, 2.01, COM, 1.9; NON-COM, 0.40). The β parameter differentiated sharply between the response tendency to say "Same" when the lines occurred in the same position and to say "Different" when they occurred in different positions, but only a slight difference between the two types of different positions (4.49 as opposed to 1.49 and 1.22). The small difference between the COM and NON-COM positions, is due to their different relations to the axis. This point will be considered below.

Signal detection analysis was also computed for the axis values. The purpose was to determine if the axis affect was due to perceptual coding differences or to a response factor. When the analysis was applied to mean hits and false alarms for on-axis as compared to off-axis trials, no differences were found. However, when the analysis was done not on axis as a factor, but rather on the axis-match (i.e., on-on; off-off vs. on-off; off-on) interesting differences for both d' and β occurred. These differences may be interpreted as shown in Table 10.2.

The perceived similarity between the orientation of the successively presented line segments is based on the congruity between the values of the axis code, on-axis versus off-axis, for the two lines. That is, line segments which match for their axis value are difficult to discriminate (they look the same) while those for which those axis values differ are easy to discriminate

TABLE 10.2
Signal Detection Analysis for Axis-Match
and Axis-Mismatch

	AXIS MATCH[1]	AXIS MISMATCH[2]
d'	1.38	1.07
β	1.06	1.28

[1]on-on; off-off
[2]on-off; off-on

(they look different). In addition, the axis match per se inclines the perceivers to say "same" while a mismatch inclines them to say "different". Note, too, that this common on-axis value for the two lines may occur when S_1 is on one axis and the S_2 is on the other.

The signal detection analysis suggests that for both the position and the axis factors a match/mismatch operation is involved both on the level of perceptual encoding (d') and response output (β). Both of these aspects then, the perceptual factors and the response bias, must be accounted for by a model of children's orientation judgments.

A MODEL FOR CHILDREN'S ORIENTATION JUDGMENTS

We have suggested that the child codes the line segment in relation to the square referent both in terms of its position in that square (*at*(x, Pp ty)) and in relation to the axis of that square, (*on*(x, Pp ty)) and then judges the orientation in terms of the congruity between those codes. But how does he relate the output of those comparisons? We showed earlier that a binary logical model of the process is inappropriate in that such a model would deliver correct responses while, in fact, children made many errors and indeed for some items, performed well below chance levels. Hence some other model is called for.

As we suggested earlier, a binary logical model is particularly appropriate for sequential comparison of conceptual representations. Perceptual representations may contain the same predicates and arguments but their mode of comparison may differ. Such a model would have the following properties:

1. a comparison of the position predicates: *at* (x, Pp ty), i.e. Line x is at a certain corner of the square y.
2. a comparison of the axis predicates: *on* (x, Pp ty), i.e. Line x is on an axis of the square y.
3. a response rule which simply translates the output of these comparison processes as follows:
   —if a match occurs, increase the tendency to say "Same"
   —if a mismatch occurs, increase the tendency to say "Different"
4. output the response with the highest response tendency.

This model is applied to the obtained data in Table 10.3. The model shows the output of the hypothesized comparison judgment and the percent errors on each of the six item types. A match on the position feature (+) produces a response bias towards a "Same" judgment (S); a mismatch (−)

TABLE 10.3
A Model for the Explanation of Error Patterns According
to Position, Axis and Response Bias

Item		1	4	6	2	3	5
Outcome of feature	Position	+	−	−	+	−	−
comparison	Axis	+	−	+	−	+	−
Response Bias	Position	S	D	D	S	D	D
	Axis	S	D	S	D	S	D
Orientation		S	D	D	D	S	S
% of errors		8	18	23	26	43	62

+ Match	S - Same
− Mismatch	D - Different

towards a "Different" judgment (D). Similarly a match on the axis feature (+) produces a bias towards a "Same" judgment (S); a mismatch (−) towards a "Different" judgment (D). As the model suggested, these two response biases are simply summed. Hence "Same" responses are easy when both features yield a match as in item 1; "Different" responses are easy when both features mismatch as in item 4. The most difficult item of all (62% errors) occurs when both features yield mismatches, thus yielding a bias to say Different, and yet the orientation is, in fact, the Same, as in item 5. Items involving one matched and one mismatched feature fall between.

This analysis then, accounts for both factors, position and axis, that were isolated in the analysis of variance and the signal detection analysis. Further it accounts for the manner in which those factors are combined in reaching a decision. Finally, this model accounts for 98.2% of the variance between the means.

We may make two further comments about this model. First, the model may be improved by differentiating the different positions into Complementary (COM) and non-complementary (NON-COM) positions and account for the fact that NON-COM are more difficult than COM as we observed earlier. Secondly, in addition to the matching factor, there is a marked-unmarked effect for the axis code; the *on* predicate was easier to assign and compare than the *off* predicate. Indeed, it is reasonable to hypothesize that the perceptual code assigned to these displays is richer than our two predicates model suggests. Of course, as the number of spatial predicates increases, the representations become more "image"-like.

Let us return finally to the hypotheses advanced at the outset. First, the evidence strongly supports the view that the line segments are assigned object-related structural descriptions: the lines were coded in terms of their relation to the properties of the reference square or relatum. Secondly, children's judgments of similarity of orientation can be largely accounted for in terms of two relational predicates, *on* and *at*, the first coding the relation between the segment and the diagonal axes of the square, the second coding the relation between the location of the line and the corners of quadrants of the square. The representations were formalized as:

on (x, Ppt y), i.e. The line x is on a proper part of the square y,
& *at* (x, Ppt y), i.e. The line x is at a proper part of the square y.

Not only do these two hypothesized spatial propositions offer an adequate account of the observed error pattern for children, they have precisely the same structure as the conceptual or form representations that we have isolated in the previous chapters of this book.

However, even if these perceptual tasks appear to make use of spatial representations possessing the same spatial predicates and spatial propositions that we find in explicit representations of space, for example, in ordinary language, they differ from them in just the ways we anticipated. First, they are not differentiated and processed sequentially but rather in parallel, and second, the outputs from those comparison processes are not related by a binary logic but rather simply summed to yield a response. We have indicated the non-articulation of these two propositions by an "&".

These results raise the question of how these processes change with development. Either the code by means of which the line segments are mentally represented may change, the procedures for comparing these codes may change, or of course, both. If we are correct in suggesting that the perceptual predicates have the same structure as conceptual ones, then we have no particular reason to expect changes in the assignment of those predicates with development. We do, however, have good reasons for expecting changes in the decision procedures by means of which the predicates are compared to yield a response. The decision procedure may come to rely on a *sequential* comparison of propositions, the outputs of which are coordinated by means of binary logic. Such procedures have been found on numerous conceptual tasks. It is indeed possible, that one of the effects of translating perceptual predicates into conceptual ones, as, for example, in learning a descriptive language, is that it permits the sequential analysis of propositions which, as long as they are purely perceptual, can be processed only in parallel.

As for the subjects in the present experiment, it appears that the judgments were made on a purely perceptual basis; there was no indication that either the children or the adults testing them were aware, at the time, of the mental code or the response rule that the children employed. When asked, they claimed that they made the comparisons on the basis of visual similarity—the lines "looked" the same or they didn't. Even if the subjects believe that they are processing the displays as visual "gestalt" patterns, they are, in fact, categorically representing the spatial relations by means of a set of spatial predicates and comparing those representations by means of an implicit set of mental operations. For adult subjects, we shall see, both the code and the operations tend to be more explicit, and more importantly, subject to voluntary control.

11 On the Mental Representation of Oblique Orientation in Adults

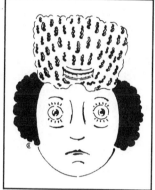

Semour Chwart, *Esquire*

We have argued throughout that spatial representations are constructed not in terms of continuous homogenous extent, but rather, in terms of the primary axes of Cartesian space. Values on these axes are expressed by propositional descriptions, such as up, down, front, back. Reliance on Cartesian dimensions makes the problem of oblique representation particularly interesting in that this Cartesian framework is not obviously relevant for the encoding of obliquely oriented lines. Children, as we have seen in the previous chapter, do not represent oblique orientation in terms of these primary Cartesian dimensions, but in terms of the particular structural characteristics of the display—their corners and their axes—and as result they make frequent errors in their judgements of similarity. The problem remains, however, to determine the way in which adults represent oblique orientation, in particular, to identify what role, if any, adults assign to the Cartesian dimensions which we have found to be so crucial to other spatial propositions.

Linguistically, obliques do appear to be represented in terms of the primary horizontal and vertical axes, for example, "up to the right" or more eliptically as "right obliques". While not every spatial proposition can be given linguistic expression, every spatial term in the language must express some spatial proposition. Hence, lexical expressions provide some evidence for the spatial predicates that are readily constructed and processed. We may, therefore, recover at least some of the spatial predicates involved in the recognition and discrimination of orientation by examining the structure of the terms used in ordinary language to express changes in orientation.

Ordinary language treats orientation basically in terms of three categories: vertical, horizontal, and oblique. While the first two refer directly to two dimensions of Cartesian space and unambiguously indicate particular orientations, namely vertical and horizontal, the third represents all orientations not describable by those dimensional terms. Thus, any line segment not strictly coinciding with a vertical or horizontal axes may be called "oblique". Some of the relations between orientations and directions of line and their lexical representations are shown in Figure 11.1. The point to

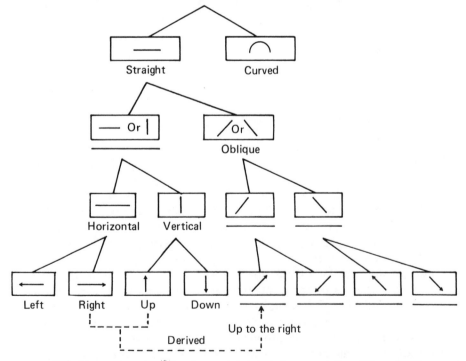

FIG. 11.1　Orientation, directions and their lexical representations (Olson, 1970).

notice from this figure is that some but not other orientations and directions are directly expressible by spatial terms. There is, for example, no superordinate term for horizontal and vertical, orthogonal is perhaps the closest, and we shall use the term in this sense. More important is the fact that while oblique lines have a general or superordinate lexical representation, *oblique*, the opposite obliques have no distinguishing terms. Further, while horizontal and vertical orientations may be differentiated into different directions each of which has a distinctive lexical representation *up, down, left,* and *right,* the similar subdivision of obliques yields four oblique directions none of which have a unique lexical representation. When we do wish to describe these orientations in ordinary language, we are forced to use a descriptive system derived from the orthogonal component such as right-oblique and left-oblique and when we wish to describe directions we are forced to use such circumlocations as "up to the right" or "down to the left", and so on.

If the linguistic expressions of spatial relations are any indication of the underlying structure of spatial predicates involved in the mental representation of space, the lacunae in English for terms expressing oblique orientations will lead us to look for peculiarities in the mental representation of obliques. However, perhaps because of these lacunae in ordinary language, formal systems have been invented to more adequately represent continuous space. Directions are often represented by the eight points of the compass thereby providing more differentiated schemes while adhering to the same principle of classification as ordinary language. Geometric measurement, on the other hand, elaborates these descriptions of orientation and direction in terms of degrees of rotation, but it does so by recourse to number concepts and to a formal technology which makes it remote from ordinary language.

But even if the expressive powers of the language seem to be biased towards primary categories of front, back, top, bottom, and the like, is there any reason to believe that the perception and memory of space is similarly biased towards these spatial relations? Perceptual asymmetries have been found in several kinds of experiments with subjects ranging from rats to adult humans. Even visual acuity of adult humans reflects such biases. Ogilvie and Taylor (1958, 1959) showed that for a fine wire to be visible in an oblique orientation, it had to be twice as wide as when it was in a horizontal or vertical orientation. Annis and Frost (1973) suggest that these asymmetries may be influenced somewhat by early experiences, yet these types of differences appear to be quite robust (see Appelle, 1972, for a review).

Much more dramatic are the experiments on the discrimination and memory of oblique orientation. Lashley (1938) found that rats could learn to discriminate a horizontal from a vertical pattern much more easily than a

45° oblique (a right oblique) from a 135° oblique (a left oblique). Sur-
therland (1969) trained octopi to respond to a rectangular bar placed in
various orientations. While they readily learned to discriminate horizontal
from vertical orientations, there was no evidence of learning when they were
required to discriminate opposite obliques.

Similar observations have been made with children. Reudel and Teuber
(1963) and Bryant (1969) found that the successive discrimination of opposite obliques is much more difficult than that for orthogonals.

All of these observations indicate that space is not "cognized" as a
homogeneous medium but rather is perceived, represented, and remembered in terms of a spatial structure, presumably having the properties we have discussed throughout this book. Moreover, the fact that these
asymmetries are not restricted to linguistically competent human adults but
to young children and other mammals as well, suggests that these spatial
representational systems are common, general, and relevant to such activities as maintaining an upright orientation, managing locomotion, keeping track of location, recognizing visual patterns, and solving spatial
problems.

In the preceding chapter we identified two of the spatial predicates that
young children appear to employ in their judgments of the orientation of
lines. Neither of these cues was orientation per se. Rather, orientation was
represented in terms of the spatial relations between parts of the line and
proper parts of the framework in which the line was presented. As a consequence, they frequently made errors in their judgments even if they
understood the requirements of the task. The present chapter is an attempt
to determine the mental representations and operations utilized by adults in
their judgments of orientation and direction of line segments.

In our early studies, the attempt was to compare aspects of the recognition and recall of oblique lines with those applied to horizontals and verticals. The hypothesis was that if tests of recognition and recall proved more
difficult for obliques than for horizontal and verticals, then that difficulty
could be attributed to greater complexity in their underlying mental
representations. The later studies attempted to spell out their precise
representational form.

Three types of studies were conducted. The first examined the relative
speed with which subjects could judge the orientations of oblique, horizontal, and vertical lines. If the representations in memory are more complex
for some orientations of line than for others, we may expect the speed with
which such judgments are made to be a function of orientation. The second
tested the hypothesis that lines which take a more complex mental representation should place a greater burden on short term memory, reducing the
number of oriented line segments which can be recalled. Thus, the second
study aimed at determining the effect of oblique orientation on memory

span. Finally, the third and most extensive group of studies examined the processes that subjects used to make judgments about the orientation of successively presented line segments which were presented in various positions on a screen. (See Olson & Hildyard, 1977). Most of the discussion will focus on the studies in this third group. Readers who are primarily interested in the theoretical implications of these studies may ignore the experimental details and go directly to the Discussion (p. 226).

1. SEARCH TIMES FOR LINE SEGMENTS OF PARTICULAR ORIENTATION AND DIRECTION

The first study tested the coding of orientation by requiring subjects to search as quickly as possible through sheets of paper containing 80 line segments with directional arrowheads for the exemplars of a particular direction. Each page contained 10 exemplars of eight directions: up, down, left, right, and the four oblique directions. The materials were counterbalanced for the order of line segments in each row, the target line segment required for a particular page, and the direction of search which the subject was required to apply: top to bottom, bottom to top, left to right, and right to left. The subjects in this study were 16 eighth grade students, with a median age of 14 years, who were tested individually on two occasions, 2 days apart.

The hypothesis was that longer search times for particular segments would indicate greater complexity in the underlying representation. Obliques, having more complex representations would be found more slowly than horizontals and verticals.

The two main effects of Orientation of Line and Direction of Search were found to be highly significant; Orientation with an F value of 31.21 ($p<0.001$) and Direction with an F value of 28.05 ($p<0.001$). There was no significant interaction between these two factors. Figure 11.2 shows the distribution of search times with respect to orientation and direction of search. Subjects found it significantly easier to search through the set of line segments for arrows bearing either a horizontal or vertical orientation than those bearing an oblique orientation (Newman-Keuls, $p<.05$). Similarly, to search the arrays horizontally was significantly easier than to search them vertically (Newman-Keuls, $p<.05$). While there was no significant interaction between these factors, closer scrutiny of Figure 11.2 shows local interactions between the direction of search and the direction of the corresponding arrows such that the arrow pointing to the right is detected more quickly when the search is left to right than when the search is right to left ($t = 1.84$, $df = 15$, $p<0.05$). The comparable interaction between arrows

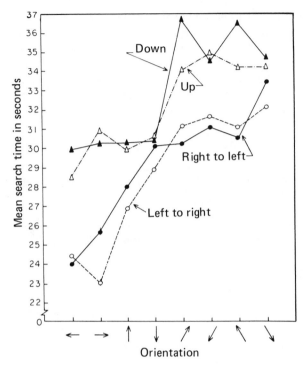

FIG. 11.2   Search times for line segments bearing various orientations and various directions of search.

pointing up and down and the vertical searches is visible in Figure 11.2 but it is not significant. It is also interesting to notice that arrows pointing down take longer to detect than arrows pointing up.

It is interesting to note as well that while not significant for the horizontal searches, *up* was more easily detected than *down* and that the obliques with an *up* feature were more easily detected than those with a *down* feature. There are some linguistic arguments to why *down* should be more complex, *down* sharing some of the features of marked adjectives. This factor becomes more relevant in later studies.

This study provides evidence, then, that the recognition of obliques involves a more complex process than the recognition of horizontal and vertical lines and that the effect can not be accounted for by the factor of direction of search although direction of search interacts with perception of orientation. The hypothesis that obliques must be matched against a more complex mental representation than horizontal and vertical lines is clearly supported by the data. Just what the structure of those representations is, remains to be seen.

2. MEMORY SPAN FOR LINES OF VARIOUS ORIENTATIONS

Because of the possible effects of the direction of search on the recognition of orientation present in the first experiment, a second study was conducted in which speed was irrelevant but which would bear on the basic hypothesis that oblique lines have a more complex underlying representation than horizontal and vertical lines. This study was modeled after the classical digit span test in that subjects were successively shown two strings of line segments in various orientations and asked to judge if the second string was identical to the first. If oblique lines were remembered in terms of a more complex representation than were horizontal and vertical orientations, fewer obliques would be remembered. More simply, memory span for obliques should be lower than that for "orthogonals".

The materials for this test consisted of pairs of sheets of paper upon which an array of one, two, three, four, or five line segments were drawn in any of the eight directions used in the previous study. Subjects examined the first member of a pair for an interval of 1 to 5 seconds, depending on the number of arrows in the array. This was removed and replaced by the second member, and subjects had to then judge whether or not the arrays of line segments on the two sheets were the same. The subjects for this study were 20 eighth grade students who were tested individually on two days.

Results

The data were analyzed by analyses of variance for repeated measures. Separate analyses were computed for all the errors, and the "different" errors (i.e., where the child failed to recognize that one of the original arrows had been rotated). Separate analyses were also computed for tasks with 2, 3, 4, and 5 lines per array.

Two of the findings will be elaborated in the following discussion. First, the ration of obliques in the array was significant for arrays having four (F (4,76) = 4.9, $p < .01$) or five (F (5,95) = 3.2, $p < .01$) line segments. This finding will be explored first by reference to the four array data. Second, there was a significant interaction between orientation (orthogonal vs. oblique) and degrees of rotation of the altered line segment (90°/180°) for arrays containing three ($F(1,20)$ = 7.03, $p < .05$), four ($F(1,20)$ = 9.19, $p < .01$), or five (F (1,20) = 10.05, $p < .01$) line segments. That is, the patterns of confusion are different for orthogonals and obliques in the more complex arrays.

The graph in Figure 11.3 shows clearly that the more obliques in the array the more errors made in the recognition of that array. The array consisting

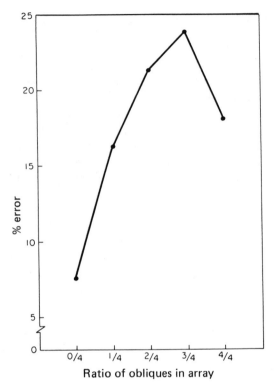

FIG. 11.3   Errors in the recognition of an array as a function of the number of obliques in the array.

entirely of horizontal and vertical lines was remembered significantly better than the array consisting entirely of obliques. With the mixed arrays, one, two, or three of the four lines being oblique, the more obliques present in the array the less likely the array was to be correctly recognized . The mixed arrays are not comparable to the all or no oblique arrays in that subjects can adopt a simpler coding for those latter patterns in two. First, they may just notice that the arrows are all oblique or all orthogonal and on that basis exclude any alternative, an effect equivalent to drawing the items from four rather than the full eight alternatives. Secondly, some subjects reported that when the arrows were all Horizontal-Vertical or Oblique, the lines formed gross patterns, such as series of parallel lines or the letter *W* and these patterns were easy to discriminate. Such patterns were largely eliminated in the mixed array lists. Hence, our consideration of the mixed and the all or no obliques arrays separately seems justified.

A pattern similar to that for 4 item arrays was found for the three and five line segment items, although they were not significant.

The findings that, within limits, the more oblique line segments in an array the more difficult the array was to remember, permit us to conclude that the memory span for oblique lines is less than that for orthogonals and hence to infer that the mental representation of obliques is more complex than that for horizontal and vertical lines.

A clue to that more complex mental representation of oblique lines is given by the pattern of errors that resuts from the interaction of the orientation of the line in the first array and the degree of rotation of the "Different" line in the second array. This interaction is shown in Figure 11.4 for all arrays combined. For Horizontal and Vertical lines a rotation of 90° was significantly more easily detected than a rotation of 180°, whereas for oblique lines a rotation through 180° was more easily detected than a rotation

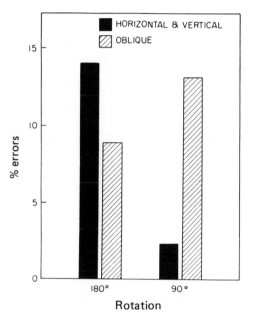

FIG. 11.4   90° and 180° confusions as a function of the orientation of the line.

through 90°. The memory representation of an arrow pointing up cannot be as simple as the feature *up* itself; for even if it is forgotten, the most likely confusion is with *down* thereby suggesting the preservation of the more general feature *vertical*. How could we most economically represent the structure of these oriented representations? By taking the embedding predicates to be qualifications of the embedded predicates, we may represent Horizontal and Vertical directions in the form:

> *direction* (orientation (line))
> *up* (vertical (line)), that is, the line has a vertical
>   orientation and an upward direction.

By assuming a systematic loss of features in memory from least to most embedded, we can account for the pattern of errors obtained for the orthogonal lines. This corresponds to the lexical fact that orientations, vertical for example, is differentiated into two directions, up and down. Hence, one may lose direction without losing orientation.

The common 90° confusion for oblique lines could result from a similar form of representation if it is assumed that they require two propositions of the form stated above. Thus, an oblique would take the description:

> *up* (vertical (line)) That is, the line has a
> vertical orientation and upward
> direction.
> and
> *right* (horizontal (line)) That is, the line has a horizontal
> orientation and a rightward direction.

By using the same procedure for deleting the least embedded feature, the description could lose the value for either "up" or "right", yielding obliques of *down to the right* or *up to the left,* respectively. In both cases, these new obliques are separated from the original by 90°, again accounting for the pattern of confusions obtained in this study.

Two further inferences seem warranted by these findings. First, such evidence appears to pose a problem for any simple imagery theory of memory in that the stimuli to be imaged are of equal size and shape and they lay in discrete positions. Why then could the new arrays not be matched against those images?

Secondly, the form of representation discovered in this last task strikingly resemble verbal descriptions of these orientations. Several studies of a Whorfian flavor have found evidence for the role of language in tasks involving memory. Events which can be economically described for others, can, as well, be economically described for oneself as an aid to remembering. Perhaps the representational system we discovered in this task is purely a post-perceptual linguistic device subjects devise as a mnemonic or aid to memory.

To avoid long term memory factors, we returned to a study of the recognition of obliques.

3. RECOGNITION TIMES FOR HORIZONTAL, VERTICAL, AND OBLIQUELY ORIENTED LINES

Experiment 1: Square Display

Our earlier study of the recognition of oblique lines, while it provided evidence for the more complex representation of obliques, was limited by the fact that it was impossible to exclude the effects of the search processes themselves on the recognition of orientation. To exclude search process effects on reaction time yet bypass the memory processes we have just considered, we developed the paradigm used in the remainder of the studies we report. The reaction time required by subjects to make same-different judgements about the orientation of two successively presented lines was measured for lines of different orientations. Overall differences in RT of Obliques relative to orthogonals would confirm their greater complexity while an analysis of those RTs would permit us to make some examination of the representations given to those displays.

In the first of these studies, line segments in one of four orientations, Horizontal, Vertical, and opposite Obliques were used. Stimuli consisted of 20 black and white 35mm slides; four of these, S_1, displayed centrally one of the four oriented lines. The remaining 16, S_2, displayed each of the four orientations in each of the four quadrants of the display, one orientation in one position appearing on each slide. This distribution was used to avoid the possiblity subjects would respond to absolute position of a constituent of the oriented line rather than to the orientation. Each S_1 was paired with each S_2 yielding 64 combinations, one-quarter of which called for a "Same" response, the remainder called for a "Different" response. The 64 pairs were presented four times in a random order fixed across Subjects. The Subjects were first required to complete an additional twenty pairs of stimuli as warm-up trials.

Subjects and procedures.   Nine adult subjects participated in the study. The first slide of each pair (S_1) appeared for one second. Following a four second delay, S_2 appeared in one of the four quadrants of the screen, and remained on the screen until the subject responded by pressing one of two telegraph keys. For one-half of the subjects the right key indicated "Same" and the left key indicated "Different"; for the remaining subjects the keys were reversed. The onset of S_2 started a timer which recorded subjects' response to the nearest 100th of a second.

Results

The mean RTs for the four presentations of each pair served as the dependent variable in the subsequent analyses. Five separate analysis of variance for repeated measures were computed, one for all the "Same" responses, and four for the "Different" responses, one for each orientation of the first slide. There was no significant difference in the time required to judge as the "Same" the pairs of lines in the four orientations ($F = 2.42$, $3/24$, n.s.). The mismatch times "Different" responses, however, were significantly different when S_1 was either oblique ($F = 18.65$, $2/16$, $p < .01$; $F = 11.91$, $2/16$, $p < .01$) The mean RTs required to judge each orientation as "Same"

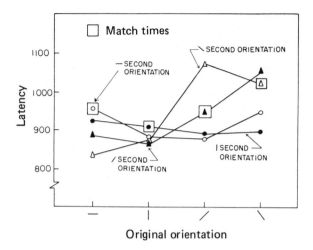

FIG. 11.5   Recognition times for the four orientations of S_2 as a function of the orientation of S_1 (square screen).

or "Different" as a function of the original stimulis orientation is shown in Figure 11.5. Mismatch times were a function of the nature of the difference between the mismatched alternative. Obliques were more difficult to differentiate from each other than they were from a horizontal or vertical. Similarly, horizontals and verticals were more confusable each other than with one of the obliques. This replicates the patterns of confusion obtained in the previous study and suggests the operation of a spatial code for representing orientation in the way described above.

However, the primary hypothesis of the experiment, namely, that match times for obliques should be longer than match times for orthogonals was not borne out by the data. A possible explanation for this failure is the powerful interaction between the orientation of the line and its position in the display. This interaction is shown in Figure 11.6.

Two features of the interaction are noteworthy. First, the two oblique lines are not of equal difficulty and second, they show complementary interactions with position. As to the first, right-obliques are easier than left-obliques, especially in some positions. As to the second, both obliques are easy in the positions which are congruent with the orientation of the line. That is, right obliques are easily judged "Same" when they occur in upper right quadrant or in the lower-left quadrant and difficult elsewhere. Correspondingly, left obliques are easily judged "Same" in the upper left and lower right quadrants.

If orientation were simply assigned a distinctive mental representation and if comparison of the lines simply involved comparison of the assigned representations, position of the line should have no effect on the process.

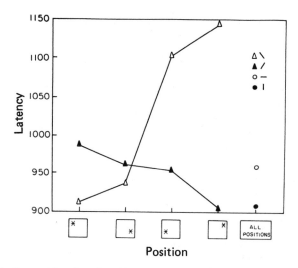

FIG. 11.6   Recognition times for obliques as a function of their position in the square display.

However, position is clearly a critical feature in making the judgment. Moreover, the position effects found here for adults are strikingly similar to those obtained for children and described in the preceding chapter. Children, it was found, encoded the oblique lines in terms of two factors, the position in the display and the relation to the axes of the display, by means of spatial propositions of the form:

> at (line, corner a) That is, the line is at corner a.

and

> *on* (line, axis) That is, the line is on an axis.

And their judgments were made by determining if the propositions representing the two lines were the same or not. However, these codes often generated incorrect responses for the children. Is it possible, then, that adults were using a structural code based on position similar to that used by the children? And if so, how did the adults arrive at the correct response?

It appears that even if position is logically irrelevant to the "Same" or "Different" judgments, even adults cannot avoid coding orientation in terms of position in the display just as the children did. Thus, the right oblique presented in the center of a square display is represented as:

> *at* (line, corner a). That is, the end of the line is at corner a.
> *on* (line, axis). That is, the line is on an axis.

As for children, if the matching stimulus has these properties, the judgment is extremely easy. Thus for the right oblique, if the second stimulus occurs in the upper right corner (or the lower left one), it falls on the axis, the judgment is easy. If both the position and the axis value are different, the right oblique falling in the upper left corner and across the axis for example, the response time required to make a "Same" response is dramatically lengthened. The corresponding pattern is obtained for the left oblique. Table 11.1 shows the response latencies as a function of the congruity/incongruity of the perceptual propositions for the compared lines. As this table shows when the two spatial propositions are congruent, it is easy to judge the lines as having the same orientations, when they are incongruent it is difficult to judge them as having the same orientation. Unfortunately, the data do not permit us to pull these two propositions apart since, for the "Same" responses, the proposition and axis features are perfectly correlated. A change in position must have a change in the axis value to remain the same orientation.

TABLE 11.1
Rts Required to Make a "Same" Judgment as a Function of Congruence
Between Perceptual Spatial Codes of the Compared Lines.

Outcome of Feature Comparison	at (lines corner)	+	−
	on (axis)	+	−
Orientation /		910	975
\		920	1125

Nonetheless, the features that make the judgment easy for the adults are the same features which, in the preceding chapter, were found to make the judgment easy for children. Conversely, the features that make the judgment difficult for children also make them difficult for adults. For both children and adults, then, oblique orientation appears to have been perceived in terms of the relation between the line and the framework by means of the spatial predicates *at* and *on*.

Here, however, the similarity between performance of adults and children ends, for when both features mismatch, children say "Different" and so make an error while adults say "Same" and so get the item correct. How are adults achieving this error-free performance? In the preceding chapter it was suggested that adults may differ from children in these spatial discrimination tasks either by altering the predicates which they assign to such displays or by altering the decision procedure applied to these predicates to make a judgment, or both.

Assuming the same predicates in terms of display position, what decision procedures would distinguish adult performance from that of the children? Children, as we discovered simply sum the outputs from the comparison process, matches inclining the children to say "Same" and mismatches inclining them to say "Different". Hence two mismatches produced a strong bias to say "Different" when in fact the obliques had the same orientation. Adults, on the other hand, say "Same" even when both features mismatch. We can account for the differences between children and adults simply by adding new decision procedures (See Table 11.2). Instead of summing the mismatches, mismatches may be kept track of by means of a "truth index", a decision procedure with two states, True and False, matches maintaining the value in the truth index, mismatches altering the value in the truth index to its opposite value. Such decision procedures are derived from propositional calculus and have been used extensively in psycholinguistic studies (cf., Clark & Chase, 1972; Olson & Filby, 1972). When this decision procedure is applied to the propositional codes described above, it would lead to the following responses: if both propositions for the two lines matched, subjects would say "Same", if one of the features mismatches, they would say "Different"; if both features mismatch, they would again say "Same". Hence, this analysis would deliver the responses given by the adult subjects. Thus it is possible that adults used the same positional code as did the children but with a decision procedure that generated correct responses. This first strategy would account for the position effects found in these data as well as the pattern of difficulty on the two cells for which we have data although it fails to account for the dramatic differences between left and right obliques.

Consequently, a second strategy is to consider a change in the assigned propositions. That is, the adult may code the orientation in terms of the

TABLE 11.2
Decision Procedure for Correctly Judging the Orientation of Two Lines on the Basis of Position and Axis Cues.

Represent first line:			
at (line, a)			
on (line, axis)			
Represent second line			
at (line, a)	at (line, b)	at (line, a)	at (line, b)
on (line, axis)	on (line, axis)	off (line, axis)	off (line, axis)
Compare 1st proposition			
+	−	+	−
	(change truth index to F)		(change index to F)
Compare 2nd proposition	+	−	−
+		(change index to F)	(change index to T)
T	F	F	T

types of representations we proposed above in the memory span study. The primary axes of the display are used as the basis for coding orientation such as:

up (V) and *right* (H) line, That is, the oblique is up to the right.

This again would account for correct responses and increased complexity of obliques as compared to orthogonals, but would assign a more restricted role to position in the display. The code for position, however, would nonetheless be automatically assigned to the display and, in certain cases, compete with the orientation code, thereby accounting for the position effects.

To better distinguish between these two coding strategies, a study was conducted which attempted to minimize the position effect by reducing the codability and hence, reduce interference effects of the positional cues. If adults were solving the task on the basis of line orientation, the second strategy, then they should be able to generate correct judgments across all positions. If display position is coded, the first strategy, than the position effects obtained in the first experiment should persist.

Experiment 2: Round Display with First Stimulus in Fixed Position

This study was designed to examine more systematically the effects of position on the mental representation of oblique orientation. Position relative to a frame of reference proved to be a powerful factor in both the preceding studies with adults and in the study with children reported in the previous chapter. Furthermore a number of researchers (Attneave & R. Olson, 1967; Attneave & Reid, 1968; Bryant, 1969, 1974; Olson, 1970a) have shown that the perception of orientation is affected by the frame of reference a subject relates that orientation to. Hence, to provide minimal reference cues and minimal interference from the spatial structure of the display, the stimuli for the present study were presented on a round screen.

Second, to determine the effects of position of the display more systematically, the eight compass points, rather than the four cardinal positions used in the previous study, were included.

The orientations of the lines, as before, were horizontal, vertical, and opposite obliques.

Subjects. Ten adult subjects, all of whom were right-handed, were paid to participate in the study.

Design and procedure. Black and white slides depicting line segments bearing one of the four orientations—horizontal, vertical, left oblique, and

right oblique—were presented to subjects on a round screen. (See Fig. 11.7.)
The slides were presented successively in pairs, the first line (S_1) appeared
for 500 msec. at the center of the screen followed by a 4 sec. pause. The
onset of S_2 which occurred in one of eight positions coincided with the activation of a timer, both of which remained active until the subjects pressed
one of the two telegraph keys on the table in front of them. The four orientations and eight possible positions for the line in S_2 resulted in 128 pairs.
Thirty-two of these formed the match condition and called for the response
"Same", while the remainder formed the mismatch condition and required
the response "Different". The 128 pairs of stimuli were presented four
times in a random order fixed across subjects.

Subjects were seated before the screen and rested their index fingers on
the telegraph keys. For half the subjects, the "Same" response was located
on the right, while for the other half it was located on the left. Subjects were
informed that they were to respond *Same* if two successive lines were of the

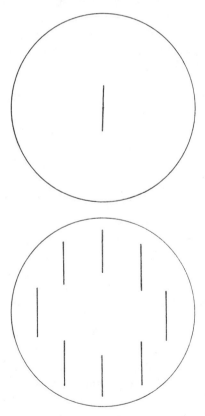

FIG. 11.7   The position of the fixed stimulus and the eight possible locations of the
variable stimulus (round screen).

same orientation regardless of the position and *Different* otherwise. They were requested to be as fast, but as accurate, as possible.

Results

The data from the 10 adult subjects were analyzed by analyses of variance for repeated measures. The dependent variable was the mean response latency for correct responses only for each distinct line pair.

For the "Match" condition the orientation factor was found to be highly significant ($F = 286.27$, $df = 3/27$, $p < .01$), as was the position of S_2 ($F = 13.66$, $df = 7/63$, $p < .01$) and the orientation by position interaction ($F = 9.31$, $df = 21/189$, .01). The "Different" responses from the mismatch condition were analyzed in two ways. In the first, one analysis for each of the four orientations of S_1 was computed: these results were almost identical with those for the "Same" responses with orientation of S_2, position, and orientation by position interaction, all highly significant. For the second method of analysis, four analyses were again computed, one for each of the orientations of S_2: in this case the effect of the orientation of S_1 was small and nonsignificant with the exception of the left oblique as S_2($F = 3.8$, $df = 2/18$, $p < .05$). Position effects were negligible when S_2 was horizontal ($F = 2.15$, $df = 7/63$, $p < .10$), small when S_2 was vertical ($F = 4.05$, $df = 7/63$, $p < .01$), and very large when S_2 was either the right oblique ($F = 43.73$, $df = 7/63$, $p < .001$) or the left oblique ($F = 53.65$, $df = 7/63$, $p < .001$). In addition, the orientation by position interactions was significant for the oblique mismatch conditions.

These analyses show, then, that the orientation of S_2, the variable position stimulus, is the major factor determining the subjects' decision time. This fact is seen even more readily in Figure 11.8 which shows the mean RTs required to recognize a line of a given orientation as a function of the preceding orientation. The time required to recognize a line, whether to identify it with a preceding line, that is, the "Match" condition, or to differentiate it from a preceding line, that is, the "Mismatch" condition, is widely and consistently longer for oblique lines than for horizontal and vertical lines. Perhaps even more striking is the difference between the two oblique lines; the left oblique takes significantly more time than the right oblique (Newman-Keuls, $p < .05$).

Position effects were highly regular for all orientations combined in both the match and mismatch conditions. In both cases, position effects occurred for both the right and left oblique but did not occur for either horizontal or vertical orientations. For the match conditions, the position N, S, E, and W are faster than NE, NW, SE, and SW. For the mismatch conditions there were additional effects in which N was also faster than S, and E was faster than W. To illustrate the position effect, the means for the orientation by

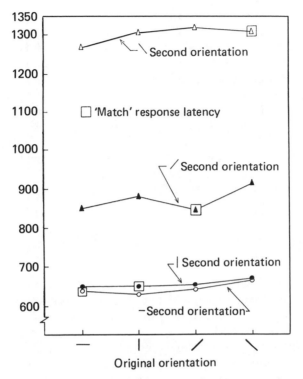

FIG. 11.8   Recognition times for the four orientations of S_2 as a function of the orientation of S_1 (round screen).

position interaction for the match condition are presented in Table 11.3.

These strong and consistent position effects are difficult to interpret. It is possible that they result in some scanning strategy, a tendency for subjects to look in some positions, such as the top or right, before looking at the other positions. That possibility is ruled out by the fact that position effects do not occur for horizontal and vertical lines. Similarly it is possible that the

TABLE 11.3
The Effects of Position on Recognition of an Oriented Line

Orientation	N	S	E	W	NW	NE	SE	SW
│	669	646	663	665	692	651	615	638
—	661	636	643	645	618	653	668	643
/	636	774	778	820	888	891	964	1040
\	1095	1166	1222	1270	1354	1369	1503	1501

direction of scanning interacts with the orientation of the lines somewhat as was reported in Experiment 1. That too appears to be ruled out by the fact that horizontal and vertical lines show no interactions with position or with direction of scan.

Rather it appears to be the case that the representation of orientation of obliques is dependent, in some way, on the representation of position while the representation of horizontals and verticals is independent of position in the display. If so, the analysis of these position effects may provide an important clue to the mental representation of oblique orientation and we shall return to this point presently. Nonetheless, to eliminate any possible effects of the direction of scanning in the judgment of orientation, a final study was conducted in which the first stimulus occupied a variable position and the second stimulus occurred in a fixed position.

Experiment 3: Round Display with Second Stimulus in Fixed Position

In the preceding experiment, the position of S_2 was found to be a significant factor in the time subjects required to determine the orientation of S_2. If the position effect is an artifact due to scanning habits—the tendency to start searching in a certain part of a display—rather than due to the structure of the representation, the effect should disappear if the first stimulus appeared in a variable position and the second stimulus appeared in a fixed position. To this end a second experiment was conducted, identical to the first one except that the position of S_1 was variable, being assigned to one of the eight positions around the screen, while the position of S_2 was fixed, always occurring at the center of the screen. As the measurement of RT began only with the onset of S_2, and S_2 was in a fixed position, any position effects due to scanning time would be excluded.

Subjects. Ten new adult subjects were paid to participate in the study. All were right-handed.

Design and procedure. The stimuli used in Experiment 3 were identical with those used in Experiment 2, with the exception that S_1 was presented in one of the variable positions described earlier while S_2 was shown in the center of the round screen.

S_1 was presented for 500 msec. followed by a 4-sec. interval. The onset of the timer coincided with the presentation of S_2 which remained on the screen until the subject pressed one of the telegraph keys. The 128 unique stimuli pairs were presented four times, in a random order fixed across subjects. All timing was controlled by a PDP-9 computer.

The subjects were seated 2 m in front of the screen, resting their index fingers on the two telegraph keys. The "Same" response was signalled by the right key for half the subjects and by the left key for the other half.

Results

The data from the 10 new adult subjects were found to be almost identical with those obtained from Experiment 2. For the "Match" responses, the effects of orientation were highly significant ($F = 328.8$, $df = 3/27$, $p < .001$), as was the position of S_1 ($F = 19.9$, $df = 7/63$, $p < .001$) and the orientation by position interaction ($F = 10.01$, $df = 21/189$, $p < .001$). The analyses for "Mismatch" responses show that the data for this Experiment differ in one fundamental way from those of Experiment 2. When the four analyses were computed, one for each of the four orientations of S_1, there were no significant effects for horizontal or vertical orientations. When S_1 was either oblique, there were significant orientation effects and significant position effects. When, however, the four analyses for each of the four orientations of S_2 were computed, the results were almost identical with those for the "Match" responses with the orientation of S_1, the position of S_1 and the position by orientation interaction all highly significant. That is, in this experiment, there were few differences between the orientations that occurred as S_2, but there were large and highly significant differences between the orientations that occurred as S_1, although it will be recalled, RT was measured beginning with the onset of S_2. Hence these results are complementary to those reported in Experiment 2. These new results are presented in Figure 11.9 (Note, however, that for Figure 11.9 the abscissa is labeled for S_2 rather than for S_1 as in Figure 11.8). As Figure 11.9 indicates, there were no significant differences between Horizontal and Vertical when they occurred as S_1; when obliques occurred as S_1 they were significantly more difficult than horizontal and vertical lines (Newman-Keuls, $p < .05$, for the match condition) and the left oblique was significantly more difficult than the right oblique (Newman-Keuls, $p < .05$, for the match condition).

The position effects in Experiment 3 were similar to those reported for Experiment 2. When S_1 was vertical or horizontal, there were no significant position effects, when S_1 was either oblique, there were always significant position effects (for the right oblique $F = 54.99$, $df = 7/63$, $p < .001$; for the left oblique $F = 44.38$, $df = 7/63$, $p < .001$), which may be summarized as follows: for the right oblique, N is always significantly faster than all other positions; N is always significantly faster than S, and E is always faster than W, though not significantly so; N, S, E, W are generally faster than NE, NW, SE, SW, but not always significantly so. For the left oblique, N is always faster than S, and E is faster than W and these differences are always significant; N, S, E, W are always faster than NE, NW, SE, SW,

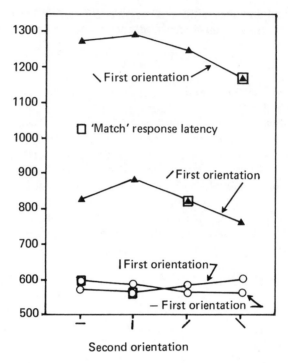

FIG. 11.9   Recognition times for the four orientations of S_1 as a function of the orientation of S_2 (round screen).

but not always significantly so. The position effects of S_1 summed over the orientation of S_2 are shown in Figure 11.10.

DISCUSSION

The findings of Experiment 3 rule out the possibility that the position effects obtained in Experiment 2 are due to habits of visual scanning, since timing did not begin until the onset of stimulus S_2 and S_2 occupied a fixed position on the display.

From both Experiment 2 and Experiment 3 we may conclude that the ease or difficulty of matching line segments depends on the particular orientation of those lines and their positions relative to the display. With respect to orientation, obliques are more difficult than horizontal and vertical lines and the left oblique is more difficult than the right oblique. With respect to position, lines falling in the top (N) position are more easily judged than those falling in the bottom (S) position, those occurring on the right (E) are easier than those on the left (W), and positions on these dimensions are easier than those that fall between these dimensions. Finally, position affects the judgment of oblique lines but not those of horizontal and vertical lines.

But how are we to explain these effects? The strong consistent interactions between orientation and position prevent us from simply adopting one of these as the preferred coding scheme as suggested in the two strategies outlined above. Obliques are coded by adults neither in terms of absolute position in the display nor directly in orientation. Let us then return to the theory of spatial relations that we have been elaborating in this volume. First, it will be recalled spatial representations are essentially relational consisting of a spatial predicate and one or more arguments and having the general form: *at* (x, y). Some of these predicates are more complex than others and more importantly, sometimes these predicates are assigned automatically while at other times they must be reconstructed intentionally by the viewer primarily for problem solving purposes. The most common predicates are those derived from the three dimensions of ego space: front/back, top/bottom, and left/right.

Secondly, the variables related by these predicates are important to a theory of spatial representations. Any object or identifiable constituent of an object may be related, by means of the spatial predicate, to any other ob-

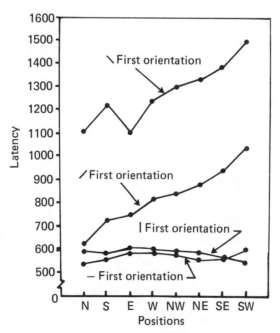

FIG. 11.10   Position effects of the four orientations of S_1 summed over the orientations of S_2.

ject, feature of object, or more general spatial framework. These latter structures (*relatum*) may vary from ego-referents, to object-referents or framework referents depending upon which relations are to be preserved as invariant.

Now, can we use this theory to account for the observations in these experiments? First, orientation, being a spatial structure, is coded not directly but relative to some relatum. As we saw in the previous chapter, orientation may be coded relative to the primary axis of the square display by means of the predicates *at* and *on*. Note that these axes are features of display and are constructed prior to the presentation of any stimuli. If the orientation of the lines can be represented in terms of these axes their representation and judgment should be relatively easy. This is the case for the horizontal and vertically oriented line segments which simply fall *on* or *parallel to* these primary axes of the display:

> *on* (S_1, V axis). That is, S_1 is on the Vertical axis.
>
> or
>
> *parallel* to (S_1, V axis). That is, S_1 is parallel to the Vertical axis.

If the second line segment takes the same description, subjects judge the lines to have the same orientation. As we pointed out, since the V and H axes are established prior to the presentation of the stimuli, the task is relatively easy and as they are general to the entire display, there is no position effect for horizontal or vertical line segments. In sum, the horizontal and vertical lines are related to the structural features of the display described by its primary axes. Moreover, each such proposition requires only one relatum either the V or H axes, but not both.

In order to distinguish direction, as we noted earlier, it would be necessary to code both orientation (right oblique) and direction (up to the right vs. down to the left). In this task however, there are no directional arrows and it is sufficient for subjects to code orientation. That is, up to the right is equivalent to down to the left; both are right-obliques.

To correctly distinguish the two obliques, it is necessary only to notice whether the top part of the line segment is to the left or to the right of a Vertical axis. The first task, then, is to find the top of the line segment, and this is done on the basis of a horizontal axes to form the proposition:

> *top* = *above* (end of the line, H-axis). That is, the end of the line above the H-axis may be coded as the top.

Second, the top of the line is related to the vertical axis by means of the predicate *left* or *right* to form the proposition:

> *right* (top, V-axis). That is, the top of the line is to right of the Vertical axis.

The problem with obliques is that subjects can most readily assign these descriptions in terms of the predominant horizontal and vertical axes of the display, what we have called "object space". However, because the position of the line segments is variable, such an assignment would lead to incorrect judgments. For example, if the central vertical axis were used to determine left or right, then the right oblique in the right half of the display would be coded as right, but the same oblique in the left half would be coded as left of the vertical axes. Such codings would therefore lead to "Different" judgments. It will be recalled that in fact young children frequently made such erroneous judgments just because they coded the orientation in terms of the invariant spatial properties of the display, its fixed corners and its fixed diagonal axes.

To successfully solve the problem, subjects must assign the horizontal and vertical axes to each successively presented line segment. Thus the judgments of *above, left,* and *right,* are based, not on the primary structural axes of the display, but on local H and V axis assigned to the particular line segments in each location.

Consider for example a right-oblique appearing in the lower left quadrant of the screen (see Fig. 11.11). As we mentioned, subjects automatically assign major H and V axes bisecting the display as a whole but these axes are inappropriate for the orientation judgment. Rather, these axes must be assigned to the particular line segment as follows. The viewer first assigns H and V axes which bisect that line segment. First the H axis is used in order to determine the top of the segment by means of the predicate *above*:

$top = above$ (end (line), H axis). That is, the end of the line above the H
axis is the top.

This top is then related to a V axis by means of the predicate *right* or *left* to form the representation for the right oblique:

right (top, V-axis). That is, the top of the line
segment is to the right of the vertical axis.

This is precisely what is meant by a right oblique and it is a code that would be common and hence appropriate for recognizing this orientation in any position. Moreover, if we accept the relative markedness of *left* with respect to *right,* than the assignment of these codes should be more difficult when the top of the line segment falls to the *left* of the V-axis than when it falls to the *right* of V.

We can summarize this theory by stating that there are two processes involved in making judgments of oblique orientation. The first has to do with locating the specific appropriate H and V axes for the line segment. The second has to do with using these axes to find (1) the *top* of the line, and (2) whether this top is to the *left* or to the *right* of the vertical.

The data are compatible with this account. First, there is an obvious

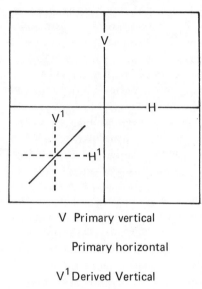

V Primary vertical

Primary horizontal

V¹ Derived Vertical

H¹ Derived horizontal

FIG. 11.11   The oblique shown in the diagram is coded as "up to the right" or "right-oblique" relative to the derived axes H¹ and V¹ even if, in terms of the primary axes, it is below the H and to the left of the V.

markedness effect for *left* as opposed to *right* oblique lines. More importantly, however, this difference between *left* and *right* obliques is constant at each of the eight positions; that is, for oblique lines, position and orientation are additive independent stages of information processing[1] (Clark & Chase, 1972; Olson & Filby, 1972). Since subjects were required to respond to orientation and ignore the position, their inability to do so suggests that position information was essential to the computation of orientation. When oblique lines occur in various positions, subjects are uncertain as to where the primary H and V axes of the displayed line are. To determine that, subjects process the position of the line to determine the location of the axes of the stimulus display and, subsequently, they describe the line orientation in terms of these axes. Put simply, the subject first examines the position to determine "Which way is up?" That decided, they determine if the top of the oblique is to the left or to the right of that vertical. The first decision takes a variable amount of time depending upon whether the position is on a primary axis and whether it is on the positive or negative pole of that dimension, as we saw earlier. The second decision requires an amount of time again determined by whether the representation employs a positive (right) or negative (left) pole of the dimension.

[1]We are indebted to Anne Treisman and Burt Rosner for bringing this fact to our attention.

An additional comment is required on why some positions (N) and some orientations (right oblique) are easier than others. Recall that the position effects are to be explained by the difficulties in finding H and V axes for the particular displays. The fixed properties of the display either facilitate that assignment or interfere with it. N, the top of the display, is the best indication of where the V axis is, S the second best, and so on. Similarly, E is at the end of the intrinsic H axis so it is the best indication of H for a stimulus occurring at E, second best at W, and so on. Stimuli occurring on either the primary H or V axis of the display are the most difficult to assign local H and V axes to.

The increased difficulty of the left oblique over the right oblique again reflect the markedness of the left-right pair. The markedness of left relative to right has been demonstrated directly by G. Olson and Laxer (1973). In these studies, left obliques are consistently slower than right obliques.

It is interesting to note too that these asymmetries between spatial predicates have "markedness" effect when voluntarily applied as in this study. In the preceding chapter, there were no significant differences between right and left obliques, but recall, however, that in that analysis the predicates right and left were not used; rather younger subjects simply noted whether or not the obliques fell on primary axis. And for that factor there was a markedness effect *on*-axis being easier than *off*-axis.

Left-Right Differences

Adults, like the child subjects described in the preceding chapter, use position information in making orientation judgments. They differ however in how they use that positional information. Child subjects use the intrinsic spatial properties of the display—its corners and sides and axes. Adults assign spatial axes to the line segment itself and then code the orientation relative to those axes. In the terms advanced in Chapter 5 children employ an object space and adults a framework space. *But,* the spatial propositions constructed to relate the orientation to those frameworks are essentially the same, consisting of a pair of propositions relating to properties of the display.

Described this way, it becomes clear that these orientation experiments have a direct similarity to the perspective and rotation tasks described in earlier chapters as well. The factor that makes those tasks difficult, it will be recalled, was not simply perceiving spatial relations, but rather in assigning the axes or frameworks derived from ego-space to other aspects of space for a particular purpose. Ego related and object related spatial description are "perceived"; they are assigned automatically in the act of perception. The higher level spatial cognition needed by these tasks involves the explicit applications of these spatial predicates to newly assigned axes—whether the application of front/back, and left/right axes to the viewpoint of another observer, as in the perspective and rotation tasks, or of the top/bottom, left/right dimensions to the spatial location of particular oblique lines in the orientation discrimination tasks. Adult spatial cognition then consists of the voluntary reassignment of the very spatial axes and predicates that were implicit and automatic in the child's ordinary perception of space.

It is just such an ability that makes the Chewart drawing with which we introduced this chapter, interesting. First, we see a man and a woman; then we see that it is the same drawing inverted; finally, we see that it all depends upon which we choose to call *top*. We can see either drawing as a man or a woman depending upon which point in the picture we decide to treat as the top of the picture. All spatial cognition involves the use of such spatial axes as top/bottom, front/back, left/right; adults simply have the advantage of being able to choose how they will be assigned.

12 Explaining Spatial Cognition: A Theory of Spatial Representation

> *"All science is reason acting/systematizing/on principles, which even animals practically know [e.g.] in balancing a body."*
> Darwin's Notebooks.

The real work of the book is now complete. In this chapter, we will identify and elaborate some of the general properties of spatial cognition and properties of the mind that have been inherent in our view throughout. To this end we will outline the structure of the theory, review its application to the tasks discussed in the book, apply it to some other tasks which have not been discussed, and finally, discuss the relationship between the view developed here and alternative conceptions of space and ultimately to alternative conceptions of the mind.

By means of a conceptual and an empirical analysis of a variety of spatial tasks that psychologists have studied over the past half century we have been able to isolate a small set of representations and operations that underlie this array of tasks. Indeed one of the surprising outcomes of the enterprise has been that such problems as the perception of patterns, the perception of spatial relations, spatial imagination, and spatial problem solving all involve a common set of mental representations and cognitive operations. Let us in conclusion review the general properties of the theory of mental representation of space that we have elaborated in the course of this book.

THE THEORY OF SPATIAL REPRESENTATION

The central properties of the theory of spatial cognition may be enumerated as follows:

1. Spatial cognitions are constructed on the basis of propositions which relate an argument to a relatum through a spatial predicate, for example,

on (book, desk), i.e. The book is on the desk

where "on" is the predicate, "book" is the argument, and "desk" is the relatum. Some spatial propositions specify the relations within an object such as that between a feature and the whole object. These "structural propositions" underlie object recognition. Some spatial propositions specify the relations between objects such as relative positions. These "relational propositions" underlie our knowledge of locations. Together such propositions serve as the mental representation of objects, patterns, locations, and events.

2. The spatial predicates are critical to the proposition. Most important of these predicates are those which are based on a three-dimensional Euclidean space defined by three orthogonal axes, producing such predicates as *front, back, top, bottom, left, right,* and so on. Others specify spatial relations on one of those dimensions such as *over, beside,* and the like. Still other predicates relate, fall within, or are derived from these basic predicates without altering their basic dimensional properties. Finally, some predicates such as *open, closed, in, out, near, far,* reflect topological relations, spatial relations which are somewhat independent of particular dimensions, and directions. We have not specifically examined these topological predicates.

3. Spatial predicates are not simply *ad hoc* lists of possible predicates but rather are organized into systems. The dimensional predicates, for example, are organized in terms of axes, planes, directions, distances, and positions in a three-dimensional Euclidean space. Not only are they related in terms of a general scheme but they may also, in some cases, be further differentiated into more basic predicates and some basic predicates may be used to generate higher order predicates. Hence, spatial predicates are structurally related. To illustrate, the predicate *top* may be constructed by applying the more basic predicate *above* to the arguments a proper part (Ppt) and the horizontal axis, as follows:

top $\longrightarrow$ *above* (Ppt, H_{axis}) That is, the top *is* the proper part
above the horizontal axis.

This new spatial predicate, *top,* may then enter into new spatial propositions. Spatial predicates, then, form orderly systems which may become elaborated by differentiation into more basic predicates and coordinated by integration into higher order predicates.

4. While the number of predicates is limited, the number of arguments

which can be expressed in spatial propositions is unlimited. Hence, the limited set of predicates can generate an infinite number of spatial propositions.

5. The relatum, the second term of the spatial proposition, falls into one of four general classes: ego, observer, object, and environment. Each of these classes provides a frame of reference within which to interpret a spatial predicate. For example, an argument, the boy, can be placed in an *ego-related* proposition:

in front (boy, ego) i.e. The boy is in front of me.

an *object related* spatial proposition:

in front (boy, car) i.e. The boy is in front of the car.

a viewer or *observer-related* proposition:

in front (boy, observer) i.e. The boy is in front of the observer.

or an *environment-related* proposition:

north (lake, town) i.e. The lake is north of the town.

Even if spatial predicates are assumed to be generated by the mind (or ego), it is not necessary to assume that they are assigned to ego before they are assigned to objects. In some ways, ego is merely another object, undoubtedly an important one. And in some ways an observer is also simply another object with such intrinsic spatial properties as, *front, back, top,* and the like. So too, environments are simply special cases of objects which are much larger than ordinary objects. Spatial predicates are readily assigned to all four; they are categories of the mind, not simply descriptions of the ego, objects, or environments. As this common set of spatial predicates is used for representing objects and observers as well as ego, and as they are so readily assigned, they frequently come into conflict. Hence, one of the more difficult problems in spatial cognitive tasks is in adopting the appropriate frame of reference or relatum for the proposition.

6. When spatial predicates are assigned to objects or events, including ego, on a more permanent basis, for example, to distinguish features or usual orientation, they may be treated as intrinsic to those objects or events. Thus, if the predicate *top* is usually assigned to a particular part of ego or to a particular part of an object such as a car, a bottle, or a room, that object will be treated as canonical, that is, as if the object intrinsically possessed the property specified by that predicate. The invariance with which these

predicates apply to the object is the major distinguishing feature between canonical and noncanonical objects. While spatial parts are permanent features of canonical objects—the top of the car remains the top even if it has turned over—the spatial predicates for noncanonical objects must be reassigned on each encounter on the basis of some other frame of reference primarily ego. Thus, descriptions like the "top of a block" or the "front of a cup" or "top of the picture frame" are temporarily assigned on the basis of current relationship between the ego or environment and that object. Environments tend to be canonical only in regard to a vertical axis; however, horizontal axes may be assigned to such properties as the front of a room or the front streets of a town or even north of town if some environmental basis for assigning the feature such as the north pole, can be found (Lynch, 1960).

7. An important consequence of the permanent assignment of spatial predicates in the creation of canonical objects is that these canonical objects then each specify a relational space to which other objects may be spatially related. Bottles, cars, rooms, houses, towns, countries, and worlds are all treated as canonical objects with intrinsic spatial properties to which objects may be related. But because their spatial properties are not congruent, all their fronts do not point in the same direction, for example, they frequently come into conflict (Harris, 1977; Pick & Lockman, 1981; Wunderlich, 1981). Water level may be tilted relative to the axis of the bottle, which may be tilted relative to the axis of the table, which may be tilted relative to the room, which may be tilted relative to the house, the hillside, the horizon, and so on. Which axes are more salient and which are appropriate for various judgments is therefore a complex issue.

8. Ordinary language yields a relatively full expression of the basic spatial predicates. The structures of this system have been described by Bierwisch (1967), H. H. Clark (1973a), Miller and Johnson-Laird (1976); Teller (1969), and in Chapter 5 of this volume. Lexical items express particular spatial predicates and hence have the same structure that mental predicates do. For example, some predicates such as *on, top, over,* and *above* express values on Cartesian dimensions but on a single dimension at a time. Representations simultaneously specifying values on more than one dimension in a single representation generally fall outside the range of single lexical items. Hence in the tasks we have examined, for example the oblique discrimination task, the representation consisted of pairs of predicates, such as *up* and *right.* Indeed, only mathematics provides for a fully explicit representation of two or three dimensions simultaneously (in terms of values on x, y, and z axes). Even these more complex predicates, however, are obviously constructed in terms of the same basic dimensions, and values on those dimensions as the simpler systems we have discussed herein. Language marks the relation *within* objects by nouns and those *between* objects by prepositions.

9. Although lexical items provide a good model of the underlying predicates that give rise to spatial propositions, the unit of mental representation of space is a proposition, not a word or a sentence. Indeed, this was one of the last points to come clear in the course of writing this book. Sentences express propositions and so the structure of a sentence serves as a model of the structure of underlying propositions. But the proposition may be constructed even if no sentence can be generated to express that proposition. Indeed, one of the most interesting aspects of spatial perception and spatial thought is the fact that so much of spatial cognition is implicit and not readily explicable in words; it is largely a form of implicit knowledge—what Campbell (1982) has called cryptic knowledge. The mental representations which so permit the perception of objects and events are obviously not confined to ordinary language descriptions; indeed it is clear that perception is nonlinguistic. While that is true, it may lead to the incorrect inference that if perceptual representations are non-verbal, they are therefore non-propositional, consisting of images, templates, traces, or the like. Perception is indeed inarticulate but the propositions constructed to represent perceptual events including spatial displays have much the same form as those which underlie the meanings of sentences. The difference we have argued, is that the former structures are implicit in object and event knowledge while, the latter are explicit as knowledge of form, that is, as knowledge of space per se. Indeed, it has been the primary concern of this book to "explicate" those implicit spatial structures.

10. While spatial perception involves the automatic assignment of predicates to ego and objects, spatial thought requires the deliberate reassignment of the predicates implicit in ordinary perception to new displays or to new aspects of the same displays. Typical of this reassignment are tasks in which the predicate *front* must be reassigned to the location of a viewer instead of its automatically assigned location, the ego. On other tasks, the horizontal and vertical axes which are automatically assigned to the major axis of the display must be reassigned to the particular aspect of the stimulus display. Although spatial predicates are automatically assigned to ego, objects and events in the visual environment, their voluntary assignment to particular aspects of displays or particular points of view is accomplished only through explicit spatial concepts.

11. Spatial development involves both elaboration and explication. Elaboration results from assigning additional predicates to a display with the effect of distinguishing that display from alternatives with which it is important not to confuse it. Elaboration also involves combining predicates to yield new predicates as described in point 2.

Explication involves the transition from implicit spatial representations which cannot be articulated into distinctive spatial propositions and which as a consequence are not subject to intentionality, into explicit spatial concepts which can be articulated into distinctive propositions and which therefore are subject to intentional assignment. To illustrate, children can assign the predicate *front* to ego and canonical objects before they can intentionally assign them to noncanonical objects. One of the last sets of predicates to become subject to voluntary reassignments are those horizontal axes, front/back and left/right.

Some Uses of the Theory in Accounting for the Experiments Discussed Herein

Let us now review briefly some of the types of problems that we have examined in the course of this book which best illustrate the explanatory value of the theory. Consider, for example, the relation between the rotations tasks and the oblique discrimination task. All of these tasks involve the identification of critical features of the display, the assignment of axes to the display based on either ego space or object space, and the construction of propositions relating the critical display features in terms of those axes. Each of these aspects of the solution is responsible for some of the complexity which differentiates the various problems.

Many of the problems examined in this volume have demonstrated that, where the critical display features are easy to identify, the problem is simpler than when the isolation of those features is difficult. This was shown by the relative simplicity of the verbal response mode compared to the pictorial in the study by Ives (Chapter 7), the verbal response designated the critical predicate *front* while the picture response did not; the relative simplicity of the known canonical objects compared to the abstract objects in the perspective task in Chapter 6, known objects have established fronts, backs and so on while abstract blocks do not; and the relative simplicity of the item questions compared to the appearance questions in the Huttenlocher and Presson Study discussed in Chapter 8, item questions designating critical predicates, appearance questions not. In all cases, the problem was easier when the critical aspect of the display was isolated for the child.

Second, the problem of assigning appropriate axes to the display, although necessary for the solution of all the tasks, is easier when the required spatial axes are congruent with the set of axes automatically assigned to the display. That is, primary axes are assigned to objects in the environment automatically, and to the extent that these axes are also the appropriate ones for the solution of a spatial task, the problem is easy to solve. Where a new set of axes is required for the purpose of solving the task, the problem is more difficult. Thus, obviously the 0° condition in the perspective task is relatively easier than the transformed conditions; the automatically assigned ego space description of the display is congruent with observer space. Also, the recognition of horizontal and vertical lines in the orientation recognition task is simple because the vertical and horizontal axes automatically assigned to the display are appropriate for the representation of these line segments.

When the axes need to be reassigned to solve the problem, the basis of that reassignment can vary, and that difference accounts for some of the differences in task complexity. Moreover, the greater the conflict between the two sets of axes, the more difficult the problem.

In the line orientation recognition task, the positions that were most difficult to represent for oblique orientation were those in which the axes in terms of which the orientation is represented, fell off the primary axes of the display. The cardinal positions N, S, E, W, were simpler than the intervening positions. That is, it was easier to reassign the H and V axes to particular line segments where the assigned axes were compatible with the primary H and V axes of the display.

While all of the spatial tasks required reassignment of major axes or dimensions, they vary in the particular dimensions that had to be reassigned. The perspective task required that reassignment of the front-back and left-right dimensions from ego space to a new observer space. For the oblique orientation task it involved reassigning the top-bottom and left-right dimensions from those appropriate to the display as a whole to those appropriate to the particular location of the oblique line segment. And finally, in the rotation task, the subject had to either assign top-bottom and front-back dimensions (in-depth rotations) or top-bottom and left-right dimensions (in the plane rotations).

In the rotations tasks, however, the axes could not be reassigned until a value for r, the angle separating the axes of the two displays had been computed, whereas in the obliques task and in the perspective task the axes could be assigned without actually computing a value for r, as the viewer already knew the point of origin of the new perspective. A value for r, however, does not call for a radical new spatial "imagery" ability; it is simply the value relating the axes of the two displays. Sometimes r is given, as when the subject is required to reconstruct the view from an alternative but given perspective and sometimes r is computed on the basis of seeing the beginning and endpoints of a spatial transformation.

Another source of difficulty in assigning appropriate axes to the display, arises from the possible conflict created by the two spatial codes, ego space and object space. This conflict is illustrated by comparing the way adults and children attempt to solve the picture description problem outlined in Chapter 5. The materials were a series of 16 pictures showing a centrally located car in one of four different orientations, and a star placed in one of the four cardinal positions around the car. The problem was to answer the question, Where is the star? For the children, each picture was given a different description in which the star was related to some invariant spatial feature of the car, for example, "At the top of the car", "At the bottom of the car", irrespective of the orientation of the car. For the adults, all pictures were described with one of four statements: The star is at the top, at the bottom, on the left, or on the right, where these expressions are determined by the location of the star *in the picture*. Thus the adults and children were locating the star within a different spatial framework: for the children the relatum was a canonical object, the car, and for the adults it was the ego space assigned to the noncanonical picture frame.

This disparity is analogous to the different solutions to the oblique orientation task used by children and adults. The children (Chapter 10), represented the orientation of the line segments in terms of some perceptually distinguishable feature of the display, and as a result, found great difficulty with certain problems and made frequent errors. The adults, however, solved the problem by assigning axes to the display, based on ego space, which could be used to consistently represent the orientation of all the line segments.

Some Applications of the Theory to Other Problems

Many tasks which appear to have little to do with the types of representation described herein are, in fact, simply disguised versions of the tasks we have analyzed. Consider Piaget and Inhelder's, (1956, p. 38) water level experiment. In this experiment young children were shown drawings of bottles tilted in various orientations and asked to draw the level of the liquid in the tilted bottles. Younger children drew the line to represent the water level on the horizontal axes of the bottle—whereas older children and adults correctly drew it on the horizontal axis of the display, that is, on the "true" horizontal.

More recently, Howard (1978) (see also Pylyshyn, 1981) showed that even undergraduates could not systematically discriminate photographs depicting correct relations between the water level and the tilt of the bottle from those representing anomalous relations; they made errors much like those made by Piaget and Inhelder's (1956) younger subjects. Pylyshyn (1981) cites this data to show that what you can imagine, visualize, or recognize depends upon what you know. What some adults know is that water "seeks its own level", what Howard called the fluid level invariance, and those subjects correctly discriminated the photographs.

But how is such a task solved? We would suggest that this problem is isomorphic to the oblique task reported in Chapter 11. Specifically, the water level orientation for all subjects is coded relative to a horizontal axis thus:

on (water level, H axis), i.e., the water level is
    on the horizontal axis.

The problem arises in determining which H axis is appropriate. The predominant H axis is derived from the object space of the bottle. To recognize a canonical object, as Rock (1973) has shown, is to discover its intrinsic spatial properties, its top and bottom, and hence its intrinsic vertical and horizontal axes. These axes may then serve in representing the orientation of the water level. This would yield the proposition:

on (water level, H axis (bottle)) That is, the water
   level is on the H axis of the bottle.

Alternatively, the primary axes of the display provide another candidate for a horizontal axis yielding the proposition:

on (water level, H axis (display)) That is, the water
   level is on the H axis of the display.

This designation, although secondary, is the correct one. But it is the correct one only because of the principle that water seeks a level horizontal to the environment. It is the conflict between these two horizontal axes that gives rise to the errors reported by Howard in his study of adults, and Piaget and Inhelder, in their study of children.

It is interesting to note that Piaget and Inhelder described the use of the first horizontal, what we have called object space, as being determined by the particular configurations presented. They claim that horizontal and vertical axes are still undiscovered (p. 382). While we agree that the child is not using "external" frames of reference, their responses nonetheless systematicy honor vertical and horizontal axes. Their axes, however, are defined on the basis of the objects themselves. The same explanation applies to Piaget and Inhelder's observations that children position fenceposts and houses perpendicular to the hill rather than perpendicular to the external frame of reference; both cases involve the propositions of perpendicular to a Horizontal axis; the only question is which H axis is relevant.

Again, the same type of conflict between competing spatial designations of H and V axes underlies the difficulty of the oblique recognition problem and accounts for the difference between child and adult responses to the picture description problem. Note, however, that while all adults were correct on the oblique orientation task, they committed errors on the water level task. In both tasks, the viewer needs to be able to assign both representations and to determine which of the two is the appropriate basis of solution. The difference between the tasks is that while all the subjects in the oblique orientation task knew which set of axes were appropriate, only those subjects in the water level task who could articulate the principle of constant water level knew which set of axes was appropriate. These differences in choice of frames of reference, we suspect, account for such differences as do exist in the spatial cognition of men and women.

Finally, let us consider a task used by Kolers and Perkins (1975) and Kolers and Smythe (1979) to provide evidence for what they called a "pattern analyzing mechanism". Subjects were shown letters, or letter sequences, which had been rotated around either a frontal, lateral, or vertical axis. Kolers and his colleagues found that letter identification is easiest with the first of these transformations, and explain the effect by claiming that the only difficulty for the first rotation is in accessing the appropriate mechanisms, whereas the difficulty for the other two rotations is complicated by the ambiguity of the rotated letter.

The strength of the explanation is that it acknowledges that the three types of transformations are quite different: the first in some sense preserves the structure of the letter while the other two violate the letter, making it ambiguous between two readings. The weakness of the explanation is that it does not express precisely the representations subjects construct for these letters nor the procedures that they use in applying them in various circumstances that would account for these distinctive patterns. An account in terms of "pattern analyzing mechanisms", therefore, is not much more explicit than the imagery theory which they reject.

Let us, then, reconsider their data in terms of the theory elaborated in this volume. Recall that all spatial arrays are represented in terms of sets of spatial propositions assigned from a particular point of view. Letters of the alphabet function as spatial arrays in that they have an internal spatial structure which can be assigned from a particular point of view. Most of the letters are canonical, which is to say that their usual orientation designates an intrinsic top and bottom and a left and right. Consider, for example, the letter *b*. The mental representaiton for the letter *b* would involve, among other things, the following spatial propositions:

above (line, H axis)
& *right* (loop, V axis)

Such propositions, as we pointed out, are implicit and linked together; they are subordinate to the higher level concept or meaning "the letter *b*". Further, these "structural descriptions" are assigned from a particular point of view, ordinarily from the perspective of the ego—the top of the *b* corresponds to the top of the ego, the right to ego's right and so on. That is, the predicate *above* can be applied only from a certain perspective, ordinarily that of ego. The point of view, as we mentioned, is specified in the *relatum* of the spatial proposition—the H axis is, ordinarily, ego's H axis.

Now let us note what happens to those representations under the different rotational transformations described by Kolers and Perkins. The critical factor is the determination of the relatum to which the constituents of the letters are related. In the untransformed letters, H axis and V axis are specified by ego and as those axes are automatically assigned to any space, the recognition procedure, finding the line is above and the loop is to the right, is a relatively straightforward matter. In all of the rotation conditions the values for each of the relatum must be recomputed before the letter can be judged in relation to them. But how could this recomputation be carried out? A letter of the alphabet is a two-dimensional, canonical object and it is represented mentally, we have argued, by means of an unanalyzed structural description, which is to say, the propositions cannot be readily analyzed into separate constituents. Thus, transformations of the letter must be treated holistically: any transformation in one proposition is tied to a transformation in the other. For the rotation in the plane of the paper, the values for the relatum for both of the propositions, namely the H axis and the V axis, may be reassigned together from an alternative point of view which we may call the "observer perspective". This reassignment creates new values for the top-bottom ends of the V axis and for the left-right ends of the H axis. Once these axes are reassigned, the recognition procedure for the letter can again go through. This is presumably what Kolers and Smythe (1979) mean by "accessing the appropriate mechanism". The procedure is illustrated in parts a and b of Figure 12.1. Note that it is the axes of the relation which were transformed, not the latter per se.

The other two transformations shown in c and d are more difficult in that the corresponding transformation is through the plane of the paper. Thus, the structural description can be applied holistically to the display only if a transformation is made of the front-back axis. But the letter has only two dimensions represented in its structural description—it has no front or back. Hence it is impossible, ordinarily, to reassign the front-back axes of the display to create a perspective from which the two propositions can be directly applied. That is, the latter two transformations are difficult in that they depend on a transformation in this third dimension which is not ordinarily implicated in our structural descriptions for letters.

It is unlikely that subjects actually carry out the reassignment of the front-back axis (with the effect of imagining what the letter would look like if it were viewed from the opposite side of the sheet of paper) although it could be done if a viewer treated the letter as a three-dimensional object with an intrinsic front and back. More likely, however, they preserve the two-dimensional structure of the displays and carry out the letter recognition process by breaking the structural description into two propositions, relating the vertical property to one relatum and the horizontal property to a different relatum. Hence, one of the propositions would be "read" in terms of the axis specified by ego and the other proposition "read" in terms of the reassigned axis described as that of the "observer" (O) in parts b, c, and d of Figure 12.1. Consider, the H-axis rotation shown in c. From the viewpoint of ego, that rotation preserves the left-right predicate but alters

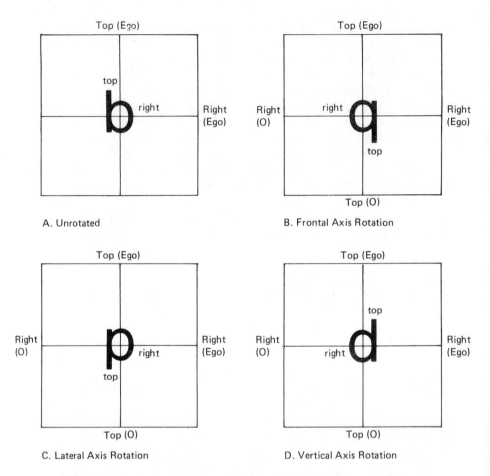

FIG. 12.1   Three transformations of the letter "b" in the letter recognition task.

the top-bottom one. Conversely, in terms of the reassigned axes, the axis representing the point of view of an observer, the top-bottom predicate is preserved but the left-right one is altered. Just the opposite occurs when the letters are rotated around the vertical, left-right axis. In that case, the ego's viewpoint preserves the top-bottom relations but alters the left-right one while in terms of the reassigned axes, just the opposite holds. In order to recognize the letters after either of these types of rotations, then, one predicate in the letter representation must be assigned in terms of the reassigned axes. For this reason, these two rotation tasks are more difficult than the in-the-plane rotations.

This distinction between two-dimensional and three-dimensional displays and the types of transformations each allows may be used to explain what may seem to be a contradiction between the findings of Shepard and Metzler (reviewed in Chapter 8) and those reported by Kolers and Perkins. Using three-dimensional objects, Shepard and Metzler found that rotations in-depth were easier than rotations in-the-plane while Kolers and Perkins, using letters, found rotations in-the-plane eaiser than those in-depth. The contradiction disappears if we note that letters have no front-back features which can be reassigned in depth rotations while solid objects do have such features. For three-dimensional objects, it appears to be the rule that left-right axis is marked relative to the front/back axis which is marked relative to the up-down axis. Consequently, transformations in primary dimensions must be sorted out prior to those in more secondary ones.

We may note two further implications of this account. If the top-bottom axis is primary, and unmarked relative to the left-right axis (Chapter 11) in cases when the two predicates come in conflict, subjects may attempt to reassign the top-bottom values before they attempted to assign the left-right ones. If so, one may predict that H-axis rotations (I) would be more difficult than V-axis rotations (M). In fact, that is precisely what Kolers and Perkins report. Secondly, it could be predicted that the children who could not break the letter representation into its separate predicates and assign them from their appropriate perspectives would not be able to discriminate confusable letters such as b, d, p, q while older children knowing explicitly the separate predicates making up the representation and the perspectives from which they are to be applied could, in fact, discriminate those letters.

While many of specific points can be determined only with additional research, they are much less significant than the demonstration this task provides for the generality of the mental representations of space we have considered. Essentially the same spatial predicates are employed by subjects in all the tasks as we have discussed herein: the oblique task, the three-mountain task, the water level task, the rotations tasks, and now the letter recognition task. The broad applicability of a small set of spatial predicates adds credibility to these structures as a mental "language" for the representation of space.

CONCLUDING SPECULATIONS

We return now to some of the conceptual issues that a theory of the mental representation of space may help to resolve.

1. Perceptual Space and Representational Space

Several writers have noted the relation between "the perception of space" and the "representation of space" (Piaget & Inhelder, 1956), between perceptual space and conceptual space (Cassirer, 1957), between perception of objects and perceptions of forms (Arnheim, 1974), between perception and conception (Miller & Johnson-Laird, 1976). What, precisely is the relation between the two? Some writers, on noting the relationship, claim that the former, perceptual space, is more complex than it was usually assumed to be. Advocates of this view were Helmholtz (1873) and Descartes (see Ree, 1975). Helmholtz argued that perception relied upon the use of unconscious inferences just as reasoning relied upon logical inferences and he described the relation between perception and thought this way:

> There appears to me to be in reality only a superficial difference between the conclusions of logicians and those inductive conclusions of which we recognize the result in the conceptions we gain of the outer world through our sensations. The difference chiefly depends upon the former conclusions being capable of expression in words, while the latter are not: because instead of words they only deal with sensations and the memory of sensations (1873, cited by Bryant, 1974, p. 3).

Furthermore, Helmholtz argued that these perceptual inferences are primary: "Just because they are not free acts of conscious thought these unconscious conclusions from analogy are irresistible, and the effects of them cannot be overcome by a better understanding of the real relations" (1866, cited by Bryant, 1974, p. 3). Descartes, too, advanced the idea that perception bears a close relationship to thought: "Human action and perception are more intellectual than they seem in that they always involve thinking, ideas or mind; and hence that they are built on structures not wholly different from those involved in what the Platonistic theory would call intellectual knowledge (Ree, 1975, p. 98).

The evidence we have reported in this volume lead to the same conclusion. The spatial structures in perception, conception and language are essentially the same. But what then is the difference?

Perceptual space, we have argued is automatic and involuntary although it is subject to some perceptual elaboration. In perception, the spatial predicates that make up the representation for an object or event are fused in a single object schema. The predicates are not articulated into separate propositions. To illustrate, in perception, a large, black block is not represented as: *large* (block) and *black* (block) but as *large* (block)
$$\& \; black \; \text{(block)}.$$

In this volume we have marked this fusion by an & thus: *large* (block) & *black* (block). That is, the two underlying propositions are fused into a single representation of that particular block. Conceptual space, on the other hand, is articulated, separated into separate propositions and subject to intentional or voluntary action and thought. But perception involves the same propositions as conceptualization. We have described the process that leads from perceptual to conceptual space as one of "explication"—making explicit and conceptual the relations that we embedded in perceptual structures, although we have given little indication of what brings that about. Once such structures are explicit, of course, they may be assigned or reassigned voluntarily for problem solving purposes. And sometimes, as in the discrimination of obliques (Chapters 10 and 11), the propositions assigned perceptually and involuntarily compete with those assigned conceptually and voluntarily. Colloquially, we could say that the obliques in different positions *look* different for both children and adults but adults know that they really *are* the same. That is, adults know that they must reassign the horizontal and vertical axes to the local space in which the oblique occurs even if the display as a whole automatically and misleadingly leads to the assignment of horizontal and vertical to the major axes of the display.

2. Egocentrism

A word on "egocentrism" may be appropriate here. Failure to grant the general availability of spatial predicates for relating things both to ego and to objects gives rise to the theory of egocentrism, a theory which we have consistently played down in this volume. Predicates are not, contrary to Piaget and others, applied first to ego and only later to objects. They are assigned to both essentially automatically. What Piaget called "decentering" results, in our view, not in the construction of object-related structural descriptions, but rather in the development of "control structures" or intentional structures which permit the voluntarily assignment of those spatial predicates to a display for particular linguistic and problem solving purposes. Nonetheless it is important to grant that it is ego which assigns these spatial predicates and, as a result, they are assigned automatically from ego's point of view. It is difficult not to see (and code) things on ego's right as on the right, things above ego as above, and so on. Similarly it is difficult not to see the top of a canonical object as the top regardless of its orientation or the top of a screen facing a subject as the top. Being automatically assigned, those are the codes that dominate young children's responses. The voluntary reassignment of these predicates is what marks "the crisis in spatial consciousness" as Cassirer called it.

But why can children recognize an elaborate display from their own point of view? Our account of how children avoid egocentrism—in which they construct another view and compare views using explicit, assigned propositional relations—is adequate to handle rotational and perspective problems but leaves us in the uncomfortable position of being unable to explain the most primitive response, which Piaget called egocentric, the recognition of a display from one's own perspective.

Referring back to Chapters 2 and 3 we would explain the processes thus.

Children automatically assign structural descriptions consisting of spatial components and relations to displays, presumably in the form of spatial propositions. But these representations being involuntary are neither subject to the novel purposes and goals of the child nor to those set by the adult. These automatically assigned descriptions would account both for the way the display "looked" as well as for its perception, both its appearance and its identity. These representations, being involuntary, are assigned in an unanalyzed, holistic fashion. Finally, being automatic, these operations are available to a child from an early age although, they are, of course, at a later stage subject to elaboration and differentiation. But more importantly, they become subject to intentional perception and action only when they become explicit.

3. Presentational Versus Representational Schemata

Piaget originated the view that sensory-motor intelligence is nonrepresentational or "presentational". That is, some mental activity may be completely dependent upon the presence of the object or stimulus; when the stimulus is removed, so is the corresponding mental activity. Such schemata may be called "presentational". For representational schemata on the other hand, mental representational activity can continue after the disappearance of the object.

But what is the status of presentational schemata? How could a representation be sufficiently powerful to accept a particular object, say a triangle, and reject a square in a discrimination task, without having as part of its "structural description" a predicate such as three vertices. If it did not have some such predicate it would also accept squares, pentagons, hexagons, and so on. Hence, it must have the requisite predicates. Why then does the representation disappear when the object disappears? Or why can a child discriminate obliques when they are simultaneously displayed but not successively displayed? Or why can a child recognize an oblique but not draw one? Our suggestion is that the difference between so called presentational and representational schemata is simply in the intentional retrievability of the representations and their manipulation in thought. These intentional structures—control structures or executive structures as other writers have referred to them (Case, in press; Pascual-Leone, 1970; Simon, 1969)—operate upon representations holding them in memory, binding them into goals, and so on, and if the intentional structures are absent, so too are the representations. Furthermore, intentional structures can act upon only those aspects of representations which are connected to meanings as we argued in the first chapter. Thus, a child may have a concept of a lollipop and thereby implicate the structural description which makes up its representation, without having access to the distinctive propositions—circles and stems—which are parts of that structural description. Or, to take another example, children may recognize and sort triangles from squares without being able to draw either of them. The child does not have independent intentional access to the predicate three-sided even if it is an implicit part of the representation for triangle.

It is for this reason that the progressive explication of the spatial propositions implicit in object perception is such an achievement. Cassirer, as we mentioned, wrote of a "genuine crisis in spatial consciousness." He argued that spatial knowledge does not reflect concrete perceptual data but reflects rather the process of symbol functions. The concrete knowledge of space, "the space of action", is replaced by the symbolization or representation of space, "the space of intuition", which breaks up the stream of experience and organizes it into conceptual systems. The conceptual system one employs to represent space depends upon which spatial determinations and relations one postulates or intends as invariant. Following the lead of Felix Klein, Cassirer argues that every special geometry is a theory of invariants which is valid across some set of transformations. Whether a triangle and a square are treated as the same or different depends upon the transformations one chooses to admit. One set generates Euclidean geometry, another projective, and still another topological geometry (Cassirer, 1957, p. 157).

But these "special" geometries are not created any more than Euclidean geometry is. They consist rather of explicating the spatial relations inexplicit in ordinary perception. Once explicit these relations can be applied intentionally to solve problems as in the studies in this book. The original explication of these structures is the achievement of the great mathematicians. It is interesting to note that the children in these studies rarely invented spatial structures; they applied those that they had already available to the task at hand. If they didn't have intentional control over the requisite predicates as for example, the H and V axes in the oblique studies or in the water level problems, they simply failed.

But mathematicians discovered the basic structural properties of the mind; they didn't invent them. Let us examine this problem somewhat more fully.

4. Spatialization and Theoretical Geometry

The treatment of spatial cognition we have developed in this book may be related to the theory of spatial cognition offered first by the Greeks in the form of classical geometry. Geometry is usually considered as a description of the structure of outer, as opposed to inner, space. The space out there, on a paper for example, was shown by Euclid to have certain properties—vertically opposite angles are equal, the sum of the angles of a triangle equal a straight angle, two triangles having two sides and an included angle equal were congruent, and so on. What is the relation between such Euclidean structures and the structure of spatial cognition?

Euclid, we suggest, worked out verbal proofs for relations that were perceptible. He provided explanations for the ways things looked. Vertically opposite angles *look* equal; he devised procedures to prove they were equal. But, we suggest, he did not invent this space, he explicated it. He developed ways for stating, consistently, what one already knew perceptually. Hence, in a sense, he was providing an explicit description of the procedures that go on implicitly in the mind. And once explicated, the rules and representation could be applied to problems for which one had no clear perceptions at all. Consider the proof that two triangles are congruent if they share particular properties. Those properties and relations which, when explicit, prove the triangle congruent are the very properties and relations implicit in their representations which make them look the same. Hence, we suggest, Euclidean geometry is an explication of the cognitive structures implicit in ordinary perception.

Furthermore, ordinary perception involves more than purely Euclidean relations. Any set of predicates extracted from perception including topological or projective relations are also subject to explication and to being taken as invariant across a set of transformations. The psychologist's error has been to assume too small a set of spatial predicates as the basis of ordinary perception. Geometry, like all fundamental mathematics, is the quest for understanding of the basic properties of the human mind (Gandy, 1973).

5. The Role of Symbols in the Explication of Spatial Structures

Earlier we remarked that the primary form of spatial development was the explication of the very spatial structures that were implicit in spatial perception. What is responsible for their explication? We would, following Cassirer (1957) and Goodman (1978), suggest that it is a consequence of the invention and the acquisition of symbols, largely the symbols of ordinary language, but also the language of geometry, and the language of art. The spatial relations that are pulled from the structural descriptions of objects depend largely upon the speaking practices of adults. We have argued that even young children automatically construct representations for objects and events utilizing spatial predicates but they have no mean of singling them out, for intentionally assigning these predicates or for intentionally reassigning them. What makes that voluntary reassignment possible is the possession of spatial concepts, categories which may be retrieved and manipulated in memory for imagining, thinking and problem solving purposes. The concepts or relations that even children can readily manipulate in memory are concepts of objects and events; such concepts make up "natural kind" concepts (Putnam, 1975); those dependent upon symbols are form concepts. These latter, many of which are "wrested from the world of language" are subject to intentionality, to deliberative cognition. With the latter, viewers can see forms, shapes, textures, sizes, patterns, not just the objects of which they are an implicit part. The fact that concepts have names, does not of course mean that they are merely verbal; words are just names for the propositions that make up fundamental structures in perception and thought. Further, these spatial concepts are wrested from perception not only through language but through geometry and through the arts.

Consider, briefly, such arts as drawing and painting. As Arnheim (1974) has pointed out each medium requires for appropriate representation an awareness of different properties of the objects portrayed. Thus, in drawing a balloon, one draws an outline. In painting a picture of a balloon, one paints a surface, the entire area of the balloon. Both of these are implicit in the perception of balloons. But the art of drawing and painting are responsible in part for the explication of these properties.

6. Spatial Cognition Versus Spatial Abilities

Traditionally, spatial cognition has been described as the *ability* to do such things as rotate an object, to comprehend imaginary movement, or to imagine displays from another point of view. Such a theory simply treats the ability as an undefined factor or a variable. It involves attempts to produce devices for measuring that ability, and it leads to the differential assignment of scores to individuals as indications of their level of "ability". The only concern with the actual structures or operations that go into or that make up that ability is of a general phenomonological sort "the ability to mentally rotate objects". Such attempts at definition and measurement may be adequate for the purpopse of predicting performance differences between individuals and for showing that children improved in their performance with age. Those attempts however are of little use for uncovering the basic operations of the mind or of structured changes that occur with development and schooling.

The problem for cognitive psychology, as we mentioned, is to describe the set of representations and operations that constitute that ability. What exactly are subjects doing when they solve a spatial problem? By approaching problems of spatial cognition and spatial development with the goal of specifying the mental representations and the operations that applied to them, it has become possible to formulate at least some aspects of a theory which is highly explicit and formal. This theory not only permits us to explain the differences between certain tasks, but more importantly to discover why certain other spatial tasks, which appear to be quite different, are in fact basically the same. Typical was the discovery that the oblique discrimination task (Chapter 11) involved the same operations as the Piagetian perspective task (Chapter 8) which in turn involved the same operations as the mental rotations task (Chapter 9); they differ only in the axis which had to be reassigned. A similar discovery, as we mentioned, was that the water level task also involved comparable operations to the letter recognition task and so on.

In addition to explaining the relation between the procedures used to solve superficially different problems, this theory has a degree of explicitness and formality that permits us to explain not only problems in general, but also specific problems in particular. True, one can still use such a theory to account for why one subject or group of subjects fail or succeed on a particular item, that is, as an indication of "ability". But in addition one would know precisely what subjects, whether passing or failing, are doing.

A common problem with specific and precise formal theories is that they may explain only a specific problem. Experimental psychology is full of such theories; the number of theories is approximately equal to the number of problems. Any economy in a theory comes from using one theory to explain many problems. As long as "ability" theory reigned supreme, it seemed satisfactory to simply have discovered a "verbal" ability and a "spatial" ability and perhaps a few others and to use this theory to "explain" performance on a large number of tasks. But as we mentioned, a general theory of this sort explains very little in particular.

Verbal ability, to take one case, reflects a general competence with some 20,000 words, the grammar, and a set of pragmatic rules; during the reign of "ability" theory there seemed to be no possibility of accounting for all those complex skills. Hence the empirical approach to this ability was to sample the domain and take the sampled performance as an indication of the verbal ability of a subject relative to a group norm. For many practical purposes such concepts and procedures were completely adequate.

But the concept of verbal ability has begun to change. Linguistic ability has been shown to involve the mastery of a characteristic and distinctive set of structures which underlie the diversity of linguistic productions. The explication of grammatical development, semantic development and pragmatic development have all begun to change our perceptions of "verbal" ability.

Much the same could be said of spatial ability. The variety of spatial tasks appeared to be infinitely large and appeared to involve an unlimited range of categories and relations. The best that could be hoped for would be to sample the domain and provide an estimate of an individual's general "spatial ability". The first clues that the domain of spatial cognition may be both finite and orderly came from the semantic analysis of adjectivals by Bierwisch (1967). H. H. Clark (1973a) and Miller and Johnson-Laird (1976) later made the important observation that L-space, that is, the lexical representation of space mapped directly on to P-space, that is, the perception of space for such terms as above, below, deep, shallow, and so on, map onto basic spatial categories. Olson (1970a), too, showed that oriented lines which were easily matched perceptually were those that took simple lexical descriptions. These observations encouraged the Fregean view that "The world of thoughts has a model in the world of sentences, expressions, words and signs" (1960, p. 123).

That attempt to recover the underlying structures of spatial cognition has continued in this volume. The research goal has been the isolation of a small set of general, perhaps universal, categories and relations which humans are highly predisposed to learn, and which are recruited in the services of an extremely large set of specific tasks. The goal then has been to translate an unspecified, undescribed "ability" into a set of specific representations and operations that could account for the variety of spatial cognitions ranging from direct spatial perception to the most elaborate and voluntary spatial cognitions.

We may take our lead from Chomsky's analysis of verbal ability (Chomsky, 1980). He points out that in the natural sciences it is common to adopt what Husserl called the "Galilean style"—that is, to construct "abstract mathematical models of the universe to which at least the physicists give a higher degree of reality than they accord the ordinary world of sensations" (p. 8). This, Chomsky argues, is the style which has led to the great achievements in the natural sciences. In addition, he argues that there is no reason to abandon that approach when one turns to the study of human beings. Chomsky's major contribution was to show that an underlying set of rules and representations could be discovered for language, and that this knowledge is in part common to humans and that it is "represented somehow in our minds, ultimately in our brains, in structures that we can hope to characterize abstractly, and in principle quite concretely, in terms of physical mechanisms" (1980, p. 5).

Of course, the structure of ordinary language is more complex by an order of magnitude than the structure of spatial concepts, but the comparison is appropriate. For spatial cognition is indeed a general and productive system which is represented in some way as internal structures in the mind and which are generatively assigned to self, others, objects, events, and so on.

The generality of spatial structures, their universality, and their ease of acquisition all suggest that the structures of spatial cognition are innate, part of the cognitive equipment passed on genetically as part of the structure of the brain. These spatial structures are involved in such general activities as maintaining erect posture, in locomotion, and in keeping track of one's location. Furthermore, these same basic structures are also utilized in pattern perception, that is, in the perception of objects and in spatial perception, that is, in the perception of the relations between objects, and in spatial cognition, that is, in solving spatial problems. Spatial structures, we suggest, have a structure analogous to that for color discovered by Berlin and Kay (1969). It is difficult to even imagine a language which did not honor the basic spatial relations we have discussed or did not express these relations by such spatial terms as *on, above, below, over, under, top, bottom,* and so on to mention only the predicates structured in terms of the vertical axes. Of course, the degree of elaboration of the spatial predicate system, their isolability from patterns and perspectives and the like are all subject to language, culture, and education. What the minimum set of predicates and operations are and the ways in which they generate higher order predicates remains to be seen. But even at the level of analysis we have considered in this volume, there is good grounds for the belief that underlying systems of spatial predicates are the building blocks for the mental representation of space.

7. Mental Imagery Versus Spatial Representations

The long and somewhat inconclusive debate between proponents of visual imagery theories such as Paivio (1971), and Kosslyn (1981) and proponents of propositional theories such as Pylyshyn (1981) is relevant to a theory of spatial cognition. Kosslyn has demonstrated a number of interesting properties of spatial imagination suggesting, for example, that subjects scan mental images in much the same way as they scan an actual event. Pylyshyn (1981), on the other hand, claims that the concept of a mental image is non-explanatory and that spatial cognition must be accounted for in terms of the viewer's implicit or tacit knowledge of the events represented.

Kosslyn's theory assumes that some visual/spatial information is stored and mentally represented in the form of mental images which are "not language-like symbolic representations, but bear a nonarbitrary correspondence to the thing being represented" (p. 46). The theory is advanced to explain such introspections as that when asked to tell how many windows there are in one's house, one imagines moving around the house, counting the windows. Further, they are called upon to explain a variety of other visual spatial tasks devised by Kosslyn and his co-workers, as well as for the visual rotation tasks described in Chapters 6–9 of this volume. Kosslyn argues that a mental image is a form of visual buffer in which the form of the operations carried out and the form of information preserved, is due to the representational medium—the mental image—rather than the structure of the beliefs about events themselves. The representational medium permits operations such as "rotate", "scan", "zoom", "focus", and the like which are completely independent of the beliefs and knowledge of the viewer.

Pylyshyn (1981) criticizes the theory by claiming that what one can do with mental images depends upon what one's "tacit" knowledge and belief about the represented events not upon some fixed properties of the representational medium.

In part, Kosslyn's imagery hypothesis is put forward to account for what subjects report as images. But as Pylyshyn (1981) notes, "a theory of underlying processes should account for *how* imagery can come to have this character, not to use this very property as an explanatory principle" (p. 28). That is, Kosslyn attempts to explain images by "hypostatizing" them; instead of explaining images, he asserts that we have them, that we rotate an image by applying a "rotate" operation, scan by a "scan" operation, and the like (p. 54).

The observations deserve an explanation; Pylyshyn makes the important point that images are "knowledge-based". To make this claim, Pylyshyn generalizes the concept of knowledge to include not just conscious knowledge and beliefs but also tacit knowledge—knowledge of what one would do if one were simulating the activity of actually observing real events. However, Pylyshyn offers no clear alternative theory of how such activities would be executed mentally; his attempt rather is to show that images do not require a particular representational format but like all behavior, should be explained in terms of knowledge, goals, intentions, and the like.[1]

While Pylyshyn's argument against images is, we believe, valid, it too fails to account for the major issues that gave impetus to image theory: image-like representations which appear to preserve whole objects by means of unanalyzed representations and on which particular retrieval operations may be applied, as for example in the rotations task, Kosslyn claims that "the primary characteristic of representations in this format is that every portion of the representation must correspond to a portion of the object...size, shape, orientation and location information are not independent in that format—in order to depict one, values on the other dimensions must be specified" (p. 50).

In the terms of the theory we have advanced in this book, the representa-

---

[1]Robert Seibel has suggested the following argument against images: "Imagine a word such as 'hippopotamus' and get a very clear image of it. Now read the letters off from your mental image one at a time, spelling the word 'hippopotamus.' Having completed that, now read the letters off backwards. There is no clearer demonstration that I know of to point out that imagery is constructed. When subjects try to read the letters off backwards they have to spell the word forward and then reconstruct the letters in reverse order. If there were a clear picture, as many imagery theories suggest, there should be no more difficulty reading the letters off backwards than forwards." Believers tend not to be swayed by such arguments.

tion corresponding to an "image" is complex and unanalyzed into its underlying propositional constituents; it is an unanalyzed structural description. But it is nonetheless composed of a set of propositions built from the same set of predicates that an explicit representation would be composed of. It differs only in that in an image-like representation, the propositions are not retrieved singly but as a complex representation of a whole object. Recall children's performance in the oblique recognition task; their representation involved a pair of propositions but those propositions could not be retrieved and compared singly: together they formed an "image" of the object. These unanalyzed structured descriptions are presumably what Pylyshyn and other authors mean by "tacit knowledge". On this point however Pylyshyn is wrong or at least misleading in suggesting that representations are "naturally" factored apart into propositions representing size, shape, and orientation. While we have argued that in "explicating" the spatial propositions implicit in the representation of objects and events one does indeed come to be able to consider size, shape, orientation, and location independently, the interesting property of "images" is that they are not analyzed into these specific forms. Indeed only a few of the predicates implicit in spatial representations are ever explicated and intentionally reassigned for problem solving purposes. Competence with the voluntary assignment of spatial predicates as is required for such "imagery" tasks as mental rotations of objects is typical of those tasks requiring intentional spatial cognition.

Thus, the debate over mental images is an interesting example of the difference between the spatial predicates implicit in the mental representation of objects and events and the explication of those spatial predicates in the form of intentional spatial concepts. But an explanation of either requires, as we have been at pains to show, a theory of the structure of the spatial predicates involved in the mental representation of space.

Kolers and Smythe (1979) criticize both "pictorialist" and "propositionalist" accounts of perception and imagination. Pictorialist accounts make the unwarranted assumptions that propositions cannot capture gradations but, as Kolers and Smythe point out, propositions can be constructed at any level of elaboration. Propositionalists' accounts assume that their propositions figure in mental activities of subjects whereas Kolers and Smythe argue, they are descriptions of the theorist imposed on behavior which is not intrinsically propositional. As an alternative Kolers and Smythe suggest that behavior is based on skilled performance regulated by "skilled pattern analyzing mechanisms", which are tacit and subject to improvement and revision with practice. In part, this is the "ability" view presented earlier, the view that mental activities can be adequately described by calling them skills, in this case "patterns analyzing mechanisms". Undoubtedly, subjects have such mechanisms, just as they have "spatial ability"; the question is what is the structure of these operations, beliefs, abilities, or skills. Propositionalist accounts are the first to take seriously the problem of what, precisely, the rules and representations underlying perception and action are.

Equivalent descriptions.   We have observed on several occasions that there are two or more equivalent ways of specifying spatial propositions. For example, in the oblique studies (Chapter 10), children may have coded the lines in terms of on/off axis but it is possible that the contrast is actually into a corner versus across a corner. For the data available the codes are equivalent. We have not in such cases tried to determine which was the correct one. Rather we have tried to construct representations which would yield appropriate outcomes. Our guess is that there are many equivalent descriptions and that with more research one may narrow the field even if it is difficult to imagine exhausting it.

More serious are the problems involving the reassignment of H and V axes. To say that the axes of Ego may be reassigned to a perspective $r°$ from Ego is equivalent in some cases to saying that the object is rotated through a distance of $r°$. For some tasks it is possible to decide which of these alternatives subjects recruited; in others they are, for the present at least, equivalent descriptions. Although with more effort we may have narrowed the range somewhat more, we have simply showed how such a theory could account for the solutions generated and the relative difficulty of the problems without determining exactly which of the equivalent descriptions subjects actually employed. That specification remains an important task for future research.

On explanation.   In explanations of human cognition, we have avoided attributing to human subjects representations or operations that we could not actually carry out ourselves. This constraint shows up in three ways. First, we have assumed, following Chomsky, that models of human cognition and descriptions of such structures as linguistic competence, or here, as spatial cognition, are of interest only if they are models of human competence. That is, the model must be a model which not only describes behavior but a model which describes the rules and representations by means of which subjects generate their behavior. That is, the rules of interest are not only the theorists' rules, but also the subject's rules; rules used by the subjects in regulating their perceptions and actions. We have perhaps gone a bit further; we have assumed that subjects' implicit knowledge possess a structure which, when specified explicitly, should, when followed literally, generate the behavior as that generated by the implicit rules and structures. In a sense that is what all theories must do; they must provide an explicit model of the events described. But a theory of the sort we have sought must characterize what the subjects themselves know but know implicitly or tacitly. Hence, even this tacit knowledge, when appropriately explicated, must be knowable and do-able in the same way that explicit knowledge must be knowable and operative. Hence, we have avoided attributing to our subjects any mysterious implicit knowledge such as point by point iconic memory because, without a camera, we could not make such an image. We have also avoided such descriptions as "spatial abilities" or "rotation abilities" or "pattern analyzing mechanisms", not because they are wrong but because they are too vague to indicate precisely what representations or operations are involved; hence they have little or no explanatory power.

The representations we have attempted to construct, therefore, have three properties: First, if the representations were literally applied, they would generate the appropriate answers to spatial problems. Secondly, as an empirical theory, the difficulties specified by the model should correspond to the difficulties that subjects have, whether measured by latencies or by developmental changes in solving the problems. And third, the representations and operations postulated as implicit structures, when explicated, should be intentionally constructable. The first two are well known in the cognitive sciences; the third should help to make the human sciences more comprehensible.

CONCLUSIONS

This theory is intended as a contribution to a computational theory of mind of the sort that is becoming common in cognitive science. It assumes that the mind consists of beliefs, wants, goals, and intentions and that behavior is the consequence of these structures. The central problems for such a theory is that of determining the structure of beliefs, how they are represented in the mind and how they are used in perception, in the formulation of intentions and in the orchestration of action. In this book we have isolated some of the representations and operations that are involved in solving a variety of spatial tasks. Ordinarily these structures and processes are implicit in higher level tasks such as perception and locomotion but, upon analysis they may be shown to possess many of the same characteristics of explicit spatial structures namely, their propositional nature, their relational structure, their alternative grounds of application.

Such a theory is clearly an inside to outside theory, a Kantian, if not a Platonic theory. The structures of space begin as structures of the mind which are utilized to construct representations of objects, patterns and events including the self. These structures of the mind are, in part, innate; others are constructed out of simpler predicates; *top*, we suggested, may be derived from *above*. These structures are the codes, categories or initial states of the mind out of which perceptions, conceptions, lexical structures and sentence meanings are composed. They are the internal structures used to model reality. They do not originate in the stimulus nor exactly in ego, they are mental machinery used for constructing and interpreting spatial relations. They are, in a sense, the internal language of spatial thinking and perceiving. Any event which can be coded in terms of the available predicates is assigned a structural description. The descriptions have the form of propositions implicit in the perception of self, others, objects and events. When differentiated from the object schema of which they are part, they form distinctively spatial propositions, or spatial forms. Not only does one construct increasingly sophisticated representations of objects and events, but the "language" of space itself develops, using some predicates for constructing additional predicates. Once isolated as spatial forms or spatial concepts, such predicates are subject to the intentional assignment to objects and events to which they would not ordinarily or automatically be assigned, for various problem solving purposes.

The spatial structures we have discussed, therefore, are part of the furniture of the mind; the rules and representations used in perceiving, and thinking about space. They are the structures of inner space.

References

Annis, R. C., & Frost, B. Human visual ecology and orientation anisotropies in acuity. *Science*, 1973, *182*, 729-731.

Appelle, S. Perception and discrimination as a function of stimulus orientation: The oblique effect in man and animals. *Psychology Bulletin*, 1972, *78*, 266-278.

Arnheim, R. Comments and discussion. In D. R. Olson & S. M. Pagliuso (Eds.), From perceiving to performing: An aspect of cognitive growth. Special issue of *Ontario Journal of Educational Research*, 1968, *10*, 203-210.

Arnheim, R. *Visual thinking*. Berkeley: University of California Press, 1969.

Arnheim, R. *Art and visual perception*. Berkeley: University of California Press, 1974.

Attneave, F., & Olson, R. K. Discriminability of stimuli varying in physical and retinal orientation. *Journal of Experimental Psychology*, 1967, *74*, 149-157.

Attneave, F., & Reid, K. Voluntary control of frame of reference and shape equivalence under head rotation. *Journal of Experimental Psychology*, 1968, *78*, 153-159.

Bartlett, F. C. *Remembering: An experimental and social study*. Cambridge: Cambridge University Press, 1932.

Benson, K. A., & Bogartz, R. S. *Coordination of perspective change in preschoolers*. Paper presented at the biannual meeting of the Society for Research in Child Development, New Orleans, March, 1977.

Berkeley, B. Towards a new theory of vision. In H. R. Herrnstein, & E. G. Boring (Eds.), *A source book in the history of psychology*. Cambridge, Mass.: Harvard University Press, 1966.

Berlin, B., & Kay, P. *Basic color terms: Their universality and evolution*. Berkeley: University of California Press, 1969.

Bierwisch, M. Some semantic universals of German adjectivals. *Foundations of Language*, 1967, *3*, 1-36.

Bogen, J. E. The other side of the brain. *Bulletin of the Los Angeles Neurological Society*, 1969, *34*, 191-220.

Borke, H. Piaget's mountains revisited: Changes in the egocentric landscape. *Developmental mental Psychology*, 1971, *5*, 263-269.

Borke, H. Piaget's mountains revisited: Changes in the egocentric landscape. *Developmental Psychology*, 1975, *11*, 240-243.

Bottenberg, R. A., & Ward, J. H. Jr. *Applied multiple linear regression.* Air Force Systems Command, Lockland Air Force Base, Lockland, Texas, March, 1963.

Bower, T. Perceptual development: Object and space. In E. C. Carterette & M. P. Friedman (Eds.), *Handbook of perception.* New York: Academic Press, 1978.

Bowerman, M. The acquisition of word meaning: An investigation of some current conflicts. In N. Waterson & C. Snow (Eds.), *Proceedings of the Third International Child Language Symposium.* New York: Wiley, 1977.

Bradley, F. H. *The principles of logic.* London: Oxford University Press, 1922.

Bransford, J., & McCarrell, N. S. A sketch of a cognitive approach to comprehension: Some thoughts about understanding what it means to comprehend. In W. B. Weimer and D. S. Palermo (Eds.), *Cognition and the symbolic processes.* Hillsdale, N.J.: Erlbaum, 1974.

Bransford, J. D., & Franks, J. J. The abstraction of linguistic ideas. *Cognitive Psychology,* 1971, *2,* 331–350.

Brooks, L. R. Spatial and verbal components in the act of recall. *Canadian Journal of Psychology,* 1968, *22,* 349–368.

Brooks, L. R. *Visual and verbal processes in internal representation.* Unpublished manuscript, 1970.

Brown, R. How shall a thing be called? *Psychological Review,* 1958, *65,* 14–21.

Bruner, J. S., Olver, R., & Greenfield, P. M. et al. *Studies in cognitive growth.* New York: Wiley, 1966.

Bruner, J. S., Roy, C., & Ratner, N. The beginnings of request. In K. Nelson (Ed.), *Children's language,* (Vol. IV). Hillsdale, N.J.: Erlbaum, in press.

Bryant, P. E. Perception and memory of the orientation of visually presented lines by children. *Nature,* 1969, *224,* 1331–1332.

Bryant, P. E. *Perception and understanding in young children: An experimental approach.* London: Methuen, 1974.

Bryden, M. P. Perceptual asymmetries in vision: Relation to handedness, eyedness, and speech lateralization. *Cortex,* 1973, *9,* 419–435.

Butterfield, H. *The origins of modern science: 1300–1800.* London: G. Bell, 1965.

Butterworth, G. Object identity in infancy: The interaction of spatial location codes in determining search errors. *Child Development,* 1975, *46,* 866–870.

Campbell, R. N. On Fodor on cognitive development. In B. de Gelder (Ed.), *Representation and knowledge.* London: Routledge & Kegan Paul, 1982.

Carpenter, P. A., & Just, M. A. Sentence comprehension: A psycholinguistic processing model of verification. *Psychological Review,* 1975, *82,* 45–73.

Case, R. *Intellectual development: A systematic reinterpretation.* New York: Academic Press, in press.

Cassirer, E. *The philosophy of symbolic forms.* (Vol. 3). *The phenomenology of knowledge.* New Haven: Yale University Press, 1957.

Chomsky, N. *Rules and representations.* New York: Columbia University Press, 1980.

Clark, E. V. What's in a word. On the child's acquisition of semantics in his first language. In T. E. Moore (Ed.), *Cognitive development and the acquisition of language.* New York: Academic Press, 1973. (a)

Clark, E. V. Non-linguistic strategies and the acquisition of word meanings. *Cognition,* 1973, *2,* 161–182. (b)

Clark. E. V. Here's the *top:* Non-linguistic strategies in the acquisition of orientational terms. *Child Development,* in press.

Clark, H. H. Space, time, semantics and the child. In T. Moore (Ed.), *Cognitive development and the acquisition of language.* New York: Academic Press, 1973. (a)

Clark, H. H. The language as fixed effect fallacy: A critique of language statistics in psychological research. *Journal of Verbal Learning and Verbal Behaviour,* 1973, *12,* 335–359. (b)

Clark, H. H., Carpenter, P. A., & Just, M. A. On the meeting of semantics and perception. In W. G. Chase (Ed.), *Visual information processing*. New York: Academic Press, 1973.

Clark, H. H., & Chase, W. G. On the process of comparing sentences against pictures. *Cognitive Psychology*, 1972, *3*, 472–517.

Clark, H. H., & Clark, E. V. *Psychology of language*. New York: Harcourt Brace Jovanovich, 1977.

Coie, J. D., Costanzo, P. R., & Farnill, D. Specific transitions in the development of spatial perspective-taking ability. *Developmental Psychology*, 1973, *9*, 167–177.

Cole, M., Gay, J., Glick, J., & Sharp, D. *The cultural context of learning and thinking*. New York: Basic Books, 1971.

Cooper, L. A. *Comparison processes in visual memory: Individual differences*. Paper presented at the 16th meeting of Psychonomic Society. Denver, 1975.

Cooper, L. A. Demonstration of a mental analog of an external rotation. *Perception and Psychophysics*, 1976, *19*, 296–302.

Cooper, L. A., & Podgorny, P. *Effects of complexity and similarity on mental transformations and visual comparison processes*. Paper presented at the 15th annual meeting of the Psychonomic Society, Boston, 1974.

Cooper, L. A., & Shepard, R. N. The time required to prepare for a rotated stimulus. *Memory and Cognition*, 1973, *7*, 246–250.

Cooper, L. A., & Shepard, R. N. Chronometric studies of the rotation of mental images. In W. G. Chase (Ed.), *Visual information processing*. New York: Academic Press, 1973.

Copley, J. *Shift of meaning*. London: Oxford University Press, 1961.

Corballis, M. C. *The nature of the left-right coding*. Paper presented at the annual meeting of the American Psychological Association, Los Angeles, 1981.

Corballis, M. C., & Beale, I. L. *The psychology of left and right*. Hillsdale: N.J.: Erlbaum, 1976.

Corballis, M. C., & Roldan, C. E. Detection of symmetry as a function of angular orientation. *Journal of Experimental Psychology: Human Perception and Performance*, 1975, *1*, 221–230.

Cornford, F. M. The invention of space. *Essays in honour of Gilbert Murray*. London: Allen and Unwin, 1936.

Cox, M. V. Perspective ability: The relative difficulty of the order observer's viewpoints. *Journal of Experimental Child Psychology*, 1977, *24*, 254–259.

Cronbach, L., & Snow, R. *Aptitudes and instructional methods: A handbook for research on interactions*. New York: Irvington, 1977.

De Lisi, R., Locker, R., & Youniss, J. Anticipatory imagery and spatial operations. *Developmental Psychology*, 1976, *12*, 298–310.

Dodwell, P. C. Children's understanding of spatial concepts. *Canadian Journal of Psychology*, 1963, *17*, 141–161.

Donaldson, M. *On judging truth values*. Edinburgh, mimeo, 1974.

Donaldson, M., & McGarrigle, J. Some clues to the nature of semantic development. *Journal of Child Language*, 1974, *1*, 85–194.

Eddington, A. S. *The nature of the physical world*. Ann Arbor: University of Michigan Press, 1958.

Elliott, J., & Dayton, C. M. *Egocentric error and the construct of egocentrism. The Journal of Genetic Psychology*, 1976, *128*, 275–289.

Fishbein, H. D., Lewis, S., & Keiffer, K. Children's understanding of spatial relations: Coordination of perspectives. *Developmental Psychology*, 1972, *7*, 21–33.

Fisher, G. H. Developmental features of behavior and perception: I: Visual and tactile-kinaesthetic shape perception. *British Journal of Educational Psychology*, 1965, *35*, 67–78.

Flavell, J. H., Botkin, P. T., Fry, C. L., Wright, J. W., & Jarvis, P. *The development of role-taking and communication skills in children.* New York: Wiley, 1968.

Fodor, J. *The language of thought.* New York: Crowell, 1975.

Ford, W., & Olson, D. R. The elaboration of the noun phrase in children's description of object. *Journal of Experimental Child Psychology, 1975, 19,* 371–382.

Frege, G. *Translations from the philosophical writings of Gottlob Frege.* In P. T. Geach & M. Black (Eds.), Oxford: Blackwell, 1952. (Originally published in 1892.)

Frege, G. *Begriffsschrift, a formula language, modeled upon that of arithmetic, for pure thought.* (1879), In Heijenoort, J. van (Ed.), *Frege and Goedel.* Cambridge, Mass.: Aarond University Press, 1970.

French, J. W. The description of aptitude and achievement tests in terms of rotated factors. *Psychometric Monograph,* No. 5, 1951.

Gandy, R. "Structure" in mathematics. In D. Robey (Ed.), *Structuralism.* Oxford University Press, 1973.

Gardner, H., Howard, V., & Perkins, D. Symbol systems: A philosophical, psychological, and educational investigation. In D. R. Olson (Ed.), *Media and symbols: The forms of expression, communication, and education.* The seventy-third year book of the National Society for the Study of Education. Chicago: University of Chicago Press, 1974.

Ghent, L. Recognition by children of realistic figures presented in various orientations. *Canadian Journal of Psychology, 1960, 14,* 249–256.

Ghent, L. Form and its orientation: A child's eye view. *American Journal of Psychology, 1961, 74,* 177–190.

Gibson, E. J. *Principles of perceptual learning and perceptual behavior.* New York: Appleton-Century Croft, 1969.

Gibson, J. J. *The senses considered as perceptual systems.* Boston: Houghton and Mifflin, 1966.

Goldstein, K., & Scheerer, M. Abstract and concrete behavior. *Psychological Monographs, 1941, 53.*

Gombrich, E. H. *Art and illusion.* New York: Pantheon Books, 1960.

Gombrich, E. The visual image. In D. R. Olson (Ed.), *Media and symbols: The forms of expression, communication and education.* Chicago: University of Chicago Press and the NSSE, 1974.

Goodman, N. *Languages of art.* Indianapolis: Bobbs-Merrill, 1968.

Goodman, N. *Ways of the world-making.* Indianapolis, Ind.: Hackett, 1978.

Greenberg, J. H. *Language universals.* The Hague: Mouton & Co., 1966.

Grieve, R., Hoogenraad, R., & Murray, D. On the young child's use of lexis and syntax in understanding locative instructions. *Cognition, 1977, 5,* 235–250.

Guilford, J. P. Printed Classification Tests. *AAF Report,* No. 5, Washington, D.C.: U.S. Government Printing Office, 1947.

Hanson, N. R. *Patterns of discovery.* Cambridge: Cambridge University Press, 1958.

Hardwick, D. A., McIntyre, C. W., & Pick, H. L. The content and manipulation of cognitive maps in children and adults. *Monographs of the Society for Research in Child Development, 1976, 41,* (3).

Harris, P. The child's representation of space. In G. Butterworth (Ed.), *The child's representation of the world.* New York: Plenum Press, 1977.

Harris, L., & Bassett, E. Reconstruction from the mental image. *Journal of Experimental Child Psychology, 1976, 21,* 514–523.

Harris, L., & Strommen, E. A. The role of front-back features in children's "front", "back" and "beside" placements of objects. *Merrill-Palmer Quarterly, 1972, 18,* 259–271.

Helmholtz, H. von. *Treatise on physiological optics.* New York: Dover, 1866.

Helmholtz, H. von. The recent progress of the theory of vision. In *Popular Scientific Lectures.* New York: Appleton, 1873.

Hoogenraad, R., Grieve, R., Baldwin, P., & Campbell, R. Comprehension as an interactive process. In R. Campbell & P. T. Smith (Eds.), *Recent advances in the psychology of language—Language development and mother-child interaction.* New York: Plenum Press, 1978.

Howard, I. P. Perception and knowledge of the water-level principle. *Perception,* 1978, *7,* 151–160.

Howard, I. P. *Human visual orientation.* Toronto: Wiley and Sons, 1982.

Howard, I. P., & Templeton, W. B. *Human spatial orientation.* London: Wiley, 1966.

Huttenlocher, J. Children's ability to order and orient objects. *Child Development,* 1967, *38,* 1169–1176.

Huttenlocher, J., & Presson, C. Mental rotation and the perspective change problem. *Cognitive Psychology,* 1973, *4,* 277–299.

Huttenlocher, J., & Presson, C. C. The coding and transformation of spatial information. *Cognitive Psychology,* 1979, *11,* 375–394.

Ibbotson, A., & Bryant, P. E. The perpendicular error and vertical effect in children's drawings. *Perception,* 1976, *5,* 319–326.

Ives, W., & Rovet, J. The role of graphic orientations in children's drawings of familiar and novel objects at rest and in motion. *Merrill-Palmer Quarterly,* 1979, *25,* 281–292.

Jenkins, H. M. Effects of the stimulus-reinforcer relation on selected and unselected responses. In R. A. Hinde & I. Stevenson-Hinde (Eds.), *Constraints on learning: Limitations and predispositions.* New York: Academic Press, 1973.

Just, M. A., & Carpenter, P. A. Eye fixation and cognitive processes. *Cognitive Psychology,* 1976, *8,* 441–480.

Kendler, T. S., & Kendler, H. H. Vertical and horizontal processes in problem solving. *Psychological Review,* 1962, *69,* 1–16.

Kielgast, K. Piaget's concept of spatial egocentrism: A reevaluation. *Scandinavian Journal of Psychology,* 1971, *12,* 179–191.

Kimura, D. The asymmetry of the human brain. *Scientific American,* 1973, *228,* 70–78.

Kolers, P. A., & Perkins, D. N. Spatial and ordinal components of form perception and literacy. *Cognitive Psychology,* 1975, *7,* 228–267.

Kolers, P. A., & Smythe, W. E. Images, symbols, and skills. *Canadian Journal of Psychology,* 1979, *3,* 158–184.

Kosslyn, S. M. Information representation in visual images. *Cognitive Psychology,* 1975, *7,* 341–370.

Kosslyn, S. M. The medium and the message in mental imagery: A theory. *Psychological Review,* 1981, *88,* 46–66.

Kosslyn, S. M., & Pomerantz, J. R. Imagery, propositions, and the form of internal representations. *Cognitive Psychology,* 1977, *9,* 52–76.

Kuczaj, S. A., II, & Maratsos, M. P. On the acquisition of *front, back,* and *side. Child Development,* 1975, *46,* 202–210.

Kunnapas, T. M. An analysis of the "Vertical-Horizontal Illusion". *Journal of Experimental Psychology,* 1955, *49,* 134–140.

Lashley, K. S. The mechanism of vision: XV. Preliminary studies of the rats' capacity for detail vision. *Journal of General Psychology,* 1938, *18,* 123–193.

Laurendeau, M., & Pinard, A. *The development of the concept of space in the child.* New York: International University Press, 1970.

Leech, G. N. *Towards a semantic description of English.* Bloomington: Indiana University Press, 1969.

Leslie, A. M. The discursive representation of perceived causal connection in infancy. In B. de Gelder (Ed.), *Knowledge and representation,* 1982.

Lovell, K. A follow-up study of some aspects of the work of Piaget and Inhelder on the child's conception of space. *British Journal of Educational Psychology,* 1959, *29,* 104–117.

Lumsden, E. A., & Poteat, B. The salience of the vertical dimension in the concept of "bigger" in five- and six-year-olds. *Journal of Verbal Learning and Verbal Behaviour,* 1968, *7,* 404–408.

Lynch, K. *The image of the city.* Cambridge, Mass.: M.I.T. Press, 1960.

Lyons, J. *Semantics Vol. I.* Cambridge, England: Cambridge University Press, 1977.

Marastos, M. P. Decrease in the understanding of the word "big" in preschool children. *Child Development,* 1973, *44,* 747–752.

Marmor, G. S. Mental rotation and number conservation: Are they related? *Developmental Psychology,* 1977, *13,* 320–325.

Masangkay, Z. S., McCluskey, K. A., McIntyre, C. W., Sims-Knight, J., Vaughn, B. E., & Flavell, J. H. The early development of inferences about the visual percepts of others. *Child Development,* 1974, *45,* 357–366.

McLuhan, M. *Understanding media: The extensions of man.* New York: McGraw-Hill, 1964.

Meltzoff, A. N., & Moore, M. K. Imitation of facial and manual gestures by human neonates. *Science,* 1977, *198,* 75–78.

Metzler, J., & Shepard, R. N. Transformational studies of the internal representation of three-dimensional objects. In R. L. Solso (Ed.), *Theories of cognitive psychology: The Loyola symposium.* Hillsdale, N.J.: Erlbaum, 1974.

Miller, G. A., & Johnson-Laird, P. N. *Language and perception.* Cambridge, Mass.: Harvard University Press, 1976.

Milner, B. Interhemispheric differences in the localization of psychological processes in man. *British Medical Bulletin,* 1971, *27,* 272–277.

Neisser, U. *Cognition and reality.* San Francisco: Freeman, 1976.

Nelson, K. Concept, word and sentence. Interrelations in acquisition and development. *Psychological Review,* 1974, *81,* 267–285.

Nigl, A. J., & Fishbein, H. D. Perception and conception in coordination of perspectives. *Developmental Psychology,* 1974, *10,* 858–866.

Norman, D., & Rumelhart, D. Memory and knowledge. In D. Norman & D. Rumelhart (Eds.), *Exploration in cognition.* San Francisco: Freeman, 1975.

Ogden, C. K. *Opposition: A linguistic and psychological analysis.* Bloomington: Indiana University Press, 1932.

Ogilvie, J. C. & Taylor, M. M. Effect of length on the visibility of a fine line. *Journal of the Optical Society of America,* 1959, *49,* 898–900.

Ogilvie, J. C., & Taylor, M. M. Effect of orientation on the visibility of fine wires. *Journal of the Optical Society of America,* 1958, *48,* 628–629.

Olson, D. R. *Cognitive development: The child's acquisition of diagonality.* New York: Academic Press, 1970. (a)

Olson, D. R. Language and thought: Aspects of a cognitive theory of semantics. *Psychological Review,* 1970, *77,* 257–273. (b)

Olson, D. R. Media, models and symbolic systems: The forms of expression and communication. In D. R. Olson (Ed.), *Media and symbols: The forms of expression, communication and education.* 73rd Yearbook of the National Society for the Study of Education, Chicago: University of Chicago Press, 1974.

Olson, D. R. On the relations between spatial and linguistic processes. In J. Eliot & N. J. Salkind (Eds.), *Children's spatial development: New research orientations.* Springfield, Ill.: Charles C. Thomas, 1975.

Olson, D. R., & Filby, N. On the comprehension of active and passive sentences. *Cognitive Psychology,* 1972, *3,* 361–381.

Olson, D. R., & Hildyard, A. The mental representation of oblique orientation. *Canadian Journal of Psychology,* 1977, *31,* 3–13.

Olson, D. R., & Nickerson, N. The contexts of comprehension: On children's understanding of the relations between active and passive sentences. *Journal of Experimental Child Psychology,* 1977, *23,* 402–414.

Olson, G. M., & Laxer, K. Asymmetries in processing the terms "right" and "left". *Journal of Experimental Psychology,* 1973, *100,* 284–290.

Ornstein, R. *The psychology of consciousness.* San Francisco: W. H. Freeman, 1972.

Page, E. B. Ordered hypotheses for multiple treatments: A significant test for linear tasks. *American Statistical Association Journal,* 1963, *58,* 216–230.

Paivio, A. Mental imagery in associative learning and memory. *Psychological Review,* 1969, *76,* 241–263.

Paivio, A. *Imagery and verbal processes.* New York: Holt, Rinehart & Winston, 1971.

Palef, S. Judging pictorial and linguistic aspects of space. *Memory and cognition,* 1978, *6,* 70–75.

Palef, S., & Olson, D. R. Spatial and verbal rivalry in a stroop-like task. *Canadian Journal of Psychology,* 1975, *29,* 201–209.

Palmer, S. E. Visual perception and world knowledge: Notes on a model of sensory-cognitive interaction. In D. A. Norman & D. E. Rumelhart (Eds.), *Explorations in cognition.* San Francisco: A. H. Freeman, 1975.

Palmer, S. E. Hierarchical structure in perceptual representation. *Cognitive Psychology,* 1977, *9,* 441–474.

Parisi, D., & Antinucci, F. *Essentials of grammar.* Translated by Elizabeth Bates. New York: Academic Press, 1976.

Pascual-Leone, J. A mathematical model for the transition rule in Piaget's developmental stages. *Acta Psychologica,* 1970, *32,* 301–345.

Perkins, F. T. Symmetry in visual recall. *American Journal of Psychology,* 1932, *44,* 473–490.

Piaget, J. *Judgment and reasoning in the child.* London: Routledge & Kegan Paul, 1928.

Piaget, J. *The origins of intelligence in the child.* New York: International Universities Press, 1952.

Piaget, J. *Science of education and the psychology of the child.* New York: Orion Press, 1970.

Piaget, J., & Inhelder, B. *The child's conception of space.* London: Routledge & Kegan Paul, 1956.

Piaget, J., & Inhelder, B. *Mental imagery in the child.* New York: Basic Books, 1971.

Pick, H., & Lockman, J. J. From frames of reference to spatial representations. In L. Liben, A. Patterson, & N. Newcombe (Eds.), *Spatial representation and behavior across the life span.* New York: Academic Press, 1981.

Posner, M. I. *Cognition: An introduction.* Glenview, Ill.: Scott, Foresman & Co., 1973.

Presson, C. C. Spatial egocentrism and the effect of an alternate frame of reference. *Journal of Experimental Child Psychology,* 1980, *29,* 391–402.

Proffitt, D. R. Structural theories in psychology and the problem of meaning. Wesleyan university, mimeo, 1977.

Pucetti, R. Unravelling the world knot: Scientists and philosophers on the mind-brain controversy. *British Journal of the Philosophy of Science,* 1978, *29,* 61–68.

Pufall, P. B. Egocentrism in spatial thinking. It depends on your point of view. *Developmental Psychology,* 1975, *11,* 297–303.

Pufall, P. B., & Shaw, R. E. Analysis of the development of children's spatial reference systems. *Cognitive Psychology,* 1973, *5,* 151–175.

Putnam, H. Is semantics possible? In H. Putnam, *Mind, language and reality: Philosophical papers.* Vol. 2. New York: Cambridge University Press, 1975.

Pylyshyn, Z. W. What the mind's eye tells the mind's brain: A critique of mental imagery. *Psychological Bulletin,* 1973, *80,* 1–24.

Pylyshyn, Z. W. Children's internal descriptions. In J. Macnamara (Ed.), *Language learning and thought.* New York: Academic Press, 1977.

Pylyshyn, Z. W. What has language to do with perception? Some speculations on the *lingua mentis.* In D. L. Waltz (Ed.), *Theoretical issues in natural language processing 2.* New York: Association for Computing Machinery, 1978.

Pylyshyn, Z. W. The imagery debate: Analogue media versus tacit knowledge. *Psychological Review,* 1981, *88,* 16–45.

Ree, J. *Descartes*. New York: Universe, 1975.

Reed, S. K. Structural descriptions and the limitations of visual images. *Memory and Cognition*, 1974, *2*, 329–336.

Reudel, R. G., & Teuber, H. L. Discrimination of direction of line in children. *Journal of Comparative and Physiological Psychology*, 1963, *56*, 892–898.

Rock, I. *Orientation and form*. New York: Academic Press, 1973.

Rock, I. The perception of disoriented figures. *Scientific American*, 1974, *230*, 78–85.

Rock, I. Unpublished lecture, 1978.

Rock, I., & Leaman, R. The experimental analysis of visual symmetry. *Acta Psychologica*, 1963, *21*, 171–183.

Rosch, E. Human categorization. In N. Warren (Ed.), *Studies in cross cultural psychology*, (Vol. 1). New York: Academic Press, 1977.

Rovet, J. *Can spatial skills be acquired via film? An analysis of the cognitive consequences of visual media*. Unpublished dissertation manuscript. University of Toronto, 1974.

Russell, B. *Human knowledge: Its scope and limitations*, 1948.

Salomon, G. *Interaction of media, cognition, and learning*. San Francisco: Jossey-Bass, 1979.

Schaller, M. J., & Harris, L. J. "Upright" orientations of forms change with subject age and features of form. *Perception and Psychophysics*, 1975, *17*, 179–188.

Seligman, M. E. P. On the generality of the laws of learning. *Psychological Review*, 1970, *77*, 406–418.

Shanz, C. U., & Watson, J. S. Assessment of spatial egocentrism through expectancy violation. *Psychonomic Science*, 1970, *18*, 93–94.

Shepard, R. N. The mental image. *American Psychologist*, 1978, *33*, 125–138.

Shepard, R., & Metzler, J. Mental rotation of three-dimensional objects. *Science*, 1971, *171*, 701–703.

Simon, H. A. *The sciences of the artificial*. Cambridge, Mass.: M.I.T. Press, 1969.

Slobin, D. I. Cognitive prerequisites for the development of grammar. In C. A. Ferguson & D. I. Slobin (Eds.), *Studies of child language development*. Toronto: Holt, Rinehart and Winston, 1973.

Smith, E. E., Shoben, E. J., & Rips, L. J. Structure and process in semantic memory: A featural model for semantic decisions. *Psychological Review*, 1974, *81*, 214–241.

Sperry, R. W. The great cerebral commissure. *Scientific American*, 1964, *210*, 44–52.

Sprat, T. *History of the Royal Society of London for the improving of natural knowledge*. In J. I. Cope & H. W. Jones (Eds.), St. Louis: Washington University Press, 1966, (originally published, London, 1667).

Sutherland, N. S. Shape discrimination in the rat, octopus, and goldfish. *Journal of Comparative Physiological Psychology*, 1969, *67*, 160–176.

Swets, J. A. The relative operation characteristic in psychology. *Science*, 1973, 182, 990–1000.

Takala, M. Asymmetries of the visual space. *Academia Scientiarumfennica Annales*, 1951, *72*.

Tapley, S. M., & Bryden, M. P. An investigation of sex differences in spatial ability: Mental rotation of three-dimensional objects. *Canadian Journal of Psychology*, 1977, *31*, 122–130.

Taylor, C. *The explanation of behavior*. London: Routledge & Kegan Paul, 1964.

Teller, P. Some discussion and extension of Manfred Bierwisch's work on German adjectivals. *Foundations of Language*, 1969, *5*, 185–217.

Thurstone, L. L. *Some primary abilities in visual thinking*. Chicago: The University of Chicago Psychometric Laboratory, Report No. 59, 1950.

Titchener, E. B. *A text-book of psychology*. New York: Macmillan, 1910.

Trabasso, T., Rollins, H., & Shaughnessy, E. Storage and verification stages in processing concepts. *Cognitive Psychology*, 1971, *2*, 239–289.

Trevarthen, C. The formulations of intersubjectivity: Development of interpersonal and co-operative understanding in infant. In D. Olson (Ed.), *Social foundations of language and thought*. New York: Norton, 1980.

Vurpillot, E. *The visual world of the child.* London: George Allen & Unwin Ltd., 1976.

Vygotsky, L. S. *Thought and language.* Cambridge, Mass.: M.I.T. Press, 1962.

Walker, L. D., & Gallin, E. S. Perspective role-taking in young children. *Journal of Experimental Child Psychology,* 1977, *24,* 343–357.

Walkerdine, V., & Sinha, C. Developing linguistic strategies in young school children. In G. Wells (Ed.), *Learning through interaction: A study of language development.* London: Cambridge University Press, 1981.

Wilcox, S., & Palermo, D. S. "In", "on", and "under" revisited. *Cognition,* 1975, *3,* 245–254.

Winer, B. J. *Statistical principles in experimental design.* New York: McGraw Hill Co., 1962.

Witelson, S. Neuroanatomical asymmetry in left-handers: A review and implication for functional asymmetry. In J. Herron (Ed.), *Neuropsychology of left-handedness.* New York: Academic Press, 1980.

Wittgenstein, L. *Philosophical investigations.* Translated by G.E.M. Anscombe, Oxford: Blackweel, 1958.

Wood, D. Teaching the young child: Some relationships between sound interaction, language and thought. In D. Olson (Ed.), *The social foundations of language and thought: Essays in honor of Jerome S. Bruner.* New York: Norton, 1980.

Wunderlich, D. Linguistic strategies. In F. Coulmas (Ed.), *A festschrift for native speaker.* The Hague: Mouton, 1981.

Zeaman, O., & House, B. J. The role of attention in retardate discrimination learning. In N. R. Ellis (Ed.), *Handbook of mental deficiency.* New York: McGraw-Hill, 1965.

Author Index

Subject Index